POLITICS AS A
NOBLE CALLING

POLITICS AS A NOBLE CALLING

The Memoirs of F. Clifton White

F. Clifton White

with Jerome Tuccille

Jameson Books, Inc. ■ Ottawa, Illinois

For sales information and catalog requests please write:

Jameson Books, Inc.
Post Office Box 738
Ottawa, Illinois 61350

5   4   3   2   1   \   98   97   96   95

Printed in the United States of America

Distributed to the book trade by Login Publishers Consortium, Chicago.

ISBN: 0-915463-64-4

For Bunny, with Love —

Friend, counselor, confidant and partner in a wonderful life for more than fifty years. You made all I achieved both possible and worthwhile.

And with eternal thanks to —

Peter and Marie Kennedy
Trygve and Lillian Tonnessen
Fred Lennon
Mike Joyce and the Harry and Lynde Bradley Foundation

Contents

Introduction

It is more than 30 years now since I met Clif White. He was organizing the Draft Goldwater campaign then and I was a novice political reporter at the old *Washington Star.* I had written a story early in 1963 quoting Barry Goldwater as saying that he wanted his backers to give him a year to think about a possible presidential campaign. White contacted me to explain why the senator's wish could not be allowed to stop the organizing efforts then getting under way.

It was the first of many conversations. Thinking back over them, I now recognize that the common thread was that I always learned something. This is, believe me, a rare experience for those who cover politics. So many politicians and political operatives think they are helping you when they utter their favorite applause lines or mouth the cliches of the moment.

Clif White was different. He was always teaching—and few people in postwar politics had more to teach than he did. These memoirs give a sense of his impact—but to appreciate his role more fully, you would have to interview all those politicians and journalists who were on the receiving end of Clif White's instruction over the years. And that would take a volume much bigger than this one.

He started out to be a teacher. And he never could shake the habit. From the classes he taught before World War II until the end of his life, he was always trying to improve people's understanding of the workings of politics and government. In our last conversation, he was as enthusiastic as he had been about Goldwater. But this time, he was excited about the work his foundation was doing in spreading the concept of democracy to nations which had long lived under tyranny. He was teaching the techniques and mechanisms that make democracy work to the emerging leaders of those lands.

It was, I can now see, the perfect way for Clif White to end his life. He had entered the political arena by helping organize the World War II veterans who had fought in the struggle to save the old democracies from extinction. He exited by bringing even deeper insight into the process to young people struggling to bring the new democracies to life.

Those experiences give a wholeness to Clif White's life that most of us would envy. But as I read these memoirs, there is another lesson that is equally important—the value of struggles that end in defeat.

Clif White lost almost as many battles as he won. But none, he says, more instructive than that first great fight for control of the American Veterans Committee, in which the man who would become the preeminent strategist of the political right found himself aligned with such left-wingers as Gus Tyler and David Dubinsky against their common enemy—the Communists.

The need for accurate intelligence and the imperative of political discipline that Clif White learned with and from them were the keys to his later success as an organizer. And yet, as we all know, his most famous organizing effort ended in what seemed to be political disaster.

When Barry Goldwater, Clif's candidate, went down to crushing defeat in 1964, the ruins seemed great enough to swallow up the hopes of the conservative movement and perhaps even end the century-old role of the Republican Party as a principal vehicle for millions of Americans' participation in politics.

It proved to be something else. Just as the battle against the Communist takeover of AVC gave an accelerated political lesson to scores of activists from Clif White to Dick Bolling, the late, great liberal Democratic representative from Missouri and congressional reformer, so the Goldwater movement seeded the careers of scores of people who went on to lead the GOP and the nation.

You can start with Ronald Reagan, who emerged as a national political figure in that campaign, and with George Bush, who gained public office for the first time as a Goldwater Republican in 1964. Of the men and women who now occupy the top tiers of Republican leadership, an astonishing percentage will tell you that they were "turned on" to politics—some of them while still teenagers—by the excitement of the Goldwater campaign.

Clif White understood this, as he understood most of the tidal forces in American politics, better than most others. Unlike most of today's political consultants, who have their eyes focused solely on the Election Day performance of their current clients, he took a long-term view of his responsibilities—and an institutional view. He cared more about the declining health of our political parties than almost anyone else I've ever known. He worried about both parties—although he was fiercely loyal to his own.

He understood, as Thruston Morton, the late senator from Kentucky and Republican National Chairman, used to say, that "the purpose of politics is the establishment of government." And he knew how difficult the challenge of governing had become in an era of splintered parties and decaying political institutions.

All this and a great deal more he imparted to me and to scores of others over a long and useful life. He did it cheerfully, never falling into the easy cynicism so many political pros affect. He was as jaunty as his inevitable bow-ties. He was special. And so is the book.

—David S. Broder
Washington, D.C.
September 1994

Prologue

Reagan. Nixon. Bush. Goldwater. Eisenhower. Dewey. This is their story as much as mine. It is the story of the American political system as I have known and lived it for over fifty years of my life. While most of my career has been spent helping Republicans get elected to public office, I have known and worked with Democrats as well, and the story I have to tell crosses party lines. This is at once a memoir and an insider's guide through the labyrinthine workings of the political system that existed during the second half of the twentieth century. By the time you finish this book, I hope you will understand as well as I do the politicians with whom I've worked and how a political campaign should be organized and structured—what works and what does not.

It is a great source of pride to me that some of the most respected politicians and political analysts in the country have had good things to say about the role I played in American politics. Theodore H. White (no relation), the renowned historian of presidential elections, once wrote: "[Clif] White became a technician of politics—one of the finest in America. As a specialist in politics—in petitions, organizations of meetings, nominations, convention tactics, floor seating, the buttoning of votes—White moved to lead, and hold the leadership of, the Young Republicans."

After I orchestrated his 1964 presidential campaign, Senator Barry Goldwater remarked, "Nobody knew as much about this country and the way it worked politically . . . as Clif White." Goldwater was a reluctant presidential candidate to the end, and it is a mark of his integrity that he blamed his loss to Lyndon Johnson that year as much on himself as on anyone else—as we will see in later chapters.

A Republican of a different stripe entirely, Governor Nelson Rockefeller of New York and vice president under Gerry Ford, referred to me as "one of the all-time greats in the political field," and former New York Senator James Buckley, brother of novelist and columnist William F. Buckley, Jr., said, "I admire Clif White's principle and high purpose every bit as much as the political skill for which he is renowned."

I recount these various accolades here not out of any sense of self-aggrandizement, but rather with a feeling of deep humility. Politics is the calling to which I dedicated my life. Today it is considered a synonym for deceit and corruption, and professional politicians occupy a level perhaps a notch or two above criminals in public esteem. It is good to know that there was a time in the nation's history when this was not the case. There was a time when politics was a noble calling, and the people who participated in it were men and women of high ideals with a genuine concern for the welfare of their fellow citizens— for the most part, at least. It is refreshing for me to know that a few people whom I admired and perhaps helped to achieve some of their nobler goals thought that I occupied a place in that better world, along with themselves.

That world is largely past. It will come as no surprise to anyone that the U.S. system of government is not working as well now as it once did; it is not working in the manner our forefathers intended it to work. Throughout the course of this book I explain a bit about why this is so, about the changes that took place along the way to derail the American dream, and about the steps we have to take to get back on track. The U.S. system of government and the Constitution upon which it is based are the noblest experiment in human affairs that the world has ever seen. We have not lost it forever—God forbid! But we have lost our way, and part of this book is about what we have to do to reclaim our birthright as free God-fearing and God-loving human beings.

Most of the people whom I served in one capacity or another over the years were decent and remarkable human beings. I cut my teeth in politics, so to speak, in the Dewey presidential campaign of 1948. Throughout the early 1950s I was part of his administration in Albany, and I worked with other Republicans around the country to elect Dwight D. Eisenhower president of the United States in 1952 and 1956. While my philosophy and temperament drew me to Republican and conservative causes throughout my life, I was also active in the American Veterans Committee—an organization that has been identified with the left wing of the political spectrum—after World War II. There I worked with Gus Tyler, an avowed democratic socialist whom I continue to respect and admire, in a successful effort to weed out Communist party members and other subversives from that otherwise excellent organization which served the interests of GIs admirably after the war.

The campaign for which I am perhaps best known, and which was simultaneously the most exhilarating and enervating endeavor of my entire life, was Barry Goldwater's bid for the presidency in 1964. In subsequent years I worked closely with Richard Nixon, Ronald Reagan, James Buckley, Gerald Ford, George Bush, and other politicians, as well as with many of their close advisers and supporters. In this book I describe their personalities, analyze their strengths and weaknesses, and shed light on why some of them were more successful than others.

Along the way I address some vital issues and questions. Why did Tom Dewey lose in 1948? What was Eisenhower really like? Kind and affable, or tough and shrewd? What did he really think of his vice president, Richard Nixon? Was Nixon popular with conservatives? What was the fatal flaw that led to his resignation from the presidency in 1974? Was Barry Goldwater refreshingly honest or self-destructively candid? What accounted for the euphoria of his supporters in 1964?

Was Ronald Reagan the intellectual lightweight his critics portrayed him to be—or a master politician with impeccable instincts? What role did his wife Nancy play in his administration? Among those who made up Reagan's inner circle—Jim Baker, Mike Deaver, Ed Meese, Bill Casey, and others—who helped him achieve his goal of launching a conservative revolution, and who held him back? Did Reagan's successor, George Bush, have any true ideological and philosophical convictions, or was he merely a political opportunist and bureaucrat as his critics have charged? Who will emerge as the Republican party leaders in the post-Bush years—Kemp, Quayle, Baker, Weld, Gramm, Powell, or someone else not currently in the running? These are just some of the people and topics I cover in this memoir.

In recent years I have served as chairman of the International Foundation for Electoral Systems, an organization dedicated to establishing democratic elections in countries throughout the world. I have advised a number of foreign governments on their own electoral procedures—among them Venezuela, the Dominican Republic, Costa Rica, Italy, Portugal, Spain, Greece, Russia and other former Soviet republics, as well as Eastern European countries formerly under Soviet domination.

The world today is undergoing some of the most dramatic and revolutionary changes that we have seen in decades. The collapse of communism has ushered in an era of tremendous opportunity, and great risk as well. In the years and decades ahead, we may witness an explosion of freedom and democracy on a scale unprecedented in human history, or be victimized by a long period of civil, political, and economic upheaval. It is up to us as human beings, calling upon the grace and good will of our Creator, to make the most of this newly discovered freedom.

This book is about the past and present, and about the future. It deals with the people who shaped the last fifty years of American history, and with the political system that has brought freedom and prosperity to so many Americans and become the envy of the world. As we face once again a critical time in our nation's history, we look toward the future with hope and optimism—and with caution. This is truly an exciting time to be alive and, like most exciting periods, it is both frightening and exhilarating.

All stories have their beginning and their end. While it is tempting to begin a story chronologically, it is sometimes instructive to start near the end where beginnings and endings come full circle. And so we begin here closer to the end, in a house in Connecticut, in the spring of a year when life began all over again.

1 A Second Beginning

My political career began back when I was too young to know any better, and it might have ended after my heart attack in 1978 were it not for a phone call from Bill Casey. I had spent the following months recuperating, not doing much of anything except trying to nurse myself back to health, when Casey called me in the spring of 1979. Bill and I had known each other off and on for the better part of thirty years at this point.

"Clif, I don't have anyone to BS with about politics anymore, now that old Len Hall is dead."

Len had been his law partner, as well as former national chairman of the Republican party and Dwight D. Eisenhower's campaign manager in 1952.

"I'll BS with you, Bill, if you're willing to buy me lunch."

"Sure, I'll buy you lunch."

Our lunch turned into a once-a-month occasion, with me traveling down to New York City from my home in Connecticut to meet him. Like me, Bill probably should have retired himself but, old war horse that he was, he couldn't let go. He belonged to every club imaginable and kept up a thriving law practice. Steeped in politics as we both were, our conversation inevitably turned to who might run for president in 1980. Even though I had recently been inactive in the aftermath of my heart attack, I did make a speech at California State University in Long Beach on October 8, 1979, during which I made perhaps the best prediction of my life: I said that the presidency was

1

Ronald Reagan's to win if John Sears didn't lose it for him. Get rid of Sears and his ill-serving advice, and Reagan would go on to win both the Republican nomination and the presidency. Those comments, I'm happy to say, were preserved on videotape.

Both Bill Casey and I felt that we were a bit too old to get actively involved in the campaign. Little did we know at the time that that was not to be the case. I was planning to attend a dinner in New York City at which Reagan would formally announce his candidacy, and Casey called me up about a week before the event and said, "Clif, I'd like you to be my guest at the dinner."

"I've already got my ticket."

"Good. You know I'm chairman of the dinner, don't you?"

"I thought we were out of politics, Bill."

"I agreed to chair the dinner, that's all."

Casey had also agreed to help out with the finances, but we both knew from past experience that you can't be only partly involved in a campaign any more than you can be partly married; either you're fully committed or you're not.

Even Ronald Reagan's severest critics acknowledged that he, among all the viable presidential candidates that year, had that certain star quality that all politicians would give their right arm to possess, but only a select few of them can claim.

I remember being at the governors' meeting in Colorado Springs after the 1966 election. It had been a great year for Republicans with Reagan elected governor of California, George Romney governor of Michigan, Ray Schaeffer governor of Pennsylvania, and Rockefeller still governor of New York. There were twenty-seven Republican governors in all.

I had worked a number of governors' conferences over the years, and I went to this one as much out of habit as for any other reason. I was standing in the reception area having a drink with broadcaster Sander Vanocur. Sandy was a good friend of mine whose politics were decidedly to the left, a bias he did not always try to hide. As we were standing there, milling around with all the other governors and media people, Ronald Reagan suddenly entered the lobby. You could feel his presence before you actually saw him and almost spontaneously, as it were, the attention of every man and woman there focused on the newly elected governor of California.

Sandy turned to me, his eyes bright and excited. "Did you see that? Did you see what happened when Reagan walked in? That's magic. George Romney was there; all the other governors were in the lobby at the time. But when Reagan entered the lobby, everyone stopped immediately and turned to him. Jack Kennedy had that magic, a few other politicians I've known have had it, and Reagan definitely has got it."

It wasn't the fact that Reagan had been a movie star. Other actors and celebrities blend into the furniture when they're off camera. It was a golden presence, a charisma, a magnetism, a *magic* as Sandy had described it, that goes beyond definition. You either had it or didn't, and it was not a quality that you could develop. Jack Kennedy had it, as Sandy had mentioned, and so did Ronald Reagan. He had just been elected governor of California, but he already had a presidential look about him—years before anyone knew that the thought of running for that office had entered his mind.

From the beginning of Reagan's 1980 presidential campaign, there were problems that were directly attributable to John Sears. Sears had managed Reagan's unsuccessful bid for the presidency in 1976, and he was brought back in as campaign manager by Mike Deaver in 1979. Sears accepted on the condition that he be given total authority, something for which I accept some blame myself. When he first got started in politics I told him that the campaign manager had to run the campaign, but I'm afraid he took that advice a bit too seriously. Reagan lost the Iowa caucuses largely because he did not campaign heavily there, on Sears's advice. Aside from Sears's mismanagement, there was also a good deal of infighting within the ranks. Mike Deaver and Lyn Nofziger had both been forced out and were to rejoin the campaign only after Sears left. The Reagan campaign had gotten off to a shaky start and appeared to be on the verge of self-destructing.

At this point I started getting telephone calls from Bill Casey as early as half past six or seven in the morning. At that hour I was usually doing laps in the indoor pool I had installed at the doctor's urging after my heart attack. Casey told me during these early-morning conversations that Reagan was talking to him about taking over as campaign manager.

"What do you think I ought to do?" Casey asked.

"Do you remember a philosophical conversation we had at one of our lunches?"

"What lunch are you talking about?"

"The one where we both decided that we were too old to do anything more in life except what we really want to do."

"Yeah, I remember that."

"So, do you want to be campaign manager or not? If you do, say yes. If not, say no. That's where we're at now."

"Well, I'll think about it."

The next time I heard from him he told me the Reagan camp was going to announce his appointment as campaign manager the day after the New Hampshire primary. I was shocked, completely stunned. I never thought he'd do it. Neither did most other political observers who understood the situation.

Many of those who staffed the campaign team that was already in existence had been part of my own organization during the Goldwater campaign of 1964. It was only natural that they would gravitate to Reagan since he offered conservatives the most dynamic and ideologically sound political campaign in sixteen years. When they heard about the Casey appointment, many of them were furious. One of my old crew, Andy Carter, had been deputy campaign manager under Sears, and now he didn't know where he stood. One by one they started calling me, asking what the hell this guy Casey was like. They had also demanded that Casey set up a strategy meeting with them in a hotel at Dulles Airport.

"Look, Casey's been around longer than you guys have," I explained to them when they called. "He likes to say that he always carried Len Hall's briefcase for him. A lot of us thought he was Len Hall's brains. I've known Bill since 1948 and he's a good guy, very competent."

They all flew into Dulles and met with Casey, and they called me between meetings for advice. I repeated essentially the same message I had been giving them all along. They were making all sorts of demands on Casey and I tried to calm them down. "He's a good guy. Give him half a chance. He knows politics inside and out."

They went back to their meeting with Casey and he apparently satisfied them the best he could. I never did tell Casey that I intervened on his behalf, but the day after the big powwow he called me up and said, "Thanks, Clif."

"What for?"

"For talking to your boys for me. They behaved very nicely in the end."

When Casey came back to New York he told me something that absolutely astonished me: the Reagan campaign did not have media people of any kind. This was another of Sears's incredible oversights. He did not have a reputation for being thorough, but it was beyond belief that he would have overlooked an area as critical as this. In this day and age you could not run an effective campaign without a media consultant.

"You've got to get one right away," I told Casey.

"Whom do you recommend?"

I told him I had high regard for both Roger Ailes and Pete Dailey. Bill asked me to set up a meeting with Ailes in New York and then accompany him on a trip to Washington to meet some other people. We had a good meeting with Ailes. On the flight down to Washington, Bill turned to me and said, "So tell me what Clif White's gonna be doing in this campaign."

"I'll be around. You know you can call me anytime you want."

"That's not good enough. You're going to have an office next to mine. First, we've got to get through the convention."

"Well, okay, I'll work on the convention for you. That's no problem since we'll have it won anyway. I know Bill Timmons and he's as good a convention man as you can find."

Timmons had been one of the young recruits who worked with me on the Goldwater campaign, and he had already signed up to work for Reagan as political director. I had a great deal of respect for him because he had beaten me in 1968 when I backed Reagan and he was Nixon's floor manager. Timmons showed me what he was capable of doing that year, and I regarded him as one of the best convention men in the country.

I agreed to work with Timmons on the 1980 convention, and I joined the campaign officially as a senior consultant, pretty much doing what I felt was necessary. The first time I went out to Detroit, some people met me on the grounds and said, "Here's your trailer, Mr. White."

"What do I need a trailer for?"

"Mr. Casey says you've got to have a trailer."

That amused me immeasurably since I had virtually invented the use of trailers at conventions, and Casey knew it. A well-equipped trailer serves as an excellent base of operations, and Casey had outfitted mine to the last detail. So I hopped aboard and orchestrated operations from inside while BT (Bill Timmons) ran the floor with his walkie-talkies. My job was easy since Reagan was a shoo-in for the nomination. When it was over, I assumed my role was over as well; I had only volunteered my services for the convention. So it came as something of a surprise when Casey asked me, "What're you gonna do now, Clif?"

"I'm going home, Bill. What else?"

"You can't do that. I just rented space in Arlington. We've got to leave tomorrow and go down there."

Bill Casey was a hard man to resist, but deep down inside those old political juices were starting to boil again. The truth was, I was spoiling for another political battle, after a few years on the sidelines. Politics is an addiction, and Casey knew it as well as anyone else. I was hooked after the convention; Casey had baited me well.

I flew down to Washington on Sunday right after the convention, and went out to Arlington, which became the official headquarters of the Reagan campaign. Casey apparently wanted to make sure I didn't get on the next plane and head back to New York, because no sooner had I arrived when some of his staff told me they had a nice apartment picked out for me.

That, too, proved irresistible, so I called my wife right away and described the view as I looked out a window of the apartment. She had always selected our living quarters ever since we were married. I might be able to run a presidential campaign, but when it came to renting apartments, that was Bunny's job. "Take it," she said. So I did, and we ended up keeping it for nine years, through the entire Reagan administration.

Casey kept his word and assigned me the office right next to his. My official title was senior adviser to the campaign manager, a function I shared with Jim Baker, who was brought on board shortly afterward. Jim had been George Bush's campaign manager, and Casey thought it would be a good idea to bring Baker aboard to incorporate the two camps into a united effort behind Reagan.

So, here I was back in the thick of things again when, only a short time before, I truly believed that my active political life had come to an end.

2 Let Reagan Be Reagan

The first time I met Jim Baker was in 1976 when Gerry Ford asked me to help him in his presidential campaign. Ford had succeeded to the presidency when Nixon resigned a couple of years earlier. Rogers Morton was Ford's campaign manager, replacing Bo Callaway, and I flew down to Washington to meet with him and the president.

"The first thing you've got to have is a delegate counter," I said.

"What do you mean?" Rog queried.

"You need one guy who does nothing but count how many delegates you've got lined up. That's absolutely essential."

They agreed, and I returned home to Greenwich. A few days later Rog called. "I've got that delegate counter. Why don't you come back down here and teach him how to do it?"

I went back down to Washington and met Rog in the campaign headquarters. After a few minutes of small talk, the door opened and a man whom I had never seen before entered the room.

"I'd like you to meet Jim Baker," Rog said. Baker had been Morton's assistant in the Commerce Department. "Jim's going to resign and become our delegate counter in the campaign."

I spent the next two days with Jim, explaining how you go out and get committed delegates and keep score on how many you've lined up. Jim was exceedingly bright. He learned quickly and performed his role well. By the time we went to the convention in Kansas City he had lined up enough delegates for Gerry Ford and had them under control. Baker and I went to our trailer, and I pointed to two facing seats—control seats—a strategy I had devised so that either of us could take over if the other was missing. I showed him the main one, the captain's or pilot's chair. "That's yours."

"No way. That's your seat. You tell me what to do."

So I did. I set up my operation there while both Jim Baker and BT, who was still political director, worked the convention floor. Gerry Ford, of course, succeeded in getting the Republican nomination and went on to lose the general election to Jimmy Carter—through no fault of Baker or Timmons. Ford lost it all by himself, and we'll talk more about that later. This was my introduction to Jim Baker, and I didn't see him again until I ran into him in a hotel lobby in 1979 when he was just starting to run George Bush's campaign for the presidency.

"How're things going?" I asked him.

"I just discovered that you can't run a presidential campaign from Houston."

"No question about that."

"So I've just moved to Washington to do the job right."

"Well, good luck." I didn't see Jim again until he walked into Reagan campaign headquarters in Arlington to share the title of senior adviser to the campaign manager with me.

Bill Casey presided over our strategy sessions every morning. Baker and I were there, as well as BT, who was now the vice chairman for organization; Pete Dailey, vice chairman for media; and Dick Wirthlin, vice chairman for research, who was essentially our pollster. Drew Lewis, representing the national committee, also attended. In addition to us, there was a traveling campaign staff that accompanied Reagan on the road. Mike Deaver was in charge of this group, and he coordinated his activities with both Casey and Wirthlin.

The campaign committee rented a large estate in Middleburg, about three-quarters of an hour west of Arlington in the lush, verdant Virginia countryside not too far from the Appalachian Trail. This became Ron and Nancy Reagan's home until after the election. The country surrounding the estate reminded me of the rolling green hills of Connecticut near my own home in Greenwich, so I felt at home out there when I went to visit. The location enabled those of us based at headquarters to travel back and forth easily, and to meet with the traveling staff and the candidate when they returned to Washington.

In early September 1980, Reagan had been on the road for a week or ten days when some problems developed, mostly with press relations. We thought it would be a good idea at this point to put someone on the plane with the candidate, someone with whom he felt comfortable, who could put him at ease. Jim Baker took me aside. "You couldn't go on the plane and ride with him, could you?" Jim knew that Reagan and I had always got along well, but ever since my heart attack my doctor had ordered me to nap in the afternoon.

"No, I'm sorry but I can't do it," I told Baker. I was truly sorry. Reagan and I had had a close relationship from the time he was governor of California. We belong to the same generation essentially; he's a few years older. Our ideas and political philosophies are close, and we could discuss events and experiences that we had both lived through. One of Reagan's chief speech writers, Tony Dolan, used to come to me to discuss an idea when he couldn't get in to talk to the candidate, and he'd go away saying, "I spoke to Clif, and I have a good idea of what Reagan would say about it." Since my health problems prevented me from assuming the role of traveling companion to the candidate, we asked Stu Spencer of California to take it on—which he did gladly.

We decided to have a meeting at the Virginia estate to discuss the campaign problems that had arisen at that time. Ron and Nancy Reagan had already relocated there from California. Our group included Bill Casey, Jim Baker, Ed Meese, Pete Dailey, Mike Deaver, BT. We sat there in the cavernous living room, forming a semi-circle around the candidate. Nancy hovered in the background, moving about and observing everything that took place. I could feel her presence, sensing her acute concern for everything that touched her husband.

The main problem, as I saw it, was that Reagan's traveling team was making him nervous and causing him to make mistakes. "If you leave him alone," I told the group, "and let him do what he wants to do, what he feels comfortable with, we won't have any problems. The problem is you guys, not him. Let Reagan be Reagan."

That was my phrase, the first time it had been used to the best of my knowledge. Jim Watt used it publicly in a speech after Reagan was elected, and that's when it caught on with the media and the public. Let Reagan be Reagan. Mike Deaver agreed with me, and so did Nancy, who always had impeccable instincts where her husband was concerned. As I recall, there was no real opposition to my position; we sat around discussing strategy for the campaign in general terms, Reagan taking it all in and flashing that famous boyish grin of his from time to time.

When the meeting broke up, I rode back to headquarters in Arlington with BT, Jim Baker, and Dean Burch, another Bush aide brought in by Baker. Suddenly Baker turned toward Burch and said, referring to Reagan, "He really isn't very smart, is he?"

"I disagree." I responded as though the remark were addressed to me. "Reagan is probably the most underrated man intellectually who's ever sought the presidency."

I knew the candidate much better than they did, and genuinely liked and admired the man. Burch and Baker had probably never met him prior to that meeting, and BT met him for the first time when the two of us flew out to California for a meeting before the convention. I had run Reagan's unsuccessful bid for the presidency in 1968, and I had known him when he was governor of California. He had the best political instincts of anyone I knew, and was bright and knowledgeable, although not overtly intellectual. My comment failed to convince Baker, however. Ironically, his association with Reagan throughout the years of his administration cemented Baker's political career. Without Reagan, Baker would most likely have returned to law practice in Texas and faded into the sunset.

Despite my misgivings about Baker's opinion of the candidate, I advised Casey to put him in charge of debate negotiations and preparations since Baker had more experience in the area than anyone else. He worked with Gerry Ford in 1976 and did a good job, notwithstanding Ford's losing effort. Casey agreed, and from that point on that was Baker's assignment in the campaign. We set up a mock television studio on the estate, where Baker rehearsed the candidate for his debates.

The first one was against John Anderson, a renegade Republican who ran as an Independent. Carter refused to participate. David Stockman had been Anderson's administrative assistant, and we persuaded him to stand in for Anderson during rehearsals. Stockman was so good at it that, at one point, he took a position with which Reagan disagreed intensely and got Reagan's Irish up. These sessions were held two or three times a day, with Baker coaching Reagan carefully.

I went out to the estate during the last practice session to observe what was going on, and saw that the candidate was handling himself well. I went up to him, put my arm around his shoulder, and said, "Now forget everything they told you during the last week. Just let your own computer regenerate the information and you won't have a single problem in the debate." I had great confidence in Reagan under those circumstances, and I didn't want him to be overcoached and tighten up.

I then went into the house and spoke to Nancy. "You'd better hide him away now. Don't let anybody talk to him between now and the debate tomorrow." Nancy had no problem with that whatsoever. She was his ultimate protector, and didn't like too many people closing in on her husband trying to tell him what to do. Letting Reagan be Reagan was something she had been doing instinctively throughout their marriage.

3 *The Troika*

Ronald Reagan was a natural performer, and most observers agreed that he was the more relaxed of the two major party candidates for president in 1980. The modern media being what they are, style unfortunately counts far more than substance in television debates. Performance—how one delivers his lines, who gets off the best one-liners—scores points with the voters. Reagan delivered the most memorable one-liner when he shook his head in his aw-shucks fashion, turned to Carter and said, "There you go again." Teaching Reagan how to play to the camera was an exercise akin to teaching a duck how to swim. Baker, to his credit, coached the candidate well, keeping him on target.

Baker's main fault, in my estimation, was that he had his own agenda which was not necessarily the president's agenda. He's an extremely bright, capable man, devoid of political philosophy or ideology. Many have described him as the ultimate pragmatist, others less charitably as a political opportunist. After the election, Jim was careful enough to avoid antagonizing Nancy Reagan and Mike Deaver, both of whom were protective of the president. He checked any ideas he had with Mike before presenting them to Reagan, but his pragmatism did eventually affect the direction of the Reagan presidency. This was a big problem for those of us who wanted to see Reagan fulfill his mandate. As we saw it, he was elected on the basis of a clearly defined sociopolitical philosophy, and this was being thwarted in too many areas by Baker.

Baker had gotten close to Reagan during those debate counseling sessions, and it seemed only a question of time before he and I locked horns. Just after the election I suggested to Casey that Reagan ought to create a position called political counselor to the president. "If you want to soften it," I told him, "you can call it public affairs counselor. But I think we ought to be right up front and say political counselor. I'd make it cabinet rank, or if not that, then this person ought to meet with the cabinet and make sure the administration fulfills Reagan's political agenda."

"That's a hell of an idea," Casey replied. "Why don't you write it up as a job description and show it to the president?"

The next time President-elect Reagan came to New York I met with him in the presidential suite at the Waldorf. I began by explaining my ideas on federalism. "This, to me, was the greatest concept our Founding Fathers instituted." I suggested that he establish a commission on federalism, with Paul Laxalt chairman. This Reagan did, putting me on the committee as well. The idea was that power is not reserved to the federal government but, rather, belongs to the states. We had drifted a long way from that notion, so I didn't expect Reagan to turn it around completely, but he did succeed in giving a lot more power back to the states. The governors were not too happy about that, nor was big business, which prefers to deal with one entity rather than fifty. This modified return to federalism, and Reagan's appointments to the federal court system, are, I believe, among the most lasting accomplishments of his administration. But Jim Baker did not care about any of that; these issues simply did not concern him.

Toward the end of our meeting, I took the political counselor job description from my pocket and handed it to the president-elect, intimating that I would be interested in the position for myself. I had told Casey that I did not want a regular job with the administration, but the role of political counselor was the only one I would have been interested in—and only for a while. My meeting was scheduled for thirty minutes, and after forty minutes or so Mike Deaver entered the room to remind Reagan that he had another appointment. As I left I had the impression that Reagan handed my job description to Deaver to look into, as most powerful people do with their aides.

Afterward, Casey asked me how the meeting went, and I told him it seemed to go well. That weekend Reagan returned to California with Deaver and Baker, Casey went home to Oyster Bay out on Long Island, and I went home to Greenwich. Sunday night I saw a report on ABC news that Lyn Nofziger was being appointed political director at the White House. No sooner did it air than my phone rang. It was Casey.

"Did you see ABC tonight?"

"I sure did."

"What the hell's that all about?"

"I have no idea. I don't know anything about it."

Before meeting with Reagan I had spoken briefly to Baker about the job. He asked to see a copy of the description—which I refused to show him. On Monday, after Baker flew back to Washington, Casey called him about the Nofziger appointment. "That was a job Clif could have done, and done well."

"You know those Californians," Baker replied. "They won't let us outsiders get too close to Reagan."

I learned later that Baker and Deaver, working together, had maneuvered to keep me out of the slot. This was a powerful post, one which gave the political counselor or director approval of personnel and other functions to ensure that the Reagan agenda was carried out. I knew Nofziger well and regarded him as a close friend, so I had no objection to his getting the job. Deaver had his own position to protect, and he knew he could work well with Baker, who was careful not to intrude on other peoples' turf as long as his own position was secure. Deaver didn't want me getting too close to the president, particularly where matters of policy were concerned, so he and Baker excluded me from the inner circle.

It was Mike Deaver who was primarily instrumental in establishing the so-called White House troika after Reagan was inaugurated. This consisted of himself, Baker, and Ed Meese, who was somewhat isolated by Deaver. Deaver was very close to Nancy, and he persuaded her that as fine a fellow as Ed Meese was, he was not as good a manager as Jim Baker, who could be trusted to serve the president's interests well. So Meese was kicked "upstairs" to become counselor to the president, a position which gave him access, but kept him away from the nitty-gritty daily activities, where the real power lay. Real power within the White House was maintained by Deaver and Baker, who were free to maneuver as they chose.

Mike Deaver established a reputation for being a shrewd public relations man, someone who invented the photo opportunity and other media events. I won't say anything against him since, I understand, he's rehabilitated himself since his downfall and is struggling to get back on his feet. But running PR for Reagan was an ideal setup for anyone, since he had perhaps the best innate publicity sense of anybody I've met.

With the troika established, Jim Baker was given a free hand in staffing much of the government. One of his appointments was selecting Rich Williamson as assistant to the president in charge of Intergovernmental Affairs. Rich was an ambitious young Republican who started out as Phil Crane's campaign manager when he first announced his own candidacy for the presidency. This position was an important post, and Rich visited me one day to discuss it.

"It's one of the most critical jobs in Washington," I told him. "You have to deal with mayors, politicians at different levels of government, coordinate policy with them, try to find common ground, and exercise a lot of influence. If you do it right, you can have a great impact on filtering Reaganism throughout the country."

"Well, I don't know much about it. I'm not sure I want it."

"In the first place, a bird in the hand's worth two in the bush. You get to move into the White House, and every time you move after that it's all upstairs. Once you put the White House on your résumé, everybody thinks you helped run the world. You'll be able to write your own ticket anywhere. I'd advise you to take it."

Baker originally liked Rich personally, recognized his skills, and actually ended up expanding the role for him. However, overly-ambitious, Rich was soon caught conspiring against Baker and was quietly eased out of the White House to a series of diplomatic posts before returning to a law firm in Chicago and an embarrassing race for the U.S. Senate in 1992.

Ironically enough for a man who had succeeded so well in two walks of life, first as an actor then in politics, Reagan had never developed a tight cadre of political advisers he could trust well enough to carry out his agenda. This made him vulnerable to political manipulation by the Jim Bakers and Mike Deavers of the world. Reagan never was a hands-on manager with a mind for detail like Jimmy Carter, who practiced it to a fault. Reagan had a grand vision centered in an ideology; he set a course, then delegated the job of following it to those around him. Unfortunately, some of those around him, the ones who accumulated most of the power in the Reagan White House, did not share the president's vision to the extent they should have.

The media made much of Reagan's so-called Kitchen Cabinet, which they thought was exercising too much influence on him. I got to know these people when I orchestrated Reagan's run for the presidency in 1968, and met with them regularly. William French Smith, Reagan's lawyer who later became attorney general, presided as a kind of chairman over the group. The money boys included Jack Hume, a San Francisco investment manager; Henry Salvatori, chairman of the Western Geophysical Company of America; Holmes Tuttle, who started as a Ford dealer in Oklahoma, made his fortune, and got along with Reagan better than any of the others; Justin Dart of Dart Drugs fame, who was as brusk and blunt and gruff as anyone I'd ever known; and A. C. Rubel, former CEO of Union Oil Company of California.

My impression was that the Kitchen Cabinet was not nearly as influential as the media feared, nor as it would like to have been. The money boys were certainly very close to Reagan, supported him, and raised a lot of the money that fueled his gubernatorial and presidential campaigns. They held meetings in California, made recommendations and, in some instances, lobbied for appointments of their own. They had some influence on high-level cabinet appointments, but virtually none on White House staffing.

Once Deaver and Baker's influence was secured, they were able to shut the money boys out, leaving the latter high and dry on the coast while the two of them, to a great extent, pursued their own agenda, which only occasionally dovetailed with that of the president.

4 Pragmatists and Opportunists

To understand a lot of what was going on behind the scenes in the White House, it helps to understand the history of the man who succeeded in maneuvering himself closest to the president. Reagan had three close political associates from California: Bill Clark, a state supreme court judge who was perhaps the closest of all in the early days; Ed Meese, who became chief of staff after Clark; and Mike Deaver.

Deaver had started off playing piano in a bar. Next he tried to sell insurance. Finally he met Bill Clark, who hired him to work in Reagan's first gubernatorial campaign. All of a sudden, Mike had a mission. Reagan became his whole life. When Ed Meese became chief of staff in Sacramento, he promoted Mike Deaver to be his assistant. It didn't take Deaver long to figure out that the key to getting through to the governor was his wife Nancy.

Nancy wanted Ron home at five o'clock; Deaver made sure he got home at five. He picked up Nancy's groceries along the way, catered to her every whim, and took care of the governor for her. Because he could play the piano, he was always fun for Nancy to have around at parties. Deaver ingratiated himself totally with Nancy and, through her, with Ron. He was her key to the governor's office, she was his to the governor. Whenever she asked him, which was fairly often, Deaver would exert pressure on Ed Meese to change Reagan's schedule to conform with Nancy's needs. Most wives think that their husbands ought to spend more time at home, and Nancy was no exception.

I don't know whether people like Mike Deaver have a congenital instinct for their role in life, or if they have to cultivate it. But Deaver had a peculiar talent. He seemed to know instinctively that no one else should be permitted to get as close as he was to his bread and butter. It's partly cunning and planning, and there's certainly enough of that to go around in the political arena. But with Deaver it seemed to go beyond mere Machiavellian maneuvering. It was almost as though existence itself depended on his lifeline to the governor. Ed Meese was not really a problem for him. Meese is very serious, and concerns himself with the serious problems of the world. He was valuable to the governor in matters of policy, but never a close social companion to Ron and Nancy.

Deaver's biggest worry was Bill Clark, the guy who rescued him from obscurity and invited him onto the Reagan bandwagon in the first place. Clark was serious, like Meese, but also socially acceptable to Nancy. Later on, after Reagan was elected president, the common wisdom had it that either Ed Meese or Bill Clark would be appointed chief of staff. I don't remember at exactly what point it was that Nancy shifted from being pro-Clark to violently anti-Clark, but there was no question in my mind that Deaver had a hand in her transformation. Her anger at Bill grew over the years, as she made clear in her memoirs, until she eventually cut him out of the Reagan inner circle. Meanwhile, Deaver established the troika in the fall of 1980, positioning Baker as chief of staff and himself as the main barrier between Reagan and those of whom Deaver disapproved.

In 1976 Deaver succeeded in keeping me out of Reagan's presidential bid, even though Ron had originally thought I would participate. I sent word to the governor that I would like to meet him for dinner the next time he was in Washington. Deaver called me to say that Reagan was coming to town, and wanted me to have dinner with him at his suite at the Madison Hotel. I assumed we would be dining alone, but when I got there Mike Deaver and John Sears were also on hand. Mike arranged to leave, but Sears remained throughout the entire affair and directed the conversation to the most inane topics imaginable.

Reagan and I enjoyed a drink, then the governor laughed and said,

"We know what you're drinking, John, don't we?" Sears's drinking problem was no secret to anyone, so he stuck to club soda for the evening in deference to Reagan. After dinner Sears and I said good-bye, then he went downstairs to the bar where he switched to scotch. I had known John ever since he had started out in politics with Richard Nixon. He was always pleasant enough, but it was abundantly clear to me that he, like Deaver, was more interested in serving his own agenda than Reagan's.

It didn't take long for the conservatives who had supported Reagan—Bill Casey, Caspar Weinberger, myself, and others—to grow exasperated with the direction in which Deaver and Baker were steering the Reagan White House. There were many who shared our views. One by one, we sent various emissaries in to speak to Reagan, but it soon became apparent that as long as Deaver and Baker were in charge over there nothing was going to happen. Finally, I asked to see Reagan myself in the spring of 1983. My request was granted. The appointment was set for 4:00 P.M., and as I entered the East Gate and started walking up the driveway, Assistant Political Director Lee Atwater came out to greet me. He looked worried and said, "My God, Clif, what happened?"

"What do you mean?"

"You were scheduled to have lunch with the president."

"No way. I'm scheduled to meet the president at four o'clock this afternoon."

"Well, the president was waiting for you for lunch."

"Well, I'm sorry, but my date is at four o'clock."

"Okay, let's go over to the reception area and see if we can get you in."

We walked across the towering colonnade that imparts a sense of history and power to everyone who passes by, and entered the lobby. Mike Deaver came out and apologized for the mix-up. "We'll go up to the residence now."

The president was there waiting for us. We were in the living quarters of the White House, and the casual informality of the setting was somewhat at variance with the historical importance of our meeting.

We said hello and sat down in chairs facing the president. I began, "Do you want to make this private, Mr. President? If so, we'll at least know who leaks it to the press." He laughed at that.

When I first met Reagan years ago, I had advised him not to let anyone come into his office with a plan for running his administration, without offering an alternative as well. "Any idiot can offer advice, but it should at least have a constructive alternative so you have a choice to make."

Here I was many years later meeting with President Ronald Reagan, trying to convince him that it would be better to reorganize his entire government. Baker, I had heard, really wanted to be secretary of state, but I thought he would be better off directing the CIA than where he was. We had enough institutional strength there to rein him in a bit. I explained this to the president. I also suggested that Bill Casey should be rewarded by being named ambassador to Ireland, something I believed he was well suited for. I had a laundry list of proposals for an entire restructuring of the administration, and I went through it as straightforwardly and as forcefully as possible. The president would be better served by appointing a person who was totally committed to fulfilling the Reagan agenda.

Breaking up the troika was, of course, my main objective, and I laid it straight out on the line, figuring this would be my one and only opportunity to present my case to Reagan. Deaver and Atwater sat there silently, squirming in their seats, while Reagan listened attentively without commenting. Finally, I motioned toward Deaver. "You've got to turn Mike out, Mr. President. Mike's got to make some money. The poor guy hasn't made any money all his life, and if he goes out there now while he's still on top, he can make a fortune. Nobody deserves that more than he does."

Deaver and Atwater were speechless as the president took it all in. My meeting had been scheduled for half an hour, and at this time somebody knocked on the door several times. We had already run beyond the allotted time. The president stood up, which was our cue to do the same. He stepped forward, extended his hand, looked me straight in the eye and said. "Clif, I really appreciate this very much."

We said good-bye, and Deaver, Atwater, and I left the room. Lee was visibly shaking; I could sense that he would rather have been any-where else than in that room during the meeting. When the three of us got into the elevator, Deaver turned to me and said, "Clif, I couldn't disagree more with what you said in there."

"Fine, Mike, that's your privilege clearly. We're all entitled to our opinions, and this is mine."

When we exited from the elevator, Deaver continued on his own way and Lee walked with me across the colonnade. He was extremely agitated. "I shouldn't have been there. I shouldn't have heard any of this. I don't want to know anything about it."

I told him I wouldn't say a word about it to anyone; it was strictly a private matter among those of us who were in the room with the president. I kept my word on that. But Mike went back and immedi-ately reported what was said to Jim Baker. I found this out later from a friend who was close to Baker. According to this source, Deaver and Baker both agreed that they "didn't want Clif White to set foot inside the White House ever again." Deaver's report to Baker made the rounds of the administration insiders, and it didn't take long before a number of them were talking about it.

As we got closer to the 1984 campaign, I called up Baker's secre-tary and asked her to put a memo on her boss's desk. "To him, from me. Subject: '84 campaign. I want it to say this: I have had perhaps more experience than anyone in dealing with incumbent presidential campaigns and the role of chief of staff. If you think this experience would be of any value to you, I would be happy to provide it. Period."

Baker called me shortly after he read it. "The last time you were down here, Clif, you tried to get me fired."

"That's not exactly accurate. I'd be happy to discuss it with you if you want to. But what I said in my memo is what I mean. I know the problems a chief of staff has with incumbent presidents running for reelection. I was there when Eisenhower did it, when Nixon did it, when Gerry Ford did it. So I'm offering my experience."

"Well, okay, I appreciate that. When can you come down?"

"You tell me. You're the busy man, not me."

"Can you be here tomorrow afternoon at four o'clock?"

"I'll see you then."

In his office the next day we sat facing each other, near the fireplace. "I didn't try to get you fired," I told him right away. "I was trying to reorganize the structure of the White House for what I considered to be the president's benefit. My only interest is what is best for Ronald Reagan. I didn't depreciate you in any way and actually suggested a more suitable role for you."

This appeared to mollify him, and I went on to discuss the forthcoming campaign. "The chief of staff has to run the campaign. He has to make sure the government and the campaign both run smoothly at the same time. You have to be on top of what the president says in his statements and speeches. If you want my best advice, let the other guys do all the mechanical things—hire airplanes and so on—and you concentrate on the key areas. Basically, let Reagan do what he does best. He knows instinctively where to go; his political instincts are impeccable. He'll win bigger than before and you'll end up being the greatest presidential campaign manager in history. You'll be the guy who put it all together."

Baker thanked me, walked me to the door, and told me to feel free to call him during the campaign whenever I felt I could be of service. I followed up on his offer, and our relationship became cordial after that. He always listened attentively and returned phone calls. But I don't have any illusions about his motivation. Jim Baker will always do what he thinks is best for Jim Baker. He remembers past grievances, but he's the kind of person who won't let them get in the way when he thinks you can help him. Pragmatist or opportunist? Hard to say. It's not always possible to understand the difference.

5 A Pioneer Spirit

Ronald Reagan was chosen by history to fill the political vacuum on the Right created by Goldwater's defeat in 1964. He happened to be the right man in the right place at the right time, and he accepted that with genuine humility. He was committed to the conservative cause first and foremost, not to the idea of being president. The roles of governor and president sought him out.

There are so many bits and pieces to a person's life, fragments of a mosaic, that it is difficult to say which are most instrumental in determining the kind of life we eventually lead. What makes some of us liberals and others conservatives, some Jews and Catholics and others Protestants, some artists and others businessmen and politicians? Our circumstances at birth have a lot to do with it, along with the myriad of experiences we encounter throughout our lives.

In the shaping of my own political career, it is not easy to identify the events that were most influential. Looking back over a lifetime which was spent, for the most part, promoting a political cause in which I fervently believed, I can point to numerous incidents that appear significant. I begin with the circumstances of my birth.

Among my ancestors are the Pilgrim Miles Standish, and Deborah Sampson, our country's first woman soldier. At the age of twenty-two, she dressed as a young man, took the name of Robert Shurtliff, and joined Washington's army. Only after she was wounded did a surgeon discover she was a woman.

My mother's father, Grandfather Hicks, fought for the Union army during the Civil War as one of the North's first volunteers, then traveled west to Montana in the war's aftermath, bringing his wife, four children, and a hired hand. This part of the country was wild and dangerous before the turn of the century, yet they traveled alone without the security of a wagon train.

When they arrived in Montana, they homesteaded a piece of land and moved into a sod hut while my grandfather built the first frame building ever seen in that part of the nation. Money was scarce. One day Grandfather reached into his pocket and produced a silver dollar, all the money they had left in the world. And they had only enough flour to last them a few days. So he left his family and went to the settlement in Billings, looking for work. The railroad was hiring men to lay track for the trains that were due to come through town, so Grandfather settled into a routine, working in town, and finishing off the family house.

They got along fine with the local Indians, who came by to trade for goods they didn't have themselves. One of Grandmother's favorite ways of disciplining my mother was to threaten to trade her to the Indians if she didn't behave herself. The family's only real threat when Grandfather was away came from other white settlers, some of them claim jumpers looking to grab someone else's property after it had been developed.

One such interloper rode up on horseback one afternoon and stopped menacingly just outside the fence. Grandmother never did learn to shoot properly, but she went outside with Grandfather's six-shooter beneath her apron and asked the stranger what he wanted. He told her they were trespassing on his claim, and he was coming in. At that point she produced her weapon and told him to move on. The man eyed her coldly, trying to intimidate her, but she stood her ground with fire in her own eyes. Finally, he reined his horse around and galloped off.

Throughout Grandfather's life he had always taken off for periods of time, weeks or months, prospecting for gold or trying to strike it rich some other way, but he had always sent money home to his family as soon as he earned it. His firstborn son was like him in spirit. He too left home at an early age to find his own fortune, wandering as far north as Alaska, looking for that elusive pot of gold. He never married or settled down. Mother's younger brother Clifton, the one after whom I was named, was a different sort entirely. Like his father he worked for the railroad. Unlike his father, he stayed home, established his roots, married, and raised a family.

My mother, Mary Eaton Hicks, was a pioneer like her parents and older brother. She was looking for adventure of her own when she met my father, Frederick Herbert White, in Montana. He had graduated from business college in upstate New York and migrated westward. Shortly after they married, they moved to New York State, where Grandfather had been born. Life had come full circle in a sense. It was not yet the turn of the century, and my father imagined that he was a farmer, a notion he would be disabused of before long.

6 _My Training Begins_

They settled on the farm that had been in my father's family for over a century. It had been granted to one of his ancestors as a reward for his services during the Revolutionary War. Many said the old soldier had been cheated, for the farm was little more than a parcel of land on a hill in a valley just outside of Leonardsville. No one had ever been able to grow anything there. Dad was no exception. Mom did manage to give birth twice before she and Dad moved into town. Leonardsville had a population of five or six hundred at the time.

After the move they had two more children. I was the last, born on June 13, 1918, when Mother was forty-eight years of age. I was more than twenty years younger than my brother Ernest Herbert and oldest sister Hattie, and a decade separated me from my older sister Arnelda. Mom and Dad had wanted to name their third-born, whom they hoped would be a son, after Doctor Arnold, the family physician, but settled on the name Arnelda after deciding that Arnoldine wasn't quite suitable. I passed Arnelda along to my own daughter as a first name later on, something for which I believe she will never forgive me.

Having demonstrated that farming—at least farming on that old patch of barren family land—would not put enough food on the table for his growing family, Father opened a general store, and later a silent movie theater, in Leonardsville. These ventures enabled him to eke out a living. After a while he got a job selling fertilizer and farm supplies to farmers in the region. His travels convinced him that we would

31

all be better off moving to a place called Earlville, which was situated between Utica and Binghamton, New York. One of the most vivid memories from my early youth is riding in a horse-drawn sleigh from the train station, where we had just arrived, through the snow to our new house. I was three or four years old at the time.

There were two trains that stopped at Earlville on different tracks on opposite sides of town. One set of tracks was laid by the Delaware Lackawanna and the other by the Ontario and Western Railroad. The state had built canals, one of which ran through Earlville. The east and west branches of the Chenango River also ran through Earlville, making it ideally situated for boat traffic on the canal. I remember playing near some of the old aqueducts around town when I was a kid. When the tracks were laid for the railroads, they tended to follow the canals because that's where the towns had sprung up. One line was built running south out of Utica, another north out of Binghamton, with both of them passing through on either side of Earlville.

At the time the largest employer in town was the Lowdown Wagon Works, which built horse-drawn wagons for milk delivery. The company got its name from the type of wagon it made—a long one built "low down" in the middle so the delivery man could easily step down to the ground with his milk bottles. Hattie's husband went to work there, and they moved right across the street from our house. Sadly, Hattie died while giving birth to her second child, a boy who lived.

My brother Ernest, married and childless, offered to adopt the boy. He and Hattie had only been a year apart in age, and they were very close. His brother-in-law agreed to the adoption, keeping his firstborn child, a girl, and giving the boy to Ernest and his wife. No sooner did that happen than Ernest's wife, who had previously been unable to conceive, became pregnant and delivered a girl before her adopted son was a year old. I was only a few years older than they were, and remember watching them grow up together.

Ernest had been teaching in Poughkeepsie, south of Albany along the Hudson River. Around 1927 he moved his family farther south to White Plains in Westchester County, where he was the head of the science department in the high school. He developed the entire concept of adult education and was referred to as the "Dean" of that field.

Initially, adult ed was little more than citizenship training for immigrants who needed to learn the fundamentals of the United States Constitution, as well as a modicum of English. During the Great Depression, Ernest expanded the curriculum to include other courses. For example, he introduced a course for teaching women how to understand sports, and invited the unions in to teach people practical skills, such as how to do repairs around the house. *Time* did a piece on him and his innovations in the field.

With his family growing up around him, my father soon tired of all the traveling he was doing. So he bought eight acres of land on the edge of Earlville and put up one of the first Socony Mobil Service Stations ever built. We all took turns pumping gas and selling oil. After a while mother made sandwiches there and served lunch and hot meals to the customers.

Dad still had notions about being a farmer, and he bought some chickens and a couple of cows for milking. Since I was a sickly kid, they nourished me by feeding me warm milk right from the cows. They used to sell eggs and milk to the neighbors who came in with their own quart cans. My chores around the family business included pumping up the gas in the morning to get the hoses flowing, pumping gas for our customers and, perhaps worst of all, whitewashing the cobblestones at the entranceway to the gas station each spring, a task that had to be completed by Memorial Day. I used to ride my bicycle to the station, since our house was only about a mile and a half away.

By today's standards, people might regard our life in Earlville as harsh, but we didn't see it that way. We did what we had to do to survive, without complaining, and everyone else did the same. There was a sense of community, a feeling that we were all part of one another's lives, all involved in a common heritage as children of a larger family that extended beyond the boundaries of our town. If parents saw neighbor children misbehaving, they didn't hesitate to speak to them about it and bring it to the attention of their own parents, something for which everyone was grateful. If parts of the whole failed to function, the entire community suffered for it in some way. This feeling of belonging and sense of community are largely gone today, along with many other values, in a predominantly transient society. I believe we are all worse off for it.

Today many parents don't begin raising a family until they're in their late thirties and early forties, so it is not unusual to see fathers in their fifties and sixties going to Little League games with their young children. In those days most women married young and were already old by thirty-five after raising a batch of children. My parents were old for their time when they had me, but Mother was as active as any of the younger parents when I was in school, attending PTA meetings and other school functions. Dad ran the gas station from six in the morning until nine at night, seven days a week, plus there was the farm to run. He was also active with the Masons. So I was fortunate in that I did not feel ostracized or deprived in any way because my folks were twenty years older than my schoolmates' parents.

The usual childhood ailments that parents take for granted today, such as measles, mumps, and chicken pox, were life-threatening when I was a kid, before serums were developed. One of the more serious ones was scarlet fever; several of my friends almost died from it. I caught it myself, was quarantined for thirty days, but got through it in good shape. The town librarian would visit me with copies of *Boy's Life* and other magazines, which could be destroyed when I finished with them. Books were taboo since everything I touched had to be fumigated to avoid contaminating everyone else.

Sickly as I was, it was only natural I suppose that I would not excel in sports. Before I graduated from high school, however, I grew to my full height, six-feet-one. Since I was tall for that period, I attempted to learn to play basketball. I studied books on the subject and practiced with a basketball my father bought me. By my senior year I made the school team and turned into a fairly decent player.

My academic record was somewhat less than admirable. I applied myself to the pursuit of girls instead of to my studies. At one point my father said to me, "Clif, you'd be surprised at what you might find between the pages of a book." Notwithstanding my lack of scholarship, my parents were determined that I was going to college. At their insistence, along with the discipline of my teachers (corporal punishment was most definitely not considered taboo before World War II),

I managed to get passing grades my senior year. I joined clubs, was elected president of my class by my third year, and eventually squeaked through.

While sports and academics didn't come naturally to me, public speaking did; I suppose I was born contentious and had a natural flair for verbal theatrics. I loved the give and take of opposing points of view, and joined the school public speaking team. The night of the finals in my senior year, Dad stayed home with a case of angina and Mom stayed with him to nurse him along. I won the finals and raced home to tell them; both of them were happy, but not unduly surprised that I had succeeded in winning at "talking up a blue streak," as they put it. Mother, in particular, always maintained a positive attitude. There wasn't anything people couldn't achieve, she believed, if they applied themselves to the task.

My lack of scholarship in high school was somewhat at variance with the record of my siblings. My brother wrote the Regents Physics textbook, taught science, and developed adult education as I mentioned. He helped tutor me in my courses. My sister Arnelda graduated from New York University and became an English teacher. Mother viewed my own lack of scholarly achievement as obstinacy on my part more than anything else, and refused to give up on me, fortunately. She had been the disciplinarian ever since I was born, and practiced what she preached. I remember once going to a movie without her permission, and coming home to find all the doors locked. I was scared and kept ringing the bell, until finally she came down and said, "Clifton, if it weren't for that doorbell, you wouldn't be allowed in tonight. Now go to bed."

My high school graduation class consisted of twenty-seven students, myself included. I applied to Colgate University, which was only six miles from our house, a distance that would enable me to live at home and help out in the family business while I commuted to classes. Fortunately, the principal of my high school was a Colgate graduate, and he intervened on my behalf. My grades were undistinguished at best, but I passed the Regents exams and the dean at Colgate said to me, "Young man, there is very little in your record that suggests I should let you enter Colgate, but I'm going to take a chance on you anyway."

Dad's angina was growing worse, and he passed away in July 1936 before my freshman year began. Mother was left with the gas station and the farm with two cows and about a thousand chickens. A couple of businessmen in town, smelling blood, tried to buy the farm at a bargain price, but the Mobil Oil Company came to her assistance. Mobil had a lease on the land, and advised her to bundle the farm and gas station together as a package and the company would go along with her. She managed to hang on for a couple more years, with me working the gas station and going to school and a hired man helping her work the farm.

Raising chickens was tricky since they are among the most stupid creatures on earth. If the heat in their shed wasn't kept at the proper level, they would pile on top of one another near the fire and smother the ones on the bottom, wiping out half of your investment. I remember having to sleep next to the shed in the winter, checking on them every once in a while to make sure they weren't about to trample themselves to death. We kept this somewhat less than ideal routine going right through my sophomore year, when Mother was able to sell both the farm and gas station at a reasonable price.

Money was scarce after Dad died, particularly in the beginning, so I borrowed from my brother and my sister Arnelda to pay the first year's tuition of three hundred dollars. After that, I put my speaking skills to work and earned a debating scholarship; playing basketball at Colgate was out of the question with the grinding schedule I had. I enjoyed college a lot more than high school, responded to the challenge, and earned considerably better grades. I joined clubs, and was elected president of the local chapter of Delta Sigma Rho, the national honors debating fraternity.

My speaking ability earned me some pocket money, too. I was paid the grand sum of forty cents an hour to tutor other students in public speaking, and made about fifteen dollars a speech hitting the Kiwanis and Rotary Club circuit. I thought I was studying to become a teacher. Little did I know at the time that I was already in training for a political career, years before it actually began.

7 *A Schoolteacher?*

It's difficult to believe now, but back then Colgate had a truly great football team. Before I arrived it had had a perfect season, and the university was criticized for emphasizing the sport too much. So the administration went to work building an equally strong debating team for balance. By the time I entered Colgate it was one of the best in the country.

The Daughters of the American Revolution needed a speaker one day. My debating coach tapped me, and offered me a piece of advice that turned out to be invaluable. "Wear your tuxedo. The old dears will love you."

He was right on the money; they loved me so much that they paid me fifty dollars. They kept inviting me back for the next two years, eventually paying me seventy-five dollars a speech, a lordly sum for a college student in the 1930s. The specter of a gangly young man all decked out in a tux and black tie had them all aquiver.

One of my predecessors on the debating team was a young man named Burdell Bixby, about whom we'll hear more later when we talk about the Dewey administration. Bix, four years ahead of me, was on the team when Colgate won all the eastern intercollegiate debating championships, a record we maintained throughout my own tenure there. I traveled around the country with the team, usually by car, and on one tour through the Midwest I surprised myself by telling our coach, who also happened to be a local Democratic politician, "Maybe I'll take a look at politics myself. I find it very interesting."

"Don't do that. Forget about taking a look at it."

"Why do you say that?" I wanted to know.

He studied my six-feet-one, one hundred and thirty pound frame. "I don't think you can handle it, son. It requires a lot of physical stamina."

That rankled me then and for many years afterward. One of my big regrets in life was that he wasn't around in 1964 when I orchestrated the Goldwater campaign for president and, in the process, somehow survived a grueling schedule that might have put some people in the hospital. Looking back now, however, his remark may well have been the spark that inspired me to prove he was wrong. There is no question that my debating experience in college spurred me on along that long, arduous, road into the political arena.

Among my courses at Colgate was one on international law, at the end of which we had to argue a case in a mock courtroom setting. The dean of Syracuse Law School was the "judge." The students were divided into teams of "lawyers," two on a side. My partner did the research, and I was chosen to plead our side of the case. We lost, as I recall, but I apparently managed to impress the dean of Syracuse Law nonetheless. My professor called me in and said the dean wanted to speak to me privately. So I drove out to Syracuse a few days later. He asked me if I had been entertaining thoughts about going to law school.

"Can't afford it," I told him. Actually, I hadn't thought about it at all, and his question surprised me.

"I think I can arrange a scholarship for you."

That got my attention in a hurry. I thanked him profusely and promised I would think seriously about it now. His offer put me in a quandary since I had already met my future wife, Gladys (Bunny) Bunnell, and we had been making plans to get married after I graduated in 1940. I had assumed, without developing a detailed scenario for the future, that I would do what all young married men do when they get married—get a job and support my wife. The notion of her working while I continued my education did not sit well with me. Bunny and I discussed it, and she was completely supportive of anything I chose to do. In the end I decided to turn down the dean's offer and pursue a teaching career. Considering the course my life has taken over the years, I couldn't help but wonder later on if it wouldn't have been smarter for me to get that law degree. In the United States at least, politicians and lawyers are practically synonymous; the two professions are bound together for better or worse (worse, I think) in a symbiotic embrace. But nobody gets a chance to rewrite history, and I'm no exception.

In marked contrast to my high school years, I graduated with honors from Colgate, and Bunny and I were married on June 22, 1940. A month earlier I had signed a contract with the Ravena public school system to teach social science and head up the department. Ravena was a small town south of Albany, a few miles inland from the west bank of the Hudson River.

Before I went to work, however, Bunny and I had a honeymoon awaiting us. We decided to drive across the country to see the World's Fair in San Francisco. Unlike my mother, who had traveled through a good part of the nation in a covered wagon, we had the benefit of motor transportation. We traded in our old cars for a new four-door Plymouth, altered to our own specifications which included a mattress in the rear instead of a back seat. These were the days before credit cards, when people had to pay for things with cash instead of mortgaging their futures. The simple fact was, we couldn't afford to stay in a hotel room every night.

We reached Chicago in time for the 1940 Democratic National Convention, without really planning it. At the time the national chairman of the Democratic party was Jim Farley, and I knew the name of his assistant. I went looking for him, hoping to use my powers of persuasion to secure a couple of admission tickets. But Bunny hit on a more novel approach. She simply went up to Vince Daley, who ran the Democratic party in New York State, told him that we were honeymooners from New York, and that it would mean so much if we could get in to see the convention. Her direct approach worked like magic. Ironically enough for someone who ended up spending most of his life getting Republicans elected to office, this was the first convention I ever attended.

The wheeling and dealing on the convention floor mesmerized me as nothing else ever did, but I continued to operate under the delusion that I wanted to be a schoolteacher. We returned to Ravena after our honeymoon. I applied myself in the classroom and also instituted a brand-new social studies program for grades seven through twelve. I continued to speak before local groups, such as Rotary and Kiwanis, and after a while our landlord and landlady began to take an interest in my activities. They were active in the Democratic party, and friends of Erastus Corning, the perennial mayor of Albany. They asked me if I would like to meet him.

It helps to understand New York State politics during that era. Albany County was run with an iron fist by the O'Connell political machine. "Uncle Dan" O'Connell was the family patriarch; nothing got done inside Albany County, no stone was turned, no decision implemented without Uncle Dan's approval. Erastus Corning was a scion of an old established, well-known family in the area. Even so, when Erastus decided that he wanted a career in politics, he needed to get the blessing of Uncle Dan, who was the political equivalent of a Mafia Don. After Dan O'Connell got Corning elected to the state assembly, Corning made the mistake of not showing up to vote on an issue that Uncle Dan deemed important. He suffered for his breach of faith, but later made peace with Dan O'Connell, convincing the old man that he had learned his lesson well. O'Connell finally tapped him to run for mayor.

Getting the Democratic nomination for anything in Albany County was tantamount to victory; Republicans, at the time, offered only token opposition. Corning became Albany's mayor and remained in that office—except for a leave of absence during World War II—until he died. Getting an audience with Erastus Corning was like being introduced to the man who sat at the right hand of God, as far as the local political hierarchy was concerned. I jumped at the opportunity and met him for lunch one day, during which he questioned me about some of the speeches I had been making to various civic organizations. Afterward, he invited me to accompany him on the walk back to his office.

"Are you interested in politics at all?" he asked me.

"I don't know. I don't know much about it, but I might be."

"Come on inside." He invited me into his office. "Do you ever go down to New York City?"

"Once in a while."

To my astonishment, Corning picked up his telephone and called Vince Daley, the very man from whom my wife had gotten those tickets to the Chicago convention, at his office in New York. "Vince, I got a young man in my office here, fellow named Clifton White, a schoolteacher in Ravena. Says he might be interested in politics. I think we ought to use him. He's a good man. I'd like him to stop in and see you next time he's down your way."

I was stunned, completely bowled over. No one had ever tried to recruit me for politics before; indeed, the only time I mentioned to someone that I found it interesting, I was told to forget about it; I didn't have the stamina. Now, the mayor of Albany was extending an invitation and opening the door for me, without my even asking. Later on, throughout my career as a Republican party operative, I had to make all the inroads on my own.

I never did take Corning up on his offer to recruit me, and to this day I'm not sure why. There's no question that had I taken advantage of his generosity, I could have made more money than I was making as a schoolteacher. My political philosophy at the time was not yet clearly defined. My father was a Republican, and I had a vague notion that that's what I should be, too. Dad voted in every election, and he believed others should exercise their franchise as well. I can still remember his shouting in celebration from the front porch of our house in Earlville when Herbert Hoover was elected president in 1928. His excitement spilled over onto me, and I thought politics must be really fascinating if Dad got worked up about it like that. But later on, as I stood in Corning's office after lunch, I had yet to develop a clear ideology of my own.

I continued to teach in Ravena, earning the grand sum of $1,200 a year initially. A raise the next year brought me up to $1,400, which I accepted even though I was offered another teaching job farther upstate for two hundred dollars a year more. On Sunday morning, December 7, 1941, Bunny and I returned from church and went to a movie in Albany. On the way home we turned on the radio and heard the shocking news that the Japanese had bombed our military base in Pearl Harbor.

My wife and I stared at each other in stricken silence. I stopped at the first open store I could find and bought special editions of every newspaper I could get my hands on to read the early news of the attack. Today the television cameras and reporters are on the scene instantly, recording historical events for posterity as they happen. In 1941 television was not yet available to the public, and the instantaneous transmission of news and information was way off in the future. People discovered what was happening slowly, over a period of days and weeks, primarily by reading newspaper accounts and listening to the radio.

I knew immediately that I wanted to enlist and fight in the war, and my wife agreed with considerable trepidation. The idea of going back into a classroom to teach the standard curriculum seemed irrelevant overnight. So did the give-and-take of local politicking. Nothing in the world at that moment was more important than the incomprehensible knowledge that the Republic of the United States of America had been shaken to the roots.

8 *The Regensburg Raid*

The United States was not a great military power in 1941. The air force did not become a separate branch of military service until after the war, so I enlisted in the Army Air Corps and was sworn in as a private. Bunny got a job teaching in nearby Coeymans, New York, and Mother moved in with her.

When my orders came in after the January semester break, I took the train to Albany and was shipped from there by train to San Antonio, Texas. The army allowed us one change of clothes for the three-day journey, but after we got to our destination we discovered that we would have to live in tents, temporarily at least, since there weren't enough barracks to house us. The army was also short on uniforms, which meant my one change of clothes had to last me two full weeks.

Everybody wanted to be a "flyboy," a pilot, which seemed about the most glamorous thing you could be in the military. I volunteered for the cadet corps, went through pre-flight training at Randolph Field in Texas, and then was sent for pilot training in Oklahoma. I was still woefully underweight and tried to beef myself up by overeating and drinking lots of water. I also suffered from asthma, which I never told them about. The flight surgeon took one look at me and asked, "Are you healthy, son?"

"Yes, sir."

"You're underweight."

"I've always been underweight, sir."

He looked me over again, apparently taking a liking to me, and smiled. "Well, you just gained fifteen pounds."

I was six-feet-one and weighed 130 pounds, but as far as the army was concerned after that I was five-feet-ten-and-a-half and weighed 145 pounds. Bunny come out to Oklahoma to visit me in June when the school year was over. Army policy stated that no wives could live nearby, but she found a place to stay anyway and we managed to get away with it. I quickly discovered that I was not destined to be a pilot. I washed out of pilot training after I went up for a test run and was unable to perform all the required maneuvers. I blamed this on my trainer, who had broken his leg and left me without any instruction for a week. So they tested me again, but I didn't do any better the second time around.

The next best thing to being a pilot was being a navigator; most of those who washed out of pilot training became either navigators or bombardiers. I finally got my wings as a navigator after completing training in Hondo, Texas, and then was sent to an army base in Washington State. Before the army moved in, there was nothing there except for about twenty-five apple farmers. Bunny stayed with me that entire summer of 1942, against regulations (as other wives did with their husbands), and she traveled with me to Washington. We arrived in town and discovered that there was not a single hotel room available. We ended up sleeping on the first-floor landing with a screen propped up around us for a semblance of privacy.

The next morning I reported to the base. As I approached headquarters a pilot stopped me and asked if I were a navigator. I answered yes, so he asked me if I would like to join his crew. "That's fine with me," I said. When I went to headquarters the brass were already assigning people to various flight crews. At first they wanted to court-martial me for being AWOL. Somehow my orders had got fouled up and, according to them, I was supposed to be somewhere else. We got that all straightened out, and the army sent me to Spokane and then to Montana for additional training before I was ready to join my crew.

The pilot who recruited me was a flying sergeant, which meant I outranked him; the great majority of pilots were commissioned officers. He had been drafted in Pocatello, Idaho, and after spending one

Christmas on KP duty, he figured there had to be a more exciting way to get through the war. He volunteered for pilot training which he completed successfully, but his behavior held him back in rank. He was a wild man, a hell-raiser and a prodigious drinker. One morning he showed up still half drunk, and we had to lift him into the cockpit and strap the oxygen mask on his face to sober him up. Nonetheless, he was a truly gifted pilot who could do things I only dreamed of doing with the aircraft.

B-17s had a ten-man crew, and ours was part of the 570th Squadron in the 390th Bomber Group. We were all set to leave for England in the spring of 1943, but as we took off we discovered that only one of our flaps was working because of a missing cotter pin. We landed in Indiana—safely, fortunately, after having gone into a nose dive—and repaired the flap. Our copilot's family lived on a farm nearby, and as we passed over it we swooped down and buzzed the place. We heard later that the chickens wouldn't lay eggs for a week.

We continued east into New York State, and I asked the pilot to head for Ithaca so we could buzz the house where Bunny was staying. On the way we flew into a thunderstorm which rocked the plane, then we went into a free fall as we hit a downdraft, so we had to abort the buzzing mission and concentrate on staying alive. Our next stop was Maine, and from there we headed out across the Atlantic toward the Irish coast. This afforded me the first opportunity since training to navigate by celestial navigation, and the pilot checked in on me a couple of times to make sure my calculations were accurate. As we reached the coast of Ireland we picked up a signal beacon and homed in on that toward Scotland.

Out over the Irish Sea the wind shifted and threw my ETA reading off by forty-five minutes. To give you some idea of the magnitude of the error, you flunked in training if you were off by three minutes and your distance were off by two miles. There was more than a little consternation aboard our aircraft when the coastline failed to materialize when I said it would. The crew began to speculate on whether we were anywhere near Great Britain and, if not, how it was possible to miss it entirely. Fortunately, the coast of Scotland came into view before our fuel supply gave out, and we landed safely in Prestwick.

From Scotland we flew next to a rebuilt air base in Framlingham in East Anglia, a bulge on the easternmost coast of England that juts out toward the continent. The Luftwaffe had bombed the base a few months before, but it had been fixed up by the time we arrived. This was where we were to begin our combat tour. A red flag outside our squadron office meant we were on alert the following morning. Typically, we'd get up at four-thirty or five in the morning and sit down to a hearty breakfast of bacon and eggs, toast, and coffee—as though this meal might be our last. Then we'd all pile into a truck and head toward the briefing room. When we got there the squadron commander would be waiting with a huge map of Europe hanging from the wall. He uncovered it when we sat down, showed us where we would be flying that day, and briefed us on the mission.

Our third mission in August 1943 would go down in history as the Regensburg Raid, one of the most dangerous of the entire war. Regensburg was situated in Bavaria, north of Munich in the southeast section of Germany, which meant we had to fly over most of the country before we reached our target. In the beginning our only fighter escorts were British Spitfires that accompanied us about halfway across the Channel. The first time I ever saw flak from anti-aircraft guns on the ground, it looked so thick and deadly I didn't believe it was possible for anyone to fly through it and live to tell the tale. I quickly learned it was—for most of us at least.

The Regensburg Raid was an especially deadly and complicated run. The map on the wall covered most of Europe and the northern rim of Africa. Our group let out a collective gasp when we saw the route we would be taking that day. It stretched across most of Germany to the southeastern region, then south through Austria and Italy into North Africa. All of it was treacherous and hostile territory. Our target was a Messerschmitt factory in Regensburg, a worthy goal with obvious benefits to the Allied forces if only we could reach it safely. But, you couldn't help wondering if the target was worth the risk to life, limb, and all that expensive hardware.

As a navigator, I had two .50 caliber machine guns at my disposal. They might have been pop guns as far as the enemy was concerned. The first time I had ever fired a machine gun in my life was out of a

B-17 over Montana at a bunch of antelopes grazing below. They looked up in wonderment at all the racket. I had never even qualified with an M-1 rifle or .45 caliber pistol. The guns in the B-17 had a big circle sight, and the way you compensated if you couldn't shoot straight was to "hose" the target. In other words, you sprayed in a circular motion around the target, "hosing" a large area, hoping you might score a hit by accident. The major problem with that technique was that it wasted a lot of ammunition. My ammunition carrier was twice the normal size, and I quickly earned a reputation as an expert hoser.

We left the coast of England in a formation developed by General Curtis LeMay—twenty-one aircraft to a group, three groups to a wing formation. His theory, much disputed at the time, was that the wing formation provided B-17s with the best protection against enemy attack fighters. Our position on the Regensburg Raid was perhaps the most vulnerable of all. We flew tail-end Charlie, way in the back, with everyone following the lead bomber. Formations tend to spread out and get ragged the farther back you fly, which leaves you more exposed than the aircraft toward the front.

We were instructed before we left that, if we missed our target the first time around, we were to circle back for another try. This increased the danger many times over since it would provide the enemy with ample time to get a good fix on our position. Needless to say, we were determined to do it right the first time. Headquarters anticipated that because of the seriousness and importance of the mission, our casualty rate would be as high as fifty percent.

On the way across Germany to Regensburg, we were under attack from enemy fighters for four-and-a-half hours straight. B-17s were going down in flames all around us, spiraling toward a fiery death. As gaps opened in the formation we moved up to fill the void, dodging enemy aircraft all the while. As we approached Regensburg one of the other navigators pulled his pistol out and pointed it at the bombardier. He said, only half jokingly, "You see that target down there? We ain't goin' around twice on this one, so make sure you hit it the first time." One measure of the success of the mission was the fact that a hospital situated just beyond the target area remained untouched. That's how accurately the bombs rained down on that Messerschmitt factory.

Mission accomplished, we headed south on the second leg of our journey toward the relative safety of North Africa. We did not encounter any more enemy aircraft, something for which we were all grateful. But the trip did take its toll in another way as, one by one, the B-17s ran out of fuel and went down into the water. We jettisoned everything we could to lighten the load—ammunition and heavy supplies mostly—on the way to Algeria, our destination.

We sighted the coast and could make out an air strip with steel mats laid flat on the sand. If there was an emergency as your aircraft approached the runway on the way back from a mission, you were supposed to set off red flares indicating you needed priority landing rights. As we got closer to the Algerian coast the sky around us was filled with red flares from other aircraft in our now chaotic formation, including our own. Everyone was rapidly running out of fuel. Finally, we got clearance to land and touched down safely. By the time we had finished taxiing down the runway, the fuel gauge read empty. Our fuel supply had run out.

9 *An Offer I Couldn't Refuse*

Our hard working, high living pilot sobered up quickly after that mission. His reputation as a drinker was largely responsible for earning us tail-end Charlie on the Regensburg Raid, and he swore he would never put us—or himself—in that position again. Our crew had experienced the horror of the mission from a unique vantage point, but it wasn't until later when we read an article in *Collier's* magazine titled "I Saw Regensburg Die," that we understood fully just how costly it was. We were truly fortunate to have survived it.

Thanks to our pilot's new sense of responsibility in the cockpit, our crew gradually worked its way forward on subsequent missions until, by the twelfth or thirteenth, we attained the status of lead crew. Lead crew was responsible for the success or failure of the entire mission, an honor in itself, and it also meant we didn't have to fly as frequently as before. Lead crew had to be briefed more thoroughly than the others because of the added responsibility, and required additional time to prepare for each mission.

Twenty-five missions constituted a completed tour of duty (it later increased to thirty-five), and we were all anxious to finish the tour and go back home. Before we did, however, a problem developed with our bombardier, who had a great record until this time. I noticed him triggering his bombs early, and sores had broken out on his arms and legs. The most vulnerable time on a mission is when you're flying straight and level, approaching your target. The flak is thickest then, and everyone's nerves are stretched out tightly. The bombardier cracked under the pressure and began releasing his bombs early. After that he had to be grounded and committed to the mental ward. His replacement was a mad little Irishman named McCarthy who couldn't do much of anything right. He was constantly jamming his guns and calling for help. Through it all we maintained our status as lead crew, and got closer and closer to that vital twenty-fifth mission.

Perhaps the most maddening time for all of us was having to wait over three weeks, twenty-three days in all, between the twenty-fourth and twenty-fifth missions. Normally, you hoped against hope that the next mission never came around; in this instance, we couldn't wait to go up again and get the tour over and done with. We lived in fear that headquarters was saving us for a really big one (big meaning dangerous). Then suddenly the wait was over. We flew number twenty-five as deputy lead with eight hundred aircraft in formation behind us. The final mission was accomplished without damage to us, and we returned to England.

The pilot was shipped home after completing the tour, but I soon learned that the war was not yet over for me. The army kept me on for thirty more days to train new lead crews, then transferred me to wing headquarters as a group navigator. By the late summer of 1944 I had had enough. I had originally enlisted because I believed in the Allied cause in the fight against nazism and fascism, but the war was gradually winding down and I was long overdue to be sent back home. I requested a transfer to stateside.

I landed in Boston on a weekend in the fall of 1944. Supposedly we would be getting orders on the following Monday to go home for thirty days, but one of the officers at the base told the commanding officer, "Look, some of these guys have been overseas for two or three years. It's crazy to make them hang around for another forty-eight hours here. Let's make it legal and give them a pass now."

We got the pass and I called Bunny in Ithaca and arranged to meet her in New York City. We spent the weekend there. Then my orders came through on Monday and I went back home with her for thirty more days of glorious rest and recreation. The war continued in Europe but my fighting days were now history. My next assignment was recruiting duty in Wilkes-Barre, Pennsylvania, where I spent most of my time singing the praises of the Army Air Corps to high school kids. One of my biggest thrills was pinning wings on football players during halftime.

After Wilkes-Barre the army sent me to Louisiana as a navigation instructor. I was promoted to flight commander and transferred again to my old base in Frederick, Oklahoma, as Information and Education officer. Every three months or so we were required to take a physical. Ever since I had enlisted the army doctors had added fifteen or twenty pounds to my weight and shortened my height. Then, one day, after all this time had elapsed, after a full combat tour as a navigator in Europe, a doctor told me I was underweight.

"Yeah," I said. "Just add twenty pounds and it'll be okay."

"I can't do that."

I had to laugh at that. I was a grizzled veteran compared to him. The army had considered me fit enough to ship me overseas and expose me to enemy anti-aircraft fire, and here he was telling me I was underweight and he couldn't do anything about it.

"You can't do it?" I replied. "The Air Corps has been doing it for the last two years, ever since I joined up."

"There's no way I can do that." He was insistent.

"You can't take me off flying status now!"

"Well, I can get you a waiver."

"I don't want a waiver. I've already served a tour in combat."

He was adamant and refused to budge, so I had no choice but to submit to one of those maddening absurdities of military life and accept a waiver to remain on flying status as I neared the end of my tour of duty. I had learned a long time before that it is pointless to argue with the bureaucratic mind. My understanding of how military bureaucracy worked (or is that a contradiction in terms?) helped me when VJ Day arrived. I was still stationed in Oklahoma. The army devised a point system to determine when we would be discharged, and my commanding officer called me in one day and asked me if I wanted to get out.

"Is this an official request?" I asked.

"No, I'm just trying to figure out when people might be discharged."

"I don't know. I'll answer that question when you're ready to ask me officially."

51

Joseph Heller's novel, *Catch 22,* had not been published yet, but I already understood that questions and answers bore no relationship to one another unless they were part of the official record. Meanwhile, as Information and Education officer, I had started a vocational education program on the base to benefit the troops when they returned to civilian life. I invited refrigerator repairmen and other skilled tradesmen to come out and train the soldiers. This program attracted some attention and a major from Randolph Field, which was training command for the Army Air Corps, invited me to be chief I & E officer at Randolph. I was a captain at the time, and the post would mean a promotion to colonel at least.

"I'd be happy to consider it."

The following morning the base adjutant called me in. "Do you want to be discharged?"

"Is this an official request?"

"Um, yes."

"You mean, you're ready to cut orders and send me home?"

"That's right."

"In that case, the answer is yes."

And so my military career officially ended. I told the major I had decided against the post, and was returning to civilian life. In retrospect, this was one of those seminal decisions—like my earlier decision not to become a lawyer—that have a major influence on the course of our lives. Had I remained in the army I might have ended up a general, retired when I was still in my forties with a generous pension, and begun a new career. But it was not to be.

My official mustering out was scheduled to take place at Fort Dix in New Jersey. Bunny and I drove east in an old beat-up Oldsmobile that needed a quart of oil every fifty miles or so. We made a stop at Princeton University, where I got in to see the head of the government department. I told him I wanted to go back to college to get my Ph.D., and I apparently impressed him enough that he offered to take me in as soon as I got my discharge.

The discharge came through in October 1945 and Bunny told me that, if it were at all possible, she would prefer to live near Ithaca so she could be closer to her family. We headed back to New York and

I went to visit Dr. Robert Cushman, who headed up the government department at Cornell. He told me that if Princeton thought I was good enough to take my Ph.D. there, he could do no less for me at Cornell. When I went to register for the quarter beginning in November, I found myself on the end of a line that reminded me of the chow line in the army. I vowed when I was discharged that I would never stand at the end of a long line again.

When I returned to my in-laws' apartment, I received one of those fortuitous phone calls that reinforced my faith in a Supreme Being who guides all our lives with a Divine plan of which only He is aware. Some people prefer to call it simply fate or coincidence, but there are times in our lives when these events occur for all of us. The caller was Leonard Cottrell, the chairman of the Sociology and Anthropology Department for the College of Arts and Sciences and the Agricultural College. He got right to the point. "I hear you were a teacher."

"That's right. I taught secondary school before the war."

"And you had a major in social sciences at Colgate?"

"Yes."

"You taught social sciences?"

"Yes."

"Well, would you be interested in teaching again?"

"I want to get my Ph.D. I don't think I'll have time to teach."

Cottrell asked if he could come to talk it over with me, and I said that would be fine. He arrived a short time later and told me that the School of Industrial and Labor Relations at Cornell would be opening that semester, and they needed someone to teach an introductory social sciences course. There was a shortage of qualified instructors in the field. He made my decision easy when he said, "We'll appoint you as an instructor with the maximum allowable salary, twenty-four hundred a year, and you can still work on your Ph.D."

It was an offer—as the saying later went—that I couldn't refuse. But I learned soon enough the age-old lesson that, if something appears too good to be true on the surface, it probably is. The job was a gift horse with complications attached. The course did not exist yet. I had to write the entire program myself, with three days remaining before classes began. Some professor had attempted to put one together before the war, and he left a file full of notes and papers for me to use as a starting point. But I was starting essentially from scratch.

Miraculously, I completed the program on time, which was an education in itself. The students signing up for it ranged in age from seventeen to over fifty. Many of them were veterans back from the war, a tough group with combat experience. They were tough mentally as well as physically, prepared for anything a university instructor could throw at them. Since I didn't have time beforehand to sort through the various textbooks on my subject, I assigned all of them—which they read without complaint. I don't think I've ever got more work out of any group in my life than I did from those vets. The course was well received, and the following year Cottrell asked me to teach it to the Home Economics Department too. After a while it became the basic sociology course on campus, taught by other professors.

The spectacle of a World War II veteran teaching other veterans the rudiments of social sciences was not without its irony. It led me into an area that I could not have foreseen earlier. It took me a while to realize it, but my instructorship at Cornell was actually the beginning of my career as a politician.

10 *The AVC*

Those who know me as a lifelong Republican are usually surprised to discover that my entry into the political arena was with an organization associated with the Left: the American Veterans Committee (AVC). AVC was founded by primarily liberal veterans at the end of the war. Its chief organizer, Gil Harrison, later became editor of the *New Republic*.

Personally, I never did like the concept of a political spectrum ranging from Left to Right. I prefer to think of political philosophy in terms of freedom on the one hand and dictatorship on the other. All my life, in all of my public activities, including my tenure with AVC, my fundamental ideology has been centered in the idea of freedom. This includes freedom to speak, and to exchange ideas without hindrance. Believing this, I had no problem whatsoever working with liberals, Trotskyites, and democratic socialists in an alliance against Communists and Fascists.

I had heard about the AVC when I was in the service, and was attracted by its slogan, "Citizens First, Veterans Second." The major problem facing vets returning from overseas was finding affordable housing on or near college campuses. Landlords were capitalizing on the situation by renting out every square inch of space they had in their basements and attics at exorbitant rates, which the veterans had to pay for out of GI benefits. In a nutshell, they were being gouged by people whose freedom they had risked their lives to protect.

As a veteran myself who was fortunate enough to be living comfortably in the aftermath of the war, I was incensed over this exploitation. To help rectify the situation I formed an AVC chapter on campus. Within a brief period our membership grew to a point where it spilled beyond the campus and encompassed all of Tompkins County. I had no experience as a political organizer at this time, but I surprised myself when I discovered that I had a natural aptitude for it.

Philosophically, I was generally opposed to rent controls, but I was pragmatic enough to realize that drastic times called for drastic remedies. As leader of the Tompkins County AVC chapter, I called for temporary rent controls to protect returning vets. It wasn't long before I got a call from the local commanders of the American Legion and the Veterans of Foreign Wars, saying they would support me. The Chamber of Commerce, however, was less than sanguine about my position, and a representative called to set up a meeting with me.

I went to the meeting with the college chaplain, who was also personally interested in the issue. I started off: "Gentlemen, I'm opposed to rent controls on principle. Therefore, I hope you can show me how we can correct this situation so that returning veterans are not being gouged to live in intolerable conditions. If you can do that I'll withdraw my request for rent controls."

Around midnight, following about four hours of rather heated discussion, the chairman of the local Chamber of Commerce finally threw his hands up in exasperation. "Well, it doesn't look like we're going to resolve this problem here."

"It doesn't look that way," I agreed. "So I'm going to go ahead and fight for rent controls in Tompkins County."

Our AVC chapter was successful in accomplishing that goal. By February 1946 the AVC was the fastest-growing veterans organization in the nation, recruiting somewhere around five thousand veterans a day. It was inevitable, I suppose, that this rate of growth would eventually be noticed by organizations that were inimical to the concept of freedom—the primary one being the Communist Party USA—which were looking to exploit our success to achieve their own ends. Our ranks were quickly swelling up with members of the CP.

My success in Tompkins County spurred me on to organize AVC chapters throughout upstate New York. We got to a point where we were large enough to forge a single statewide chapter, pooling our resources with other chapters in New York City and the surrounding suburbs. In the process of doing this I met Gus Tyler, who had been training director for the International Ladies Garment Workers Union, and later became the union's vice president of Public Affairs. His assignment was to work as an organizer of the AVC, along with Dave Dubinsky, another union leader. Both Gus and Dave were old-line socialists. But they were anti-Communists as well, and knew how to fight them better than anyone else.

The three of us decided to combine our efforts and organize the state of New York together. I set up an office in Albany, and went to see my old friend, Erastus Corning, who was once again mayor after the war. He was an AVC member himself, and thoroughly supportive of our efforts. I was in charge of the committee responsible for organizing the first statewide convention in AVC history, and I announced my candidacy for chairman of the New York State Chapter. In doing so, I learned firsthand what lengths the Communists would go to in order to achieve their own ends. Any remaining illusions I may have had about the tactics they were capable of adopting were forever laid to rest.

Dave Dubinsky had given the AVC fifty thousand dollars toward the cost of putting on the convention. The Communists in our ranks lost no time in accusing me of using the money for my own candidacy, which was totally untrue. They also accused me of living with the woman I had hired to run the Albany office, another distortion of the facts. We had rented an apartment for the AVC in Albany instead of an office, to save money, but the Communists, with their expert use of the smear tactic, twisted it to look as though we were having an affair. I knew their accusations were falsifications, and I was naive enough to believe that the other delegates would recognize them as such. But this was not the case. Gus Tyler was my floor leader at the convention, and he said to me at one point, "Clif, I'm afraid we just don't have the votes."

"What can we do?"

"We have a chance of electing George Spiegelberger. It's our only hope." Spiegelberger was a law professor at New York University who had written the constitution and bylaws for the organization. He was an impressive speaker and generally well liked. I had little choice but to go along with Gus; the alternative was losing everything to the Communist contingent. I sat there in the balcony, feeling as violated as I ever had in my life, and watched Gus go to the podium to announce that I had authorized him to withdraw my name from nomination. He substituted Spiegelberger's name in place of mine.

The plan backfired, not through any fault of either Gus Tyler or George Spiegelberger. The simple fact was the Communists were nonpareil organizers, and they had lined up the votes beforehand. The outcome was predetermined. Afterward, I went down to the bar at the hotel, the Dewitt Clinton, and saw Gus sitting there at a table. He waved me over.

"I'm finished, Gus," I lamented. "I have no future."

"Nonsense. These experiences are always valuable. Learn from them. I've been fighting these bastards for a long time. The first thing you need to know is whom you can trust, who will stand up with you, whom you can work with. I'm gonna beat them yet—we are, because you're gonna help me."

His words were a tonic for me. I had felt utterly helpless after our defeat, but Gus was offering hope. The battle was not over. Gus and I remained lifelong friends despite our political differences. All of us meet certain people who have lasting impact in our lives. Gus was one of those in mine. He was right. I had learned valuable lessons that day. The first was that the Communists did not play by the same rules everyone else did. They had no concept of fair play, and believed instead that the end justified the means—any means. The second lesson I learned was not to take anything for granted. Two delegates from my own chapter, whose votes I assumed I could count on, had voted with the Communists.

I called one of the leaders of our organizing committee before I left Albany and predicted, "This is never happening to me again." I told him I wanted to meet with all our delegates when I got home. When I returned to Cornell I got my people together and laid down the law. "We're going to organize this American Veterans Committee chapter in Tompkins County with one man in charge of ten. Each leader will be personally responsible for his ten men, and he's going to tell them that when we have an AVC meeting they all have to attend. I don't care what else is going on, short of death. When there's a critical vote coming up, everyone has to attend and cast his vote against the Communists."

That's exactly how we set things up from that moment on, and it worked without a hitch. About a year later I was up for reelection, and the Communists of course were out to unseat me. I lined up all my people before the meeting, which took place in an old assembly hall at Cornell. I had even gone so far as to prepare slips ahead of time instructing the delegates to vote for me and others on my slate. The Communist leader rose to his feet immediately. "I assume you're going to relinquish the chair."

"You assume incorrectly. I have no such intention."

He made an impassioned plea for "fair play," and I ruled him out of order, following Roberts Rules of Order to the minutest detail. Everyone who wanted to speak had to state his reason for rising, and if it wasn't germane to the business at hand I ruled him out of order. If it was to the point, he stated his piece succinctly and sat down. We proceeded in this fashion until the vote tabulation. We succeeded in shutting out the Communists. Every single one of our people was voted into office. When it was over the Communist leader rose to speak.

"For what purpose do you rise?" I asked.

"Come off it, Clif. It's all over. You've won. I just wanted to congratulate the chairman on the best railroad job I've ever seen."

"The chairman accepts your congratulations." I banged the gavel. Victory was sweet, and it assuaged to some degree the bitter defeat of a year earlier. But it was only the latest battle in a continuing war. The Communists intensified their nationwide efforts to gain control of the AVC. The battle lines were clearly drawn, with both sides digging in deeper for a protracted struggle that would not end until many years later.

A favorite ploy of the Communists in the AVC was to drag out a meeting until one or two in the morning, when most of the delegates had had enough and gone home. The Communists alerted their own people beforehand to stay around for a critical vote. The following morning, the delegates who left would read in the newspapers that a quorum of delegates in the meeting they had attended passed a resolution endorsing Stalin, for example, in the wee hours of the morning. The Communists utilized this tactic at our first national convention in Milwaukee.

Gus Tyler was aware of what they were doing, and he devised a strategy to fight it. He reserved a block of hotel rooms for our people to stay in when the meetings ran late, so that the delegates didn't have to travel away from the hotel. When the Communists called a vote, we rang their rooms and told them to come down. We fought the Communists tooth and nail in this period right after the war, when there were a considerable number of fellow travelers—if not outright Communist party members—in our ranks and throughout the country.

One of the AVC leaders on the far Left at the time was Mike Straight, whom everyone thought of as just a rich ultraliberal. Tyler spent a considerable amount of time playing tennis with him out on Long Island, trying to bring him closer to the center. Later on it was revealed that Straight was a Communist party member and more. He admitted to me in 1985 that he had been recruited by the KGB when he was a student at Oxford during the war.

Word circulated at the Milwaukee convention that Elliott Roosevelt, the late president's brother, was also working with the Communists. If he was not actually a Communist, he was at least decidedly more left-wing than the president had been. We took care of that problem by bringing the matter to his mother's attention. The family matriarch told Elliott in effect, "Behave yourself, Elliott. Don't go messing things up." Elliott did as he was told.

FDR had been on the AVC committee along with Orin Root, the founder of the Willkie clubs in 1940. This was the only post Root had ever been elected to, something I accomplished by running him on the same ticket with Roosevelt. I was also responsible for the votes of the upstate New York delegation at the convention. I had learned my lesson the hard way that the most important thing at any convention is to be able to count correctly. You have to line up all your delegates and make sure they'll vote the way you want them to. I thought I had accomplished this when I got a message from the chairman of the Erie County delegation. He apologized and informed me that he had a defector in his group. We were a vote shy of the total I had anticipated. The buck stopped with me, so I called up Gus Tyler to tell him the news.

"What's his name?" asked Gus.

I told him and Gus startled me by laughing out loud.

"What's so funny?"

"He's a Trotskyite. Don't worry about him. When the time comes, he'll vote with me against the Stalinists."

I was getting a crash course on factional infighting on the Left. The various splinter groups seemed to hate one another even more than they hated capitalists. "Good God," I said to Gus. "Don't tell my delegates they've got a Trotskyite in their ranks. The chairman's a member of the Junior Chamber of Commerce. As far as he's concerned, a Communist is a Communist. They're all bad."

"He's not bad in this context," Gus replied. "He's a fervid anti-Stalinist and he'll vote with us."

One litmus test we devised for weeding out the Communists in AVC was to propose a resolution condemning Nazism and Communism. The Communists routinely refused to back these measures, preferring instead to limit the target to Nazism and Fascism. Stalin had been our ally during the war, was their standard argument, and his excesses should be overlooked. After a long struggle the battle for control of the AVC was won by the anti-Communists, but the organization was permanently tarnished by its reputation as a Communist front. Sadly, the AVC never developed to its full potential.

11 *The Most Exciting Profession*

Because of my AVC activities, as well as my efforts to create a nondiscriminatory fraternity house at Cornell where everyone—Christians, Jews, blacks, and whites—could live together (a radical proposal at the time), some Republican party leaders came to me in 1946 and asked me to run for Congress in the 37th Congressional District. With the first taste of political combat under my belt, the notion had great appeal. I was too naive to realize that the people who approached me were a group of dissidents looking to take on the entrenched party regulars, and I was to be their stalking horse.

I announced my candidacy, only to discover when I went to the courthouse to get petitions that there was none available. This should have been my first clue that the party machine was not going to make it easy for a challenger to get on the ballot, let alone succeed in toppling the incumbent. But I would not be deterred. I got hold of a copy of the state election laws, read it thoroughly, and printed up my own petitions according to the letter of the rules and regulations laid out by the establishment.

The incumbent in the congressional district, which included five counties, was Republican W. Sterling Cole, another Colgate man. "Stub" Cole was a staunch conservative with anti-union propensities. I regarded myself as reasonably conservative on many issues, notwithstanding my AVC and integrationist activism, but I was decidedly pro-union and won the support of the Machinists Union, the largest in Ithaca. Unfortunately, its support did not include financial assistance. Instead, the union printed up pamphlets for me at its own expense, a strategy that allowed it to slant the rhetoric to suit itself.

Still, this was heady stuff for me, a young college instructor back from the war being courted to run for Congress. I eked out enough signatures on the petition to earn a spot on the ballot in the Republican primary. Bunny, pregnant with our son, was by my side much of the time, and I have no doubt that a lot of voters sympathized enough with the plight of this gawky young candidate and his pregnant wife to cast their votes for me. I lost to Cole, but I did make the strongest run against him that anyone had until then. After my defeat I vowed that I would learn what politics was all about, how it worked from inside and out. I was determined from that moment on to pursue a political career.

I learned a lot from Stub, a consummate politician, during the course of the campaign. About a week before the election he ran a newspaper ad with the ominous headline, "The Deadly Parallel." On one side of the ad he itemized all his accomplishments, and on the other side under my name he printed "Unknown." Anyone reading it would have got the impression that I wasn't qualified for anything, including sweeping the street. I felt an obligation to respond to it with an ad of my own, which cost me every last nickel I had. Essentially, I reprinted his ad, substituting the word "True" for "Deadly" in the headline, and then listing my own accomplishments.

Of course, it was too late and ineffectual to do me any good. I was a neophyte in the art of politicking and I had spent my savings for nothing. Despite the beating he gave me, Stub and I became friends afterward. I hired him to work as congressional liaison in the 1964 Goldwater presidential campaign, and later I hired his son in the successful 1970 Jim Buckley campaign for the U.S. Senate. But in 1946 there were no books on the nitty-gritty of politics, no guides on how to run a successful campaign for public office. The only way to learn was to go out and do it. Trial and error. And that's exactly what I did.

I volunteered for all the jobs nobody else wanted to do. One of my assignments was to drive a group of old ladies into the city from the country to vote. Many of them had no other means of transportation and would otherwise not have been able to cast their ballots. After a while, a bunch of them got into my car and asked me, "Well, whom are we voting for today?" The proverbial light bulb went on inside my head. It occurred to me that this was what politics was all about— getting out the vote. I was these ladies' contact with the political world. They trusted my judgment. I was more sure of their votes than I was of my wife's. By volunteering for a job many others viewed as a nuisance, I had learned a great lesson. Politics is the art of earning people's trust, becoming their de facto political leader, and swaying their votes. Without enough votes to win an election, everything else is academic.

My determination to pursue a political career attracted me to the Young Republicans, as well as the regular party organization. I attended my first New York State YR convention in 1948, and my first national YR convention a year later in Salt Lake City. I flew with a group from New York City in a DC-3, and we had to make an unscheduled landing in Denver to fuel up again for the flight over the mountains. This was a more adventurous undertaking in 1949 than it is today.

I mentioned earlier that the first national political convention I ever attended was the 1940 Democratic one in Chicago when Bunny and I stopped there on our honeymoon. The first one I participated in was the 1948 Republican convention in Philadelphia that nominated Thomas E. Dewey for president. I was on the national board of Youth for Dewey and performed two functions that had a decisive impact on me. The second also had a lasting impact on politics at large.

The first was orchestrating the Dewey floor demonstrations, which were the purview of the delegates at the time. You were permitted to bring in a band, in addition to the delegates, but no one else as far as outsiders were concerned. I bent this rule considerably when I paid off a guard at the door and sneaked in twenty or twenty-five Young Republicans from upstate New York to flesh out our forces. Robert Taft had been nominated first, and his demonstrators cavorted for about twenty-five minutes. My instructions were to make sure that the Dewey demonstration lasted at least a few minutes longer.

In 1948, air conditioning was not exactly a universal commodity. The convention hall was stifling, with throngs of sweating delegates flooding the aisles, screaming at the top of their lungs. The sergeant at arms kept yelling, "Clear the aisles! Clear the aisles!" I was determined to keep the ruckus going for a full half hour, five minutes longer than the Taft demonstration, and the only way to do that was to keep the band marching and playing and drowning out the sergeant at arms. We stretched it out for thirty minutes before we quit. By the time it was over my suit jacket was soaked through with perspiration. I wrung out one of the sleeves and could see water dripping to the floor. Dewey, of course, won the nomination and went on to lose the election in a photo finish to Harry Truman.

My second major function at the convention had a lasting effect on the way future conventions were organized. Dewey set up his headquarters, along with most of his brain trust, at the Bellevue-Stratford Hotel. Protocol dictated that the candidate never appeared on the floor of the convention until after he was nominated. Meanwhile, it was imperative that a line of communication be maintained between the candidate and his staff and his people on the convention floor.

The only effective means of doing that was to literally hog a telephone line and secure it against all attackers. So, Yours Truly sat in a telephone booth right off the floor with a mountain of nickels in front of me, which I fed one at a time every three minutes into the insatiable machine to keep a line open to the Dewey suite. In view of all the electronic wizardry at our disposal today, it's hard to believe that there simply was no other way to stay in contact as recently as 1948. Whoever succeeded in tying up all the available telephone lines had a distinct advantage over the competition. Maintaining one's composure in the face of all sorts of threats from other delegates—to say nothing of angry reporters looking to file a story with their newspapers—bordered on the heroic, particularly for a gangling appleknocker like me.

Even I, with my inexperience, realized that this was no way to win a nomination, let alone an election. So, by the time I ran Goldwater for President in 1964 I had developed the most sophisticated telephone communication system ever seen on a convention floor. It played no small part in winning the Republican nomination for Goldwater, and became the model for other candidates from both parties for years afterward. But 1964 was still a long way in the future in 1948, and keeping a death grip on my telephone was the only way to stay in contact with our candidate.

I met the governor for the first time during the convention. I had a message to deliver in person, so I went up to his suite and sat in the anteroom with a bunch of other people who were also waiting to see him. This was the way Dewey liked to conduct his affairs; he had a formal manner about him, and a meeting with him took on the aspects of an audience with the pope. While I was sitting there with the others, one of his aides opened the door to his suite and said, "You're next, governor."

Five men in the room rose to their feet. I suddenly felt overwhelmed. Here I was, this gawky kid whose job was manning a telephone booth when I wasn't making signs and hiding them from the opposition, sitting in a room with five governors waiting to see Tom Dewey. These politicians, powerful enough in their own realm, all looked like ordinary human beings to me. I still didn't know the first thing about politics, but I did know just enough to realize that, for me at least, it was the most exciting profession in the world.

12 *My Course Is Set*

When I attended my first New York State Young Republican Convention in 1948, my enthusiasm was perhaps exceeded by my naiveté; I announced my candidacy for chairman of the board without realizing that you could not be elected chairman without being a member first. Since I was not a member, I was forced to withdraw my name.

By 1950 I had learned a thing or two, and ran this time for president of the Association of New York State Young Republican Clubs. I did this at the behest of a group of people who were eager to wrest control of the organization away from New York City. During the previous two years I had done a lot of work for the YRs and established a bit of a reputation as a result. My hard work paid off, and this time I stayed the course and won.

I was not interested in power for myself, but rather in a way to get things done through work and organization. In 1949 we had succeeded in electing our own candidate as national chairman. A powerful midwestern faction controlled the national organization, and it was imperative that we come up with a midwesterner of our own to succeed at that level. We approached John Tope of Michigan, who had been interested in being elected treasurer up to that point, and asked him if he would like to be national chairman instead. Tope thought it might not be a bad idea. I told him it was possible as long as he had the support of his own state, plus one other from outside the Midwest caucus. We could deliver New York, which would be all he needed to put him over the top. He agreed, and the strategy worked.

With our own man as national chairman and me in control of the New York chapter, we were now in a position to implement a strategy for the future. As it turned out, my term in office lasted from 1950 to 1952, but the "Clif White Era"—as it was referred to later on—continued for six years beyond that, a total of eight years. The technique I developed for maintaining control depended on three basic strategies: a trusted corps of loyal workers at the center; continuing analysis of the weaknesses, strengths, and objectives of our opponents; and an efficient information-gathering network with good lines of communication between the members of our group. Every successful organization relies on these three elements; no group, political or other, can survive without dedicated workers, careful analysis of the facts, and good information passed along through efficient lines of communication.

Congressman Bill Pfeiffer, who was state chairman of the Republican party in New York in 1950, the year I was elected president of the Association of New York YR Clubs, asked me to work with him on the Republican state committee following our convention. My tenure at Cornell was running out, so I was more than a little interested in working full time in politics.

"What would I be doing?" I asked.

"Basically, I'd like you to organize more YR clubs around the state."

There was nothing I wanted to do more, so I agreed without hesitation.

"When can you start?"

"I've got about a hundred students at Cornell who'd like to get their final grades. How about the first of July?"

"Fine."

So I began by organizing YR chapters throughout the state as Pfeiffer requested. The first real test of power we faced occurred at the 1951 YR national convention in Boston. It was shaping up to be a big battle between the Eisenhower and Taft forces—Eisenhower the popular former general and war hero, and Robert Taft the standard-bearer of the conservative wing of the Republican party. Taft had been a presidential candidate since 1940, and his people were largely in control of the YRs.

Tom Dewey had essentially created and developed the Eisenhower camp, and he made it clear that he was counting on me to defeat the opposition. Without Dewey, there would have been no Eisenhower organization in New York, and Taft would have been largely unopposed. Defeating Taft meant replacing his delegates with uncommitted delegates and electing our own chairman of the Young Republican National Federation. Since I had spent the past year consolidating my own forces within the national organization, this would be a test of just how well I had done my job.

I was living in Ithaca at this time, and I had the distinct impression that it was going to be an extremely difficult fight. I wanted to be as well prepared for it as possible, so I called the governor's office and asked for an appointment. Dewey's New York City headquarters was a suite at the top of the Roosevelt Hotel near Grand Central Station, and I arrived shortly before the scheduled time. Dewey was nothing if not precise; his entire demeanor from his carefully tailored suits to his groomed hair to his neatly trimmed mustache spoke of precision, and he expected others to be precise as well. He rarely kept people waiting long to see him, and I was ushered into his office within minutes.

"You've got to be quick. We squeezed you in between the chief justice of the appellate division of the supreme court and the commissioner of education. What can I do for you?"

"I have only one request, Governor. I'm going to Boston next week for the Young Republicans convention."

"Yes?"

"I ask only that while I'm up there for the four days, nobody else can speak for the state of New York but me. Everyone'll be trying to go around me to get to you, to get to the national committeeman or the state chairman or somebody else to put pressure on the delegates. I can't run things properly unless I have authority to speak for the state."

"Of course not. That's understood."

"That's all I have then. I appreciate that very much, Governor." I left and that was the end of it. Dewey was true to his word right down the line. I went to Boston early to get my bearings in anticipation of a tough fight, and in that regard I was not disappointed.

71

The opposition was both experienced and well organized. It knew every trick imaginable and tried them all. Republican party leadership in Washington involved itself in every step of the proceedings, even going so far as to hold a caucus of Taft forces off the floor of the Senate and place telephone calls to delegates in Boston, to the governor, and to his right-hand man Russell Sprague, who was national committeeman. Russ was the real Dewey strongman as far as the national nomination was concerned. However, each time the opposition called someone—Dewey, Russ, whomever—the message was the same: the one to clear things with was some kid in Boston named Clif White. Clif who? Hardly anyone had heard of me at the time, but Dewey delivered as he promised he would. He gave me a job to do, and he gave me the authority I needed to do it properly. His word was his bond; it was a question of integrity with him, one of his greatest strengths. He backed me all the way despite the many cries of protest from Republican party leaders.

The strategy succeeded. We won after five ballots, electing my candidate, Herbert Warburton of Delaware. This was a major relief for me since Dewey was also a tough taskmaster. He gave you what you asked for to get a job done, but once he did that he expected you to succeed. He demanded results from those who worked for him, and had little patience with inefficiency. Following Warburton's victory, I put together my own slate of delegates to the national convention and got them elected as well. I learned a lot from Dewey by observing how he operated. He was a master politician who understood that there was no such thing as power without control. You can't run any organization effectively unless you control the majority of those connected to the voting process. Everything else is academic. Dewey's success was all the more remarkable considering that New York Republicans were not well liked nationally. He (and the rest of us New Yorkers by association) was considered to be arrogant and autocratic—traits not well suited for making friends. Understanding this, it was important that we not gloat over our victory in Boston. We were careful to run candidates from other states—Sully Barnes from South Dakota in 1953, for example—for national office. It was not important where they came from, so long as they were committed to us.

Gaining their loyalty was not all that difficult. We had the votes and could deliver what they wanted as long as they agreed to cooperate. "How would you like to be chairman of the Young Republicans Federation?" I would ask a prospective candidate. If he were interested, the rest was academic; I'd explain how we could secure the post for him and what we expected in return. From that point on the candidate was committed to us.

The convention in Boston turned out to be a crossroad for me in a way I had not anticipated. Working with Dewey and learning from him was exhilarating, and our victory enabled me to make a few major decisions about my life. Throughout the convention I had been an important player behind the scenes, and I enjoyed the action as well as being at the center of activity. Everyone who wanted to know what was going on—including the press—had to speak to me.

Then, suddenly, Warburton was elected and the spotlight turned to him. I went up to my room alone and, for the first time in days, my telephone was silent. I turned on the television and there was Warburton, an unknown candidate from Delaware just a few days before, whom we had handpicked to run, taking his bows before the camera. A dark loneliness descended upon me, infusing me with gloom. I became uncharacteristically depressed and felt sorry for myself. I was the one who made it all happen, and no one seemed to care any longer. I called Dewey to report on our victory, and he said, "Fine." That was it, nothing else. No "Thank you for a job well done." As far as the governor was concerned, I had done what was expected of me. Anything less would have been unacceptable to him; Tom Dewey did not keep people who disappointed him around very long. I was looking for some sort of acknowledgment for the role I had played—a pat on the back, if you will—but none was forthcoming.

This incident was a great lesson to me. Prayer has always got me through my darkest moments, and this time was no exception. The lesson I learned was that the candidate gets all the credit in the end. The starring role is reserved for the individual elected to public office; he is the one the public and the media lionize—or vilify, depending on the circumstances. I learned that the Almighty selects all of us for different roles in life, and mine was to be not the star but rather the man behind the scenes who gets things done. We are asked to perform a job the best we can because it is right, not because it will lead to fame, fortune, and personal glory. All rewards come from God. Whatever talent we have comes from Him, and we have to use our gifts for others without expecting any more in return than what is actually given to us.

This was a tough lesson, to be sure. But praying for guidance and understanding was what got me through this youthful ordeal. Accepting the message inherent in it elevated my spirits and gave me a new perspective on life. I made a decision there, in that hotel room in Boston, to do whatever job I felt called upon to do, without expecting any public recognition for it. Any acclaim would be a bonus from the Lord, a measure of His grace. In any event, I was thoroughly hooked on politics as a career. The taste of it that I got during that convention in Boston was all I needed. I was going to devote my life to politics in one form or another. If I did not command center stage, I would put everything I had learned about hard work, organization, and political infighting to work for a cause in which I believed.

In 1951 I ran for county chairman of the Republican party in Tompkins County, and won. It seemed academic to me that, in order to operate effectively in that post, it was essential to understand the county committee bylaws. Since no one I asked seemed to know anything about them, I went to Albany and got a copy from the office of the secretary of state. Then I had them printed and posted on the wall in our headquarters.

"My goal," I told committee members, "is to run the county effectively. This means getting good candidates to run for office, and getting them elected so they can produce good government. If that doesn't happen, then it's my fault and the answer is to get rid of me." I meant that accountability is the cornerstone of good government. One of the major problems we face today is that no one wants to be held accountable for anything that goes wrong.

In December 1951, following close on the heels of our victory in Boston, I created the Youth for Eisenhower Committee. Governor Dewey endorsed this effort wholeheartedly in private, but he did not want his name officially associated with it. Since everyone knew by now that I was part of Dewey's organization, it followed that my name would also be omitted from the organization's literature. As a result, we ended up appointing Henry Cabot Lodge as chairman. Lodge was debonair, handsome, and charming when he needed to be. He was so polished, in fact, that he succeeded in camouflaging his considerable intellectual deficiencies—Lodge was not the brightest individual I had ever met, nor was he even in the running.

It was interesting to speculate why Dewey was so adamantly opposed to Robert Taft. At this point, Taft and Dewey had been battling each other for twelve years going back to 1940, and Dewey had been beating him consistently. As a former presidential candidate, Dewey was the acknowledged party leader, the man whom the press sought out to discover what was going on. He virtually *created* Eisenhower as the Republican candidate for 1952. Some believed that Dewey objected to Taft's conservative positions as the leading spokesman for the right wing of the party. In retrospect, however, I think Dewey would have opposed Taft out of habit. I don't think it was Taft's ideology in and of itself that bothered him. In fact, if Dewey had one major shortcoming, it was his own *lack* of ideology. He was a pragmatist first and foremost, a man who believed in good government—honesty, integrity, and getting things done efficiently.

Dewey had made his mark as an impeccably honest district attorney who had fought corruption and won. He considered himself to be a modern man and an effective governor, and in a non-ideological way I'm sure he thought of Taft as an anachronistic mossback, a throwback to an earlier era, who failed to understand the problems of the contemporary world. In Dewey's mind Taft was a loser without a chance of winning the presidency, and that was reason enough not to support him under any circumstances. Dewey wanted to back someone who he believed could win.

A man with such an abiding intolerance of losers had to be deeply affected by his own unsuccessful attempts to win the presidency. Virtually everyone, including the nation's leading political analysts, had been telling Dewey since 1940 that it was only a question of time before he was elected to the highest office in the land. Dewey had even gone so far as to pick his cabinet in 1948, some members of which put down payments on houses near Washington in anticipation of serving in the first Dewey administration. When Dewey lost to Truman in the historic photo finish that year, his personal physicians monitored him closely for signs of psychological side effects. But Dewey was tough, and he rallied quickly in the aftermath of the 1948 election.

Dewey convinced me that Eisenhower had a better chance than Taft did of securing the White House for the Republican party; indeed, that he was the *only* serious candidate who had any chance at all. As a member of the Dewey organization, I had little choice but to go along with the governor in his support of Eisenhower even though I was closer to Robert Taft ideologically. You are either on the team or off it in politics, and this was especially true when you served in any organization headed by Tom Dewey. He was the man in control at all times, and he demanded loyalty of those who worked for him. So, my course was set clearly for the foreseeable future. I was hooked on politics, and the prospect of working closely with Dewey and the Republican party in New York State was all the more auspicious for a political neophyte like me.

13 *Ike*

The Dewey machine ran efficiently enough most of the time, but the governor was only human after all, and he was capable of committing an occasional blunder. During his gubernatorial reelection campaign in 1950, he embarked on one of those whistle-stop tours across the state that were considered to be essential at the time. As his train pulled into Rochester, Dewey got up onto the train platform and informed the crowd that he was "tickled pink" to be in Buffalo! This type of faux pas was completely out of character for him, but it had been a rugged day on the campaign trail and he was understandably tired. His indiscretion only served to prove that, beneath his steely demeanor, Governor Thomas E. Dewey was as human as the rest of us. Nevertheless, the local voters were infuriated and the press seized the opportunity to build the incident into a major story.

I mention this here as a backdrop to Dwight D. Eisenhower's whistle-stop tour of New York State during his 1952 presidential campaign. We held a rally for Ike in Albany where Dewey introduced the candidate to the electorate. At each stop along the way there was a rally, and the crowds grew progressively larger. Onward we rattled across the state, stopping in Schenectady, Utica, and Syracuse. Finally we were due to arrive at the scene of Dewey's 1950 blunder, Rochester.

The local dignitaries aboard the train approached the national committeewoman Judy Weiss, who also happened to be from Rochester, and suggested that it might be a good idea for someone other than Dewey to introduce Eisenhower in Rochester since the governor was not overly popular there. She relayed the message to Bill Pfeiffer, who was in the first car of the caravan, and he came back and told me.

"Well, I'm not going to tell the governor that," I said.

"I don't want to either."

"Let's get Len to tell him," I suggested, referring to Len Hall, Eisenhower's campaign manager.

Len looked horrified when we told him what was going on. He certainly wasn't going to tell Dewey anything like that. We were at an impasse; none of us had the courage to confront Dewey, and the campaign train was rapidly approaching Rochester. Fortunately for us, Senator Frank Carlson of Kansas, one of Eisenhower's chief advisers, who was also from his home state, rode to the rescue. He saw the three of us New Yorkers with our heads together, almost quivering in our boots. He asked us if we had a problem.

"We don't think Governor Dewey should introduce Ike in Rochester," I responded, "but there isn't a Republican on this train with enough guts to tell him."

"Would you like me to tell him?" Carlson asked.

A feeling of overwhelming relief descended upon the three of us. "You sure would be taking a bunch of New Yorkers off the hook if you did," was my reply.

Without hesitating, the good senator strode manfully up to the head car, went right up to Dewey and informed him that he wanted Judy Weiss to introduce Ike in Rochester since that was her home town.

"Fine," Dewey said, and that was the end of it—no questions, complaints, or recriminations.

It was somewhat ironic that Dewey had the ability to intimidate just about everyone who came in contact with him, considering his diminutive stature. Most people could not tell by looking at campaign photographs that Dewey was actually shorter than Harry Truman. The governor rarely allowed visitors to photograph him in front of his desk. His official desk was set upon a raised platform, and when he stood behind it he appeared to be as tall as everyone around him. He compensated for his lack of height by adopting that forbidding, steely demeanor that characterized his public persona. His critics accused him of lacking warmth and, the truth is, he could be abrupt and short-tempered at times. He turned his sarcasm on me on more than one occasion, when he was less than elated with some of my suggestions. However, he was equally tough on himself. If there was one word that summed him up, it was *competence*. He demanded it of himself, and he backed his people up a hundred percent when they did their jobs well.

I worked closely in New York City with Bill Pfeiffer, the state chairman of the Republican party, on Eisenhower's 1952 presidential campaign. At the end of each day Bill and I usually sat down together and discussed the day's activities. One evening he said to me, "I had dinner with the governor the other night and he mentioned that it would be a good idea for you to get some government experience. 'If we win this thing,' he said, 'Clif could be of help working either down in Washington, or right here in the state.'"

This was a great compliment coming from Dewey. You never really knew where you stood with him until he offered you a job. If he did, that meant he had a high regard for your ability. He never actually told anyone he liked the job you were doing. He simply moved you up within his organization to reward a performance well done.

I mulled Bill's remark over for a minute. "I really don't want to go to Washington. I'd prefer to remain in New York."

One of the New York jobs Dewey had in mind, according to Pfeiffer, was with the State Liquor Authority, which he promptly described as a "rats' nest where you could forget about getting anything done." The second position he mentioned was executive assistant to the commissioner of the Department of Motor Vehicles.

"I'd be more interested in the second spot," I said, then pretty much forgot about it in the heat of the campaign.

It was still only the spring of the year, and we had a long campaign ahead of us. Eisenhower had entered politics almost by accident as it were. He was a war hero, there was a vacuum in national leadership in the aftermath of the war, and Ike was called upon to fill it. Like Dewey, he was more of a pragmatist than an ideologist. Both of the major political parties had approached him about running in 1952, and he could just as easily have run as a Democrat as a Republican. Eisenhower genuinely loved people—all kinds of people from every stratum in society—and that accounted for his appeal and his strength as a leader. Not all politicians have that quality. Many of them are introverts who neither like nor understand people, and they manage to overcome that weakness and become leaders despite themselves; Richard Nixon is a classic case in point. But Eisenhower did not have to pretend. He was genuinely warm and outgoing, and the public responded to him.

Ike was not a rich man from the start. However, he had written a book, *Crusade in Europe,* that was enormously successful and made a lot of money for him. As a result, he called upon the services of several investment advisers, foremost among them a wealthy Wall Street broker named Clif Roberts, who had created the famous golf course in Augusta, Georgia.

Roberts idolized Eisenhower and was determined to see him become president. One of the things he did for Ike was lobby Congress to pass a tax law permitting those who had received inordinate amounts of money in a single year to average out the income over several years to alleviate the tax bite. That law remained in effect until the Reagan years when it was swept aside with other loopholes. Today few people realize that it was originally passed because of Roberts's efforts to help his friend Ike avoid the pitfalls of overnight success with a single book.

I had first met Roberts myself about a year before the Republican convention. At the time he wanted to fly delegates over to Paris to meet Eisenhower, who had yet to return home from the war. He said he would raise the money himself to pay expenses. Roberts knew the world of finance, but he was a neophyte when it came to politics. The problem with his idea was that there was no way to know that far in advance just who the delegates would be. I explained the situation to him, and he was genuinely upset.

I remembered this incident months later after I started the Youth for Eisenhower Committee. As I mentioned earlier, we appointed Henry Cabot Lodge chairman for reasons that had nothing whatsoever to do with his level of competence. I wanted to bring some young Republicans into Washington from different parts of the country, and I went to Lodge's office to get the money to pay for it. This was a simple request, but as I learned on many occasions over the years, nothing was ever simple where Lodge was concerned; the man was incapable of making a decision on his own, and he told me to take the matter up with Dewey or . . . somebody, anybody but him. At that point I recalled Roberts and his fund-raising abilities, so I called him.

"How much do you need?"

"About five thousand dollars."

"Can you cover it yourself for the time being?"

At the time I was earning about twelve thousand dollars a year working for the Republican State Committee, and five thousand dollars was a small fortune to me. "I'm afraid not," I said, gulping hard.

"Well, okay then. Call this phone number in twenty minutes and tell them where you want the money delivered."

He gave me the number and a name to ask for, and in no time at all an envelope containing the money was hand-delivered to me. It did not take me long to catch on that Clif Roberts was a man who delivered what he said he would. He had the money and the connections to get things done. From that moment on, I did an end run around Lodge and went directly to Roberts whenever I needed something.

The National Guard Armory in Philadelphia was the scene of the official opening of Eisenhower's campaign. A tremendous crowd waited outside anxiously, packed together like so many sardines in a can. Ike took an elevator up to the tower, stepped out onto the parapet and flashed his trademark "V for Victory" sign. The people below roared themselves hoarse, as they would do throughout the campaign whenever Eisenhower did that. The gesture was more eloquent than words, and it became a symbol of hope for a nation looking to regain its footing in the aftermath of the war.

Ike waved to the crowd, then rode the elevator down to ground level. It opened onto a driveway where cars and limousines pulled in to pick up people or drop them off. I was standing out front with Ike's press secretary, Jim Hagerty, and other members of the campaign staff. The crowd behind us pressed against the police barricade, straining to get a closer look at the war hero who was now a candidate for president. Somehow, a scruffy-looking kid wiggled through the cordon of police and the phalanx of Secret Service agents protecting the candidate, and walked right up to him. Without missing a beat, grinning from ear to ear, Ike reached down and picked him up. He smiled into his face, which was level with his own. "What're you doing out this time of night, little fellow?"

It was a totally spontaneous gesture made all the more touching because of Ike's genuine warmth and humanity. I turned instantly to Hagerty, "Where are the photographers when we need them?" There was not a single cameraman around to record the event. This was 1952; television was just beginning to find its way into American households. Today the world has grown accustomed to seeing a veritable forest of television cameras and an army of media types on hand to record history in bite-sized segments for easy consumption. Nothing goes unnoticed and unrecorded today. In fact, it is not beyond the political consultants to go out and hire a kid for their candidate to hug and then stage the whole thing as a media event. But, for Ike, it was a perfectly human response. Staging a moment of warmth for posterity was the furthest thing from his mind.

Eisenhower was particularly fond of young people. It did not come up during his presidential campaign, but I learned later that he favored a law permitting eighteen year olds to vote, which put him way out front of most public figures on the issue. After he was elected he wanted the Young Republicans to pass a resolution endorsing this position. At the time I was opposed to the concept, as was our national chairman, Herb Warburton, but Ike was so adamant about it that we went along with him and got it passed. He told Herb and me privately that we needed to do more to involve young people in politics and get them elected to public office. The nation needed new blood, he explained, in order to remain fresh, vibrant, and dynamic. He believed that the youth of the country—any country for that matter—were coming up with new ideas constantly, and everyone could benefit from listening to them.

Another episode that exemplified Ike's genuine concern for people—young people in particular—occurred about a year later after he agreed to speak before the Young Republican National Convention. Sully

Barnes, who had replaced Herb Warburton as national chairman, was introduced to Ike and spoke to him briefly. Shortly afterward, Sully injured his back and had to be hospitalized in South Dakota. He asked me if I could take some of the Young Republicans to Washington to meet the president—something he would ordinarily have done. I agreed to do it, and waited outside the Oval Office with Ike's appointments secretary Tom Stevens while the president met with them. When the meeting ended, Ike came out and pulled me aside.

"How's Sully?"

"I think he'll be all right." I could not help but wonder how he knew Sully was in the hospital since I had not mentioned it. It just didn't seem important enough for a president to be concerned about.

Ike inquired further. "Is he getting good care out there? We can transfer him to Johns Hopkins if you think it'll do any good."

"I talked to him this morning and he says he's all right."

"Well, if he needs anything, let me know."

I was stunned. Today, after decades of political perks and assorted abuses of the public trust by elected officials, this would probably be criticized as "special privilege" by the media, but in the more innocent age of the 1950s it was an expression of heartfelt concern. Eisenhower actually *cared* about the condition of some young man he barely knew who was lying in a hospital bed in South Dakota. Among his successors in the White House, only Ronald Reagan—who was similar to Ike in this regard—would have exhibited a similar concern. This genuine love of people is perhaps the foremost trait of someone born to lead.

In many respects, Eisenhower stands out as perhaps the most apolitical of all the post-war presidents. It is not so much that he was politically naive as that he truly did not care about the subtleties and nuances of political maneuvering. In most instances, politicians have to learn the art of politics—how to get elected and remain in office—but Ike's natural appeal kept him in the White House for eight years. To a great extent he rose above politics, and he was one of the few who could do that and get away with it. What the public saw on display was the real man, someone who followed his feelings and basic instincts without worrying about public opinion polls. Virtually no serious politician today would dare operate in that fashion.

It is worth noting that Ike's wife Mamie had as much disregard for the political profession as he did. She did what was expected of her on the campaign trail and as First Lady and, for the most part, she did it well. But it was a great effort for her to rein in her temper— something I experienced firsthand when I inadvertently woke her up at two o'clock one morning. It was during the 1952 campaign. I had to contact Ike's campaign train, which was sitting in the yards in Cleveland, and someone handed me the wrong telephone number. (Later on I came to believe that it was not done accidentally, but rather deliberately by someone playing a practical joke. I never found out for sure.) I dialed the number, believing it would ring in the compartment of one of Ike's aides, only to find out the hard way that it was the number for Mamie's compartment. Her indignant response left me speechless. I knew instantly that it was far better to have Mamie as an ally than as an opponent, and went out of my way on many occasions afterward to work my way back into her good favor.

14 Political Patronage

I had forgotten all about Governor Dewey's job offer, conveyed to me through Bill Pfeiffer in the spring of 1952, in the midst of the campaign. But when the election was over and candidate Dwight D. Eisenhower became president-elect, Pfeiffer and I packed up our files in New York City and boarded the train to Albany. On the trip north he asked me, "What're you going to do now?"

"The same thing everyone else is doing. I'm heading down to Florida for a little vacation."

"Yes, well don't forget you've got a job in Motor Vehicles when you get back."

I was elated. This was yet one more indication that Dewey made good on his promises, rewarding those who served him well. Many politicians promise all sorts of things to people during the course of a campaign, but you never know if they intend to follow through when all the excitement is over. Since I had made up my mind to pursue a career in politics one way or another, this was an ideal opportunity for me.

When I returned from Florida I went to the New York Republican State Committee headquarters in Albany and, with considerable embarrassment, asked someone for directions to the Department of Motor Vehicles. Then I drove out and announced my name to the receptionist. Instantly, a rather gruff, intimidating man whom I recognized as Jim McDuff, chairman of Otsego County and the commissioner of Motor Vehicles, stepped out of his office and bellowed, "What the hell are you doing here?"

"I came here to work." I was considerably put off by his manner.

"Well, we've got an office for you around here somewhere, but I told Bixby I didn't want you showing up here for another week."

"Nobody told me anything about that."

R. Burdell Bixby, the man he referred to, had preceded me at Colgate by four years, graduating in 1936. I had been regarded as a pretty good debater by our coach, but according to him Bixby was the greatest, the role model for all of us to emulate. During my four years there I had grown accustomed to hearing the coach measure our performances against Bixby's standards—how Bixby would have handled every topic we debated—and I had grown tired of being compared unfavorably with him. But there was no getting away from him and the long shadow he cast. After college Bixby worked part-time for Irving Ives, majority leader of the state assembly, while he attended law school. With his law degree in hand, Bixby worked for a brief period with the Republican state committee before moving into the governor's office as a kind of executive assistant in charge of patronage. In time, Dewey acknowledged his considerable talents by making him his closest associate. It was virtually impossible to get in to see the governor without going to Bixby first. Later on, when Dewey left office in 1954, Bixby joined Dewey at his law firm, Dewey, Ballantine. Much as I admired him and respected his achievements, I resented to some degree being constantly overshadowed by him. Now here I was, reporting for my first day of work at the Motor Vehicles Department and feeling pretty good about it, being told that Bixby was supposed to be supervising my time of arrival.

My first day on the job was an education in bureaucratic gamesmanship. I had been appointed as assistant to the commissioner. This was allegedly a notch above deputy commissioner, of whom I learned quickly there was a grand total of five, none of them inclined to take his marching orders from a neophyte like me. I discovered that the only way to assert yourself in a bureaucracy is to create a title with considerably more clout than everyone else's. Without requesting permission from anyone, I had a sign posted on my door that read: EXECUTIVE DEPUTY COMMISSIONER OF MOTOR VEHICLES OF THE STATE OF NEW YORK—a clear signal to everyone that I was truly a Grand Potentate of the Highest Order. While Jim McDuff was ostensibly my boss, a position he achieved by working his way up the bureaucratic ladder, I was in effect the governor's "man" in the department, and my newly created title clearly reflected that. I learned my lesson well from this experience, and made sure I had awe-inspiring titles wherever I went throughout the rest of my political career.

Perhaps the closest thing to a compliment I ever received from Dewey occurred a year later. As I mentioned earlier, we succeeded in electing our own candidate, Sully Barnes from South Dakota, as chairman of the Young Republicans National Federation in 1953. I returned to New York afterward just in time for the annual bash at the farm of Mallory Stevens, chairman of the Ways and Means Committee. Dewey was there nibbling on an ear of corn and eating steak with his jacket off and his sleeves rolled up—a rare informal moment for him—when I arrived. I went up to him somewhat proudly, "We won on the first ballot with seventy percent of the vote."

He looked up from his corn smiling broadly. "You'd better be careful, Clif, or you might turn out to be a politician." In most circles today, that comment would be construed as an insult. However, coming from Dewey, who considered politics to be a high calling and practiced it accordingly, this was saying a lot.

Dewey demanded honesty as well as efficiency from himself and his people. There was a Republican state senator from Orange County named Arthur Wickes, who was majority leader at the time. He ran his district well and was generally effective. However, a problem developed when the unions went out on strike while they were building dams for New York City. Many people were out of work and the voters were upset. Wickes decided to solve the problem as expeditiously as possible, without regard for the finer moral distinctions. He asked a labor racketeer named Joey Fay, who was serving time in Sing Sing, to help him out. Unfortunately for Wickes, somebody saw him visiting Fay in jail and alerted the press.

Dewey was incensed when the story broke. To him the mere appearance of impropriety was unacceptable, regardless of whether or not Wickes had done anything wrong. He was adamant about protecting not only his administration, but the New York State Republican party as well, from any hint of scandal or corruption. Dewey called a special session of the legislature and replaced Wickes with Walter Mahoney, chairman of the Senate Finance Committee. This may sound like summary justice to some, but Dewey treated everyone the same; there was no second chance where integrity was concerned. Once you stepped over the line, you were out.

The word *patronage* has taken on a negative connotation today, but in those days it was virtually synonymous with good government. Good Government is Good Politics was a maxim Dewey lived by. Politics, to him, meant getting things done and, as far as he was concerned, there was nothing wrong with rewarding those who helped you accomplish your goals. No one got a political job in any county in New York, including mine, unless the county chairman who answered to the governor approved it. It was understood that anyone recommended for a post had to be qualified for it; rewarding people indiscriminately was out of the question under Dewey. Every candidate for a state position was checked out by the state police. Dewey rejected all candidates who had blemishes on their records. He kept his patronage system clean, unlike many other administrations, and it functioned well because of that.

I became chairman of Tompkins County in 1954, a year when Jacob Javits was running for attorney general. Being from New York City, Javits was unfamiliar with the way things worked upstate. Without checking with anyone, he picked his own man to run his Jewish committee in Tompkins County. When I heard about it I called Bill Pfeiffer and told him that Javits never cleared his man with me or the governor, and we had problems with his selection.

"Let me handle it," Pfeiffer said.

Shortly afterward, I got a call from the candidate himself. "I understand you have a problem with my appointee in your county."

"I think you've picked the wrong guy. We checked him out and he hasn't seen the inside of a synagogue in ten years. If you need a chairman for Jewish affairs, we know somebody who's a staunch Republican and he's religious as well."

Javits agreed and that was the end of it. This was a good example of how the political patronage system worked under Tom Dewey. He ran a tight ship, as the saying goes, but it was done in the interests of Good Government, of keeping his administration clean and making sure that the political jobs in the state were filled by the best people available. Everyone was handpicked, either by Dewey or the county chairmen—candidates for mayor, town supervisor, alderman, county attorney, all the way down the line. Each county chairman wielded power through the support of the governor and the strength of the organization. In my own county, I would approach a prospective candidate for office myself, and tell him, "I want you to run for this particular office. The party can get you nominated and elected. I ask only one thing in return: whenever there's a vote that's going to affect the welfare of the Republican party, I retain the right to discuss that issue with you. That doesn't mean I tell you how to vote, only that you listen to my thoughts on the matter." Each county chairman in New York during the Dewey years operated pretty much the same way.

Tom Dewey told me about a discussion he had with his son one night, which summed up his theory of Good Government pretty well. His son had been attacking the notion of political bosses as inherently corrupt, and wondered how his father could defend it. The governor looked at his son and said, "It's not the idea that's corrupt, it's some of the people who practice it. In my case I put good people into jobs, and we make commitments to one another that we know we'll keep. That way we know where we stand with one another at all times. I like political bosses who uphold their end of the bargain."

Dewey had learned something about patronage from the Democrats when he was first elected governor as an incorruptible "racket-busting" district attorney. There were two powerful Democratic machines in New York at the time—Ed Flynn's Bronx County organization in New York City, and the veritable fiefdom based in Albany presided over by Uncle Dan O'Connell. One of Dewey's big campaign promises was that he would break up both machines if he were elected. In the beginning the former DA and newly elected governor tried to do exactly that. O'Connell was known to be a late-night carouser, a drinker and a womanizer, and Dewey had a secret camera set up to take a picture of Uncle Dan leaving a brothel one night. The camera worked exactly as planned; it snapped a marvelous picture for posterity of Dan O'Connell staring directly into the lens, thumbing his nose at Dewey and his minions.

The Republican governor learned quickly that it would be more effective to deal with Uncle Dan and Ed Flynn in the Bronx, instead of attempting to topple them from their thrones. O'Connell, in particular, was tough, shrewd, powerful, a gutsy street fighter who was honest enough in his own fashion—which was not exactly Dewey's fashion, but something he had to live with. Under Uncle Dan, organized crime had a place in New York State as long as it was *orderly*. He accommodated the entrenched mob bosses, who worked with him to keep out the "independents" and preserve the public peace. There were no shootouts in the streets of Albany; everything from prostitution to gambling was run like a proper business.

While this was morally repugnant to Dewey, he realized that a working arrangement with O'Connell was better than all-out war. To govern effectively, he required some votes from the Democratic side of the aisle, and Uncle Dan had the ability to deliver them—or to deny them and foster a state of political gridlock. Dan O'Connell ran the cops and the wards, and therefore the streets, like a benevolent dictator. He paid for votes with jobs. The big joke in Albany was that you could always tell when an election was coming up by counting the public employees. Uncle Dan manufactured jobs by the hundreds when he needed to get out the vote. There were times when he seemed to be counting the leaves falling off the trees, since there was at least one person assigned to pick them up—one for each leaf on the ground.

Dewey learned his political lessons well by observing O'Connell and Flynn, studying the way they ran their respective organizations. He saw what worked and what did not, and adapted their techniques accordingly to suit his purposes. By weeding out corruption from his own administration and preserving what he deemed to be the best elements of the political patronage system, he was able to create a powerful political machine of his own in New York State.

Dewey's proudest achievement as governor was the construction of the Thomas E. Dewey Thruway—later referred to by its unofficial name, the New York State Thruway—which he began in 1950 and completed in 1954. In one of his speeches Dewey had predicted that people would be able to drive from New York City to Chicago some day without hitting a traffic light. He remained in office long enough to see it happen.

There was a certain irony in this, since Dewey did not want to stand for reelection as governor in 1950 after his unsuccessful bid for the presidency two years earlier. He stated this publicly, which opened the door for his lieutenant governor, Joe Hanley, a veteran of the Spanish-American War from upstate New York, to seek the nomination. Hanley was unsuitable from every conceivable perspective. He was basically a political hack, controlled by Kingsland (King) Macy, the boss of Suffolk County on Long Island, who had always despised Dewey. Macy would do anything to further his own interests, including running an unfit candidate like Hanley who could be counted on to do his bidding.

Without consulting Dewey, I told Bill Pfeiffer and Bill Rusher, who was a young conservative activist with the YRs at the time, that I wanted to push through a resolution drafting Dewey at the YR board meeting in Buffalo. Rusher and Pfeiffer both admired Dewey and had little regard for Hanley. Pfeiffer gave me the green light as he rolled his eyes toward the heavens, and said, "Let 'er go, let 'er go."

It was not an easy fight, but I did manage to get the resolution passed after a considerable amount of arm-twisting and deal-making. The Erie County delegation supported Walter Mahoney, majority leader of the state senate, in the absence of a Dewey candidacy. Mahoney's backers argued forcefully and with great conviction that Dewey would not accept a draft, and the Republican party would be stuck with Hanley as its 1950 gubernatorial candidate. I had to convince them that the governor would indeed respond to a genuine draft—a gamble on my part since I had no assurances of any kind from Dewey. I did feel strongly, however, that a showdown between Mahoney and Hanley (with Macy's backing) could easily result in a victory for Hanley.

As it turned out, Hanley's own venality got the best of him. Pfeiffer and a few other party leaders convinced him to withdraw his name, according to Hanley, in return for an offer to "take care" of him by, among other things, supporting him in a bid for the U.S. Senate.

Pfeiffer's version of the story was that they did everything from begging him to withdraw to threatening to throw him out of an airplane if he didn't; but the idea of running Hanley for the U.S. Senate was patently absurd. Hanley made the mistake of discussing the alleged offer to "take care of me" in a letter to Macy, who lost no time in releasing a copy to the *New York Times,* which printed it on page one. He did this to embarrass Dewey and his people, but Dewey defused the issue with an ironic stroke of high political satire. He held a press conference at which he stated that he had the highest regard for Joe Hanley, and would do anything he could to help him. But the matter was already resolved because he fully expected Hanley to be elected to the U.S. Senate, if that's what he wanted.

Hanley was suddenly adrift with nowhere to go and no one to turn to. A man of limited intelligence who cut a rather pathetic figure, he had overreached himself and self-destructed in the process. Macy would have nothing to do with him from that moment on, and he was no longer a problem for us. Any promise to back him for the U.S. Senate—if it ever took place—was a gift horse at best and a cruel joke at worst, apparent to everyone but Hanley. With a final touch of irony, Dewey did take care of him in an appropriate fashion, as he did all those who served him. He rewarded him with the directorship of Veterans Affairs for the state of New York, a position that gave him job security and a pension in return for his years of loyalty—notwithstanding his dalliance with Macy.

It was the best solution for our side. Dewey had little choice after this near-fiasco but to run again in the best interests of the Republican party. We wound up with the candidate we wanted, and he went on to build his thruway and serve out his final four years in public life.

15 *The Right to Know*

Eisenhower's presidency was, in many ways, a disappointment for conservative Republicans. His major drawback as a politician was that he knew nothing about the Republican party organization beyond the national level: he had no experience in the world of state and county chairmen, committee people, and other local functionaries. He *was* cooperative about getting out on the hustings and speaking before local groups—particularly, as I mentioned earlier, where young people were involved. His primary appeal to Dewey, and consequently to other rank-and-file Republicans, was that he was eminently more electable than his main opponent, Robert Taft.

An important element of Dewey's plan to secure the nomination for Eisenhower was winning Richard Nixon over to the Eisenhower camp. Nixon ran for Congress in 1946, the same year I had made my own misguided bid for a congressional seat. Nixon won, of course, and quickly established his reputation as a leader of the new wave of young, post-war politicians. They banded together in an organization they called the Chowder and Marching Club, which still meets once a year or so. Nixon became a YR hero as a congressman, a position he solidified when he was elected to the U.S. Senate in 1950.

Dewey was among the first to recognize Nixon as an up-and-coming young Republican, and he invited him to speak at a hundred-dollar-a-plate state committee dinner in New York City. Nixon gave one of the most forceful and dynamic speeches of his young career that night, and he impressed Dewey and everyone else who heard him.

Dewey invited him to his suite afterward—the first time, as I recall, that they sat down privately for an in-depth political discussion. In the course of that meeting, Dewey convinced Nixon to get off the fence and come out squarely for Eisenhower in the Republican primaries.

This was no small achievement for Dewey. Unlike New York under Dewey, California lacked a cohesive statewide Republican party organization. Power was decentralized, and auxiliary groups ran things pretty much as they saw fit on a local level. This was a state of political anarchy, which was all the more horrifying from an organizational standpoint since California and New York were the two pivotal states for any would-be president. Dewey knew that he needed California if he was going to secure the nomination for Ike. No one really controlled the California delegation, although Governor Earl Warren assumed he did as the leading Republican in the state. But Nixon was also a force to be reckoned with, and Dewey needed him on his side.

In many ways, the 1952 Republican convention was the last truly competitive one we've had. The nomination was up in the air, and both Eisenhower and Taft had a good chance of securing it. What made the fight all the more competitive was that there were warring slates of delegates from Texas and other essential states, some committed to Taft and others to Ike. Dewey reached down into his grab bag of political tricks and came up with something he called the Fair Play Amendment, which he managed to get passed. The net result was that more Eisenhower than Taft delegates were seated. Later on Harold Stassen, who still had credibility as a presidential contender, took credit for nominating Eisenhower when his home state, Minnesota, cast the deciding vote. But it was Dewey who orchestrated the winning strategy, and Stassen merely decided that it was prudent to jump aboard the bandwagon.

As an integral part of this strategy, Nixon delivered the powerful California delegation for Eisenhower, and in doing so positioned himself as a leading candidate for the vice presidential nomination. The YRs loved him, Dewey wanted him, and Eisenhower had no objection to him. Eisenhower, the quintessential *un*politician, had never really given that much thought to the entire process and depended on party leaders like Dewey to work out all the details. Vice presidents at that time were much less an issue than they are now after an assassination and a resignation (Nixon's ironically enough) that propelled two of them into the Oval Office. As long as Nixon had no skeletons rattling around in his closet, that was good enough for Ike.

Nixon turned out to be a strong asset in the campaign. He was a consummate politician even then, with an instinct for political infighting and no-holds-barred campaigning. Not content to ride into office on Eisenhower's coattails, he developed an efficient organization with his own manager, press secretary, and advance men. He was an indefatigable campaigner, energized by his entry into the national political arena.

Eisenhower did not go down in history as an innovative leader, but rather as more of a reassuring father figure who came along at a time when the country needed stability. He did, however, make some dramatic changes in the structure of his administration that have lasted until today. The major one was his designation of Sherman Adams as his chief of staff, a position previously known only in the military. In military fashion, Ike appointed people to various posts under the directorship of the chief of staff. Ike's press secretary was Jim Hagerty, who wielded a good deal of power and used the royal *we* when speaking for the administration. Hagerty was sometimes referred to as "the assistant president." This was not an abdication of responsibility on Eisenhower's part, but rather a career general's way of surrounding himself with flak catchers and remaining above the fray to some extent.

As chief of staff, Adams functioned as a kind of Amanuensis for All Seasons, and Hagerty was extremely effective in his role as liaison with the press. He had served as Dewey's press secretary—a testimony to his fitness for the role—prior to joining the White House staff. As a result of that experience, he possessed political skills that the new president lacked, and about which he was genuinely unconcerned. Hagerty introduced television cameras into the White House, thereby setting the stage to some extent for the man who succeeded Eisenhower, John F. Kennedy, the nation's first "media president."

Over the years much has been said about Ike's relationship with his vice president, Dick Nixon. The major problem between the two was that they were basically incompatible. Ike was open and spontaneous; Nixon was guarded and calculating. There was nothing natural about the man. He adopted whatever personality and played whatever role he thought were suitable for the occasion. He drank with his supporters, he even uttered an occasional profanity or two in the privacy of the back rooms of politics because he thought he should be acting out the part of a fun-loving "regular guy," one of the boys. This was partly due to his own fundamental insecurity, something that was even more apparent in 1952 than it was in later years.

In the beginning Nixon's wife Pat was excited about her husband's rising political stature, but she grew disenchanted over the years. I remember accompanying the Nixons during the campaign on a train tour through upstate New York. We switched tracks in Utica and I spotted fifty people or so—fifty *voters* to me and anyone else who thinks like a politician—waiting for Nixon to show his face at the rear of the train. Nixon was at least as stiff as Dewey, and rarely appeared in public without a jacket and tie. I went to Pat and got her to convince him to remove his jacket, roll up his shirtsleeves, put on his "regular guy" face and wave to the crowd.

The Nixons had little money then, a condition that plagued them most of their lives until after he resigned the presidency in 1974. Knowing this, a bunch of Dick's friends and supporters put together a so-called Nixon Fund to help finance his campaign. PACs were illegal at the time and, when the press found out about the fund, it tore into the issue with gusto. Newspaper people were not too fond of Nixon to begin with, partly because of his defensive posture with them, but primarily because of his crusade against Alger Hiss and his hard-hitting campaign against Helen Gahagan Douglas, another darling of the Left. Even Nixon's friends had a tough time talking to him, and they used to joke that Jack the Ripper and the Boston Strangler got better press than he did.

Ike, in true statesmanlike fashion, kept himself above the fray. Unlike his running mate, he was popular with everyone, and there was no talk of tarnishing him with Nixon's peccadilloes. But the general was privately annoyed. He was completely honest himself and insisted that everyone on his team be "as clean as a hound's tooth," to use his expression. Nixon had definitely roamed over into the gray area of morality, if not beyond it, and there was talk of dumping him from the ticket—talk that Ike did not discourage. Nixon had little choice but to face the issue squarely and exonerate himself, or resign.

What followed has been immortalized in history as Nixon's famous Checkers Speech, which received its name from Nixon's maudlin comment that he refused to return a cocker spaniel named Checkers that was given as a gift to his daughters by an admirer. Historians of the era failed to note, however, that Nixon borrowed heavily from Franklin Delano Roosevelt in his half-hour address to the nation. Nixon, himself, was an avid student of history, and he used a 1940 Roosevelt speech as a model for his own. FDR had been attacked for taking his own dog, a black scottie named Fala, for a ride on a government airplane. When he defended himself in a nationwide radio address, he said something to the effect that, "I understand the attacks on me. I don't even mind the attacks against Eleanor. We've gotten used to that. But when you pick on my little dog Fala, that I resent." FDR's histrionic ploy had been eminently successful, and no one was more aware of that than Dick Nixon.

Nixon's presentation was cloying to say the least. He ranged from a teary-eyed appeal for forgiveness (quintessential Nixonian hypocrisy, according to some) to a somewhat thuggish suggestion that Ike's opponent Adlai Stevenson—and, by implication, Eisenhower as well—come clean about his own finances. Overlooked in all the critical analysis, however, was that Nixon's speech *worked;* it accomplished what it was designed to do. I watched the speech on television in a hotel room in Binghamton, New York, with Louis Lefkowitz, a candidate for attorney general at the time, and a few other New York Republicans. Nixon was not popular with this group, to understate the case, and the people sitting around the television that night did not expect him to survive the ordeal—nor did they particularly want him to.

When the half-hour address, which the Republican National Committee paid for with a check for seventy-five thousand dollars, was over, there was a consensus that Nixon succeeded in pulling his fat out of the fire. We all felt that he had gambled and won, and telephone calls to Dewey and other party leaders reinforced this view. The following day, Nixon flew from California to West Virginia to meet with Eisenhower, and all eyes were on the general to see his reaction. In front of a cheering crowd, with the television cameras rolling, Ike threw his arm around Nixon's shoulders, flashed that famous ear-to-ear Eisenhower grin, and said, "You're my boy." That was the icing on the cake for Dick Nixon. If he were good enough for Ike, he was good enough for the country. The Checkers Speech was history and Nixon's place in the American political arena was, for better or worse, secure.

As far as the morality of Nixon's relationship with his fund-raisers is concerned, most legal experts agree that he had gone right up to that line separating the appearance of impropriety from illegality, but not crossed over it. The idea that Nixon associated with rich and influential people who were corrupting him is nonsense. However, he had created an impression of vulnerability in this area, and it plagued him for the rest of his life. This, again, was due to his basic insecurity. Where Nixon really erred was on the issue of full disclosure. He should have informed Ike and the public of the existence of the fund, and let everyone make up his mind about whether or not it constituted a problem. Honesty was never Nixon's strongest virtue, and he eventually paid dearly for this shortcoming.

The tragedy of Richard Nixon is related to a broader problem endemic in politics today. We have lost sight of the fact that democracy is basically a messy form of government. Churchill understood this, and he also understood that, with all its failings, democracy is better than all the alternatives. Democracy entails choices and the truth is, people don't always choose the best among all possible alternatives; that's the risk inherent in freedom. Unfortunately, crooks thrive in a free environment, and we have certainly had our share of crooked politicians over the years. James Michael Curley was convicted of mail fraud after he was elected mayor of Boston, and served five months in jail; Jimmy Walker was a thief and the voters elected him to public office in spite of it. In a democracy people have a right to decide for themselves whom they want to represent them, but there is the assumption that all the facts are available before the voters make their decision.

Nixon's mistake was failing to supply people with the facts. The voters have a right to know that a candidate is receiving money (in Nixon's case, it amounted to eighteen thousand dollars from seventy-six contributors, mostly Southern California businessmen) from one group or another, and then decide if there is anything wrong with it. Certainly, Nixon should have discussed the matter with Eisenhower, just as Thomas Eagleton should have told George McGovern about his psychological problems in 1972. Democracy works best when there is full disclosure from all the candidates, and it runs into problems when they try to keep sensitive issues secret. When Ronald Reagan was elected governor of California, his so-called Kitchen Cabinet bought him and Nancy a house because the executive mansion was located on a busy street, and it had actually been condemned as a fire hazard by the fire department. Reagan later donated the house to the state. The question of whether or not his backers were buying influence was left for the voters to decide once the details were made public.

In an effort to purge dishonesty from our system of government, we are contemplating the adoption of all sorts of remedies, including abolishing PACs. But these types of solutions do not get to the heart of the problem; they are invariably aimed at treating symptoms. The real issue is making politicians accountable for their actions. Nixon was not completely honest and forthcoming about his personal involvements. His problems in this area were compounded throughout his tenure as vice president. It was apparent that he had his sights set on the presidency. His ambition, per se, was not wrong, but it was a palpable thing with him. He exuded something that went beyond ambition—a kind of psychic lust for power, acceptance, and recognition. The young vice president was straining at the proverbial leash and Eisenhower, recognizing his craving as an unhealthy thing, reined the presidential leash in tight and barely utilized Nixon's talents.

In the end, no one ever got to know the real Richard Nixon because he himself had never been able to figure out who he truly was. He was a man for any and all occasions—tough guy, sycophant, moralist, utterer of profanities—any man you wanted him to be, condemned to lead the life of an actor because of his monumental insecurities. Sadly, the nation suffered as a result. He had the ability to become a great leader. But with all of Richard Nixon's high intelligence and political vision, his own fatal flaws drove him from the highest office in the land after he had finally been able to attain it.

16 *Snowed Out*

It was during Dewey's final term as governor of New York, and Eisenhower's first as president, that my own career as an upstate New York political "boss" reached a pinnacle of sorts. I received my education primarily by observing Dewey, trying to emulate on the county level what he was doing statewide. When a local newspaper dubbed me the "Republican Boss of Tompkins County," I thought I finally belonged to the same political class as Uncle Dan O'Connell and the governor himself. Of course, I justified my new-found political clout with the belief that it served the cause of Good Government.

There was (and is) only one way to learn the art of politics—go out and *do* it. I volunteered for every job imaginable and discovered first-hand exactly what could and could not be accomplished on each level of government. My eyes were opened wide when I found out that elected politicians, for the most part, did not know the fundamentals of practical politics; they simply did not know how things worked or got done. What they were good at was shaking hands, giving speeches, and going through the motions of campaigning. Others took care of the details that put them in office—the million-and-one things that had to be accomplished at the grass roots level for the campaign to work as a whole and be successful. Real power rested with the people behind the scenes who planned and orchestrated the entire event. This was perhaps the single most important lesson I learned in all my years in politics.

I put this lesson to work during a mayoralty race in Ithaca. A Democrat had just beaten a weak Republican candidate—someone I had not chosen myself. Three days after the election, the Democratic mayor-elect died and, according to New York electoral law at the time, we had to hold a special election the following February. This time it was my job to select the candidate, so I approached a man named Stan Shaw, a popular retired assemblyman in town, and got him to run. Shaw won the special election, and I felt pretty good about my own role in his victory.

Stan was from the old school, however, and we had a falling-out immediately after his inauguration. He was an elderly gent, originally elected to the state assembly before Dewey came into power, and he put his own team in place. Stan insisted on going his own way, making appointments I did not approve of and voting against party interests on other issues. I wanted the same deal with him that I had with other candidates we ran for office—not the right to tell him how to vote, but to discuss issues with him that were important to the party. He refused to compromise, so I decided to replace him with another candidate when his two-year term was over.

"You can't do that," he informed me. "I want to run for reelection."

"We can't work together. I have to run somebody else."

"I'll run against him in the primary."

"We'll beat you if you do. It won't look good for you."

"I don't suppose you'll tell me whom you want to run."

"You're right about that."

A few weeks later Stan called me up to say he was thinking of dropping out, but he was curious about who my candidate was. He was a crafty old devil, and I knew that he just wanted to see if he had a chance to beat my candidate before deciding whether or not to run.

"You'll find out who he is when we file," I answered. Stan was getting on in years, and I was gambling that he didn't have the energy left to assemble his own organization and mount a campaign without party support. The job was a nice sinecure for him, but he really didn't need it at this stage of his life. The gamble paid off. Stan left the scene quietly, and we won the mayoralty again with a wider margin than before. This time we were in firm control of the city of Ithaca and the county. Thirteen of the fourteen aldermen were Republicans, handpicked by me. My position as "political boss" of Tompkins County was now solidified.

The appellation came in handy when I went head-to-head with a local sheriff who had similar ideas about his own independence vis-à-vis the party hierarchy. I had to discuss an issue with him, and he said to me, "Why should I cooperate? The Republican party never did anything for me."

"Things are different now. We'll raise money for you, manage your campaign, and support you down the line. All we ask is that you listen to our positions on key issues."

"I can probably win without your help."

"We'll run somebody against you if you try."

"What makes you think you can beat me?"

"The only way to find out for sure is to test it in a campaign. Are you sure you want to take the chance?"

He thought it over and decided in the end that it was not worth bucking the party organization. If he cooperated with us he was virtually assured of keeping his job; if we beat him, he would lose everything. The deal I worked out with him was that he could select his own deputies, but I retained the right of approval. In return, we supported his reelection bid. It was a fair exchange all around, and this was the approach I took with everyone we ran for office. The quid pro quo for party support in a campaign was an open channel of communication, especially on matters of importance to the Republican party.

I realize that the modus operandi might strike some people as cynical—politics as usual—but I make no apologies for it. It was both an efficient and an effective way of running an administration, and it remains so today. The benefit of this type of party system, including all the patronage and horse-trading that go with it, is that you always know who is responsible for everything that happens. You know whom to go to when you want something done, who gets credit when a job is done well, and who is responsible when mistakes are made. As long as the people in various positions are free of corruption and further the interests of Good Government, the system works. If it breaks down and fails to function as it should, the voters have the final say in the matter; they can exercise their right to kick out the rascals and replace them with a new team.

This, to me, is the essence of democracy. Politics in a democracy is the art of compromise; there is no way around that. Ideologues usually don't care to hear that. They are so convinced their brand of utopia is the only correct way for everyone to live that they want to force it on others. True believers of both the Left and the Right are the most dangerous people in any society. They want to legislate every belief they hold into law and, in doing so, run the risk of fragmenting the country into warring camps. In the end, their way of doing things undermines the democratic process and leads to dictatorship. Over the years I've made no secret of my allegiance to the conservative wing of the Republican party. This is a matter of principle and philosophical belief. But I have never been comfortable with fire-breathing ideologues of any stripe who fail to respect the ideas of others. People in power—whether conservative, liberal or somewhere in between—should lead by example without trying to enact every idea they have into law.

I have always believed that the two-party system is the best that democracy has to offer. When it is working properly, it is more efficient than a parliamentary or multiparty system. Politics is the art of getting things done, and this involves compromise and cooperation with others of similar interests, at least in selected issues. My conservatism did not stand in the way of friendships and working relationships with other politicians with whom I have disagreed. As I mentioned before, I worked with Gus Tyler in the AVC after World War II. When he and Dave Dubinsky started the Liberal party in New York, their primary strength was in New York City, with only limited contacts upstate. They were both concerned about keeping Communists from infiltrating their party—a concern that I shared with them—so they would ask me to do a check on various candidates they ran for office in my neck of the woods. I was only too happy to let them know if a prospective candidate was a genuine liberal, or a closet Red masquerading in liberal clothing. If liberals or conservatives knew that Clif White was screening candidates for the Liberal party, there would most likely have been an uproar!

The point is, Gus and Dave respected me and I respected them despite our political differences. They relied on my judgment in this instance to make sure that they were fielding the best of all possible candidates, and this dovetailed with my interests as well. If one of their people got elected in my bailiwick, at least I had the satisfaction of knowing not only that he was honest, capable, and qualified for the office, but also that he was not working secretly to undermine the democratic system.

What I had against Communists in our society—and it should be noted that Tyler, Dubinsky, and other democratic socialists were just as strongly opposed to them—was once again the question of disclosure; they refused to acknowledge exactly what their goals were, namely, the overthrow of democratic processes and the establishment of a dictatorship. Joe McCarthy disgraced himself and, indirectly, the anti-Communist cause with his lists of names and his other asinine tactics. What was overlooked in the ensuing effort to discredit McCarthy and drive him out of government was the subversive, totalitarian nature of the enemy in our midst. No other free society on earth permits terrorists and others committed to violence to operate openly and without restraints. For a democracy to flourish, it is imperative that the people be given all the facts available. If a candidate for public office believes in God and attends church or synagogue regularly, the voters should know that. Likewise, if his opponent is against the freedoms outlined in our constitution, and wants to create an atheistic utopia on earth instead, that information ought to be broadly disseminated as well. But the Communist party did not believe in honesty and full disclosure. It engaged in subversion, secrecy, and distortion of the facts—The Big Lie as it was called—and that was reason enough to uproot it from society.

The Dewey era came to an end with the gubernatorial election of 1954. On June 3 of that year, the governor announced that he would not seek a fourth term. "After twenty-four years in public office, I should like a little private life for a change." Privately he told Clare Boothe Luce that the time had come "for me to pass from the scene."

Dewey's handpicked successor was Irving Ives, former dean of Cornell's School of Industrial and Labor Relations, who was elected to the U.S. Senate in 1946, a beneficiary of Dewey's landslide gubernatorial victory. The Democratic candidate was W. Averell Harriman, who was regarded as a "virtuous stiff" by many observers, including Eisenhower, who also referred to him as a "nincompoop" and a "Park Avenue Truman." Unfortunately for the Republican party, Harriman's patrician and somewhat prudish manner made him appear more conservative than Ives, who was identified more with the liberal wing of the Republican party. Ives was the one who tried to portray Harriman as anti-union in the campaign.

The election was close. When I analyzed the results afterward, I was convinced that a sudden snowstorm gave Harriman the victory that year. A blizzard swept into New York on the morning of the election, which made it difficult for many voters to get to the polls. We usually gave party workers the day off so that they could drive Republican voters to the polls and otherwise "get out the vote." In 1954, however, the plan backfired when cars were buried in snow all over the state, I ended up commandeering automobiles equipped with tire chains from the sheriff's office, a questionable procedure at best from a legal perspective. However, I reasoned that, in the event of a Republican victory, our party was unlikely to investigate the issue; and if the Democrats won, they would be so flush with new-found power that they would overlook it. As it turned out, even these vehicles were not up to the job. We really required Sherman tanks. When the final votes were tabulated, Ives lost by one vote per precinct—less than ten thousand votes statewide. I lost upwards of two hundred votes in my county alone because of the weather.

After the election, it was just a question of time before the new regime cleaned house and appointed new people to various posts, mine included. I benefited to some extent in that the Democratic party had been out of power for so long that it literally did not have a grasp on how things worked in the state. There was confusion at various levels of government, and I actually served as Harriman's commissioner of Motor Vehicles for three months while he got around to appointing a replacement. Harriman's executive assistant was a feisty young Irishman named Daniel Patrick Moynihan, the same flamboyant raconteur who was later elected to the U.S. Senate. (There is some irony in that the man whom Moynihan defeated in 1976 was the incumbent James Buckley, whose successful 1970 race I had managed myself.) Notwithstanding our different party allegiances, Moynihan and I got along extremely well. He had a devilish sense of humor even then, and a love of good cheer and hearty good fun—in sharp contrast to his puritanical boss. We were kindred spirits in more ways than one, another example of the adage that politics does make for strange bedfellows indeed.

17 Teaching Politics

One measure of Pat Moynihan's effusive nature was his child-like appreciation of so mundane a matter as the distribution of license plates and medallions. Shortly after Harriman's inauguration Moynihan asked me how he could get some medallions.

"What medallions?" I asked.

"The medallions politicians put on their cars so people know who they are."

"We don't do things that way up here. We print up business cards for politicians instead."

He was genuinely upset. "I think we need medallions. Why don't we make some up?"

"Let me look into it."

In anyone else this concern for privilege and rank would have been objectionable, but with Pat it had an almost endearing quality. I had a bunch of medallions stamped with various political titles for the incoming Democrats to fasten onto their cars. Satisfied that their rank and position would not go unnoticed by the public, Moynihan then asked me how we went about issuing distinctive license plates.

"The governor ordinarily approves them for major contributors."

"Can you make some up for us?" He handed me a laundry list of names and requests.

License plates in those days were made by prisoners in state penitentiaries, so I ordered dozens of them for big Democratic party contributors. Leo Durocher, then manager of the Brooklyn Dodgers, received three of them for his Cadillacs—LD1, LD2, and LD3. Milton Berle requested TV1, representing his self-designated rank as the presiding King of Television (a slap at Arthur Godfrey who had notions of his own about who was Top Banana). There was a problem with Berle's plate in that designer plates for television personnel could only be issued to technical people, such as cameramen and electricians, and reporters, so that they could cross police lines to cover a story. Berle was furious when we turned him down and, when he received an award for being the outstanding television performer of 1955, he quipped that he could get an award like that, but he couldn't get the license plate he wanted in New York.

Moynihan was like a kid in a candy store with his medallions and license plates—he literally could not get enough of them. However, the total number we could issue was limited since, in those days, license plates contained only four digits.

"Suppose we expand the digits to six?" he wondered. He asked a friend of his, a Catholic priest who was also a mathematician, to calculate how many extra plates we could issue if we increased the number of digits. I never did learn the outcome of this project since Harriman finally appointed a new commissioner to replace me in April 1955. I was sorry to be out of a job, and could only hope that my replacement had half as much fun working with Pat on license plates as I did. Many years later, whenever Pat and I ran into each other, he always pointed at me and remarked to anyone who was listening, "Clif White and I used to have a corner on all the distinctive license plates in New York."

With Dewey gone and a Democratic administration now entrenched in New York, the idea of returning to teaching after all those heady years in the political arena held absolutely no appeal for me. Clearly, my path through life had arrived at a crossroad of sorts. I knew I wanted to remain in politics, but I didn't know how or in what capacity. I had a major decision to make, one that would affect the direction my life would take for years to come. As always, whenever I came face-to-face with a situation such as this, I turned to the voice within— to the Lord and maker of us all—for inspiration.

My tenure as Republican party chairman of Tompkins County ended early in 1956. As I analyzed the changes that had taken place on the political landscape during the past five years or so, it occurred to me that the arrival of television had revolutionized the art of politics permanently.

As recently as 1948, it had not been a factor. Television was still a novelty—few families could afford to buy one. There was a single, immobile camera at the Republican convention that year, trained implacably on the speaker of the moment at the podium. This worked to Dewey's advantage since he came across best when he was photographed by himself, giving a speech or answering questions. But even then the press secretary of the New York Republican State Committee, Harvey Call, recognized television's potential as a campaign tool, and served as Dewey's media adviser later on.

Most likely Dewey would not have been as successful a politician as he was had he come along a generation later. The camera would not have been as kind to him as it was to, say, John F. Kennedy or Ronald Reagan, both of whom used it to great advantage. Dewey had his height against him, which I discussed earlier. There was also a problem with his mustache and his cigarette holder. He bore an unfortunate resemblance to Charlie Chaplin with that clipped-off black brush above his lip, but he was decidedly not a comedian. He refused to shave it off on the grounds that he liked it, and "Mrs. Dewey likes it too." His ever-present cigarette holder gave him a somewhat sterile appearance, but here too he refused to make a concession to his public image. The doctor told him he could continue to smoke as long as he used a filtered cigarette holder, he said, and that was the end of it. Whether or not any of these surface "liabilities" cost him the White House is impossible to say, but surely they did not further his cause.

All of this was not as clear to me in 1955 as it was years later with the benefit of 20/20 hindsight. No one could foresee completely the insidious effect television would have on the political process, but it was apparent that dramatic and far-reaching changes were taking place. Over the years television has succeeded in trivializing the art of debate, particularly in a political campaign. Dewey with his high intelligence and sharp wit excelled at it. Today, five-, ten-, and fifteen-second sound bites have replaced substantive discussion of the issues. The most photogenic and relaxed candidate is usually proclaimed to be the "winner." How a message is delivered is more important than the message itself. One-liners and zingers get aired over and over on prime-time television. I believe that television has seriously impaired the entire democratic process; it has the ability to undermine competitive, democratic elections to the degree that it substitutes performance for intelligent deliberation.

Along with the advent of television and its impact on politics came the development of what has come to be known as the public affairs movement, and it was in this area that I established a base of operations. One of my main concerns at the time was that businessmen, for the most part, did not understand politics and the mechanics of the political system, while the unions did. I had nothing against unions organizing for political goals; in fact, I supported the concept wholeheartedly. But I did think that the lack of political activism in the business community created an imbalance in favor of the unions, and I decided to do something about it.

A group of young professionals had formed a pro-Eisenhower organization called Young Men in Government during the 1952 campaign. One of the leaders was Bruce Palmer, president of the Mutual Benefit Life Insurance Company in New Jersey, and there was a large contingent from California. The West Coast faction entertained somewhat grandiose notions about what its role in government should be; some of them took the name of the organization quite literally, believing they should receive cabinet appointments after the election. When the cabinet posts failed to materialize, they flew into a snit and threatened to disband.

It came to a head at a meeting I attended in Chicago. The Californians made good on their threat and left the fold, but Palmer stayed on and created a new organization which he named the Effective Citizens Organization (ECO). His stated goal as president of ECO was to get businessmen more involved in politics—something that dovetailed perfectly with my own growing interest. I spoke to Robert R. (Randy) Richardson, a good friend of mine and the son of the founder of the Richardson Foundation, and persuaded him to supply ECO with its first grant to help it get started.

Palmer hired a public relations man named Joe Eley, and he and I developed a seminar for businessmen outlining exactly how the Amer-

112

ican political system worked. Since Bruce Palmer had considerable influence as the president of a large insurance company based in New Jersey, we decided to hold our first seminar at Princeton University. We obtained lists of businesses from the various Chambers of Commerce and sent out mailings. Getting commitments to attend from the business community was not an easy task. In those days business was wary of any kind of political involvement; anti-business sentiment was rife in Washington, and most corporate heads were loath to raise their political profile, notwithstanding the growing clout of the unions. They would not agree to attend our seminar unless we assured them that our organization was bipartisan. With this in mind, we invited the county chairmen as well as pollsters—Gallup, Roper, Lubell, etc.—from both political parties.

It was difficult work in the beginning, but we caught on gradually and attendance grew from seminar to seminar. Making refinements along the way, we took our dog-and-pony show on the road, traveling from Princeton to Michigan State to the University of Southern California. We tightened our conferences from four days to three, and changed the name of them from Political Action to Public Affairs since the former was identified largely with the unions. Public Affairs Seminars had a less-threatening sound to the ears of most businessmen. Political Action was synonymous with organizing political precincts and getting out the vote—a distinctly union activity in those days. The AFL-CIO had even put together a book on the subject, *How to Win,* the most comprehensive one available at the time. Of course this was precisely what we were teaching our business people to do, but never mind. They learned political action under the rubric of public affairs, and thus the public affairs movement in the United States came into existence.

We had been doing this for about a year when Bill Merryhew, a vice president at General Electric who later became president, asked us to create a similar seminar for his company. We worked out an agreement and signed a contract, and our GE seminar was successful enough to attract the attention of Harry Bradley, chairman of the Allen Bradley Company. We did the same for him and, suddenly, a new industry—the public affairs seminars market—was born, and we had a corner on it. Eley and I established Public Affairs Counselors to market our concept, eventually doing business with just about every sizable company in and around Milwaukee, where Bradley was based. Successful businessman that he was, Harry Bradley suggested that we change the word *Counselors* in the name of our group to *Council* on the grounds that it sounded more prestigious. Whether or not this had anything to do with our ensuing success is difficult to say, but our council (consisting of two *counselors,* Eley and me) prospered beyond our wildest hopes. Today, virtually every corporation in the United States has its own public affairs department, a direct result of our early efforts.

I had always believed in free enterprise over socialism without fully analyzing why, but this experience taught me more than any textbook ever could about how entrepreneurship and hard work could create a profession where none had existed before. It all developed from an idea born of a desire to teach others the political skills we had learned over the years—and make a living, if possible, doing it. The only opposition we had along the way was from corporate lobbyists who felt that we were treading on their turf; they believed that, if we became successful, we might one day replace them. Joe and I won them over by convincing them that their fear was unfounded. We were actually broadening their horizons to a great degree by drumming up grass roots support for their efforts. By involving business people more deeply in the political process, showing them how to function as precinct committeemen, county chairmen, even state legislators and congressmen if they wanted to run for public office, we were creating legions of important allies for corporate lobbyists on every conceivable level.

Through it all we were careful to maintain a bipartisan balance in our seminars. The original reason for this, as I mentioned earlier, was to overcome corporate reluctance to raise its political profile. As we gained acceptance from the business community, however, an altogether different kind of a problem arose; the unions grew suspicious that we were out to increase the power of big business at their expense. It was a damned-if-you-do, damned-if-you-don't situation. We put on a seminar for GE in Lynn, Massachusetts, and the president of the electrical workers local, a tough group by any measure, demanded that he be allowed to attend along with the executives of the company. We agreed, and when it was over he paid us the best compliment he could. "I came here to take you guys apart," he said in front of everyone, "but I want you to know this is the best program I've ever seen. It's much better than the one our union sponsors." We all went out for drinks afterward, and both the union leader and the company's labor negotiator admitted that it was the first time they had been able to look at each other across a table without arguing. This, to me, is the heart and soul of politics—negotiation, compromise, getting things accomplished for the greater good of all—and I felt we were on the right track after that.

The essential lesson to be learned by anyone interested in politics is that all *good* politics is local. It all starts at the grass roots level and works its way up from there; nothing happens unless you get the people in the precincts and on the planning and zoning boards to agree on issues first. Each state has its own bylaws, each county committee across the country is organized in its own unique fashion. Unless you understand how things get done in each community, you won't accomplish anything on the state level.

Each time we conducted a seminar, I wrote a booklet outlining the political structure of that region. Since no one had ever done this before, the attendees at our seminars went away knowing more about the politics of the areas in which they lived than anyone else. In every state I visited I went to the headquarters of both parties and requested a copy of their bylaws. Incredible as it sounds, the state of Missouri at the time did not have any bylaws at all detailing how the political system should be organized. Traditionally, the parties had petition drives to get proposed legislation on the ballot, and each party had its chairman, secretary, treasurer, and so on—but there was no *legal* basis for how and why they did those things. I explained to them how anyone could run candidates for public office and propose legislation without going through a petition drive, and there was no legal way to prevent it. This stirred things up pretty well; both parties got together pronto and adopted sets of bylaws—the first time Democrats and Republicans had been able to agree unanimously on anything in Missouri, or anywhere else for that matter.

Shortly afterward we conducted a seminar in Hamilton County, Ohio, inviting the county chairmen of both the Republican and Democratic parties to speak. When they finished I presented both of them with copies of a guidebook I had written, containing the bylaws for their county. They both looked stunned.

"Where did you find these?"

"It's public information," I told them. "Anyone can get them. All you have to do is ask."

Neither one had ever seen them. What was even more astounding was that neither county chairman of the two major political parties had even thought to *ask* for them. This was akin to running a company without knowing how decisions were made and who was responsible for what, or driving down a highway with no knowledge of the traffic laws. Local political bylaws are the rules under which we operate and govern, yet few politicians and political appointees know the first thing about them. The ones who do, control the levers of political power, and have a great advantage over everyone else.

When I understood fully how ignorant most people were of the political process, I decided to have a little fun. In the front of every guidebook I left space for the conferees to fill in their names, election district, ward, state legislative and congressional districts, and other pertinent political data. I asked them to fill in the information now, and when the vast majority stared back at me blankly, I offered them the option of doing it at home—after they did a little homework and found out what districts they lived in. To ease their collective pain, I informed them at that point that the answers were inside the booklet; all they had to do was look up their street addresses to find the election districts. The spirit of fun in this exercise had an obvious purpose behind it. If nothing else, the people who came to our seminars went home knowing whom to contact when they wanted something done.

What Joe Eley and I did at these seminars did not require any special kind of genius; it was basically good common sense reinforced with hard work. Our fundamental assumption was that, if you were planning a career in politics, you sure as hell ought to know how the system worked. Even if you weren't, it was in all of our best interests to understand how elected officials operated. Whoever knew the rules was in a position to create an organization and get candidates elected to public office. Power started in the streets and filtered up to the top—an axiom that the New Left latched on to in the late 1960s. As things stood, however, a lot of people were getting elected without really understanding why. They left it all to chance, which meant that the opposition had as good a chance of winning as they did the next time around.

Leaving things to chance, as any good, seasoned politician can tell you, is no way to run an organization.

18 *Meeting the People*

We knew that we had finally arrived when the U.S. Chamber of Commerce sent someone to one of our seminars to take notes. He duly copied down everything he heard, mistakes and all, and then the Chamber printed them up into a guidebook of its own and sold millions of copies of what was little more than a flawed reproduction of our product. The Chamber proceeded to sponsor public affairs seminars taught by politicians who, in many cases, could not tell you what their own bylaws were. While it may be true that imitation is the sincerest form of flattery, Joe Eley and I did not much appreciate at the time this type of competition from such a formidable organization. Looking back from the perspective of several decades later, however, I can honestly say I am pleased that the Chamber of Commerce was able to profit from our idea. It is a fine organization that deserves everyone's support.

Corporations today, as I mentioned, all have their own public affairs departments as a result of these early efforts, but this turned out to be a mixed blessing when the lawyers decided to get in on the act. Lawyers, as is their wont, figured that they ought to be involved in anything new that comes along, and skirmishes erupted between the legal and public relations departments at many companies when they tried to incorporate public affairs into their own separate bailiwicks. Eley and I were called in often to resolve these disputes. We usually took the diplomatic (not to say cowardly) way out by suggesting that the company hire an outside consultant for the job.

But this solution, reasonable as it may have sounded on the surface, was not ideal. Corporate decisions are ordinarily made by committees, and collective bodies are not known for creative thinking. Many of them hired former public officials and retired politicians as their outside consultants, assuming that they knew the political process pretty well—a naive assumption at best, as I have already noted. There were exceptions, however. Clark MacGregor, a former congressman from Minnesota, was an extremely effective public affairs officer who later became Richard Nixon's campaign manager. He was largely responsible for creating the PACs that prospered with the reform laws of the 1970s, and are an integral part of the political landscape today. Say what you will about the PACs, no one can deny their effectiveness.

Personally, I don't think there is anything inherently evil in PACs. Their original function was to get people more involved in the political process; they were an offshoot of the public affairs movement itself. Sadly enough, PACs have transmogrified over the years into vehicles for raising obscene amounts of money, usually for the incumbents of both major political parties. Money has gained supremacy over hard work and commitment. As vehicles for funneling incredible sums of money into the war chests of powerful politicians, the PACs have destroyed the very idea of good citizenship and become a threat to democracy. Voters have grown cynical because of that, becoming increasingly alienated from their own political system.

While the Republican party has taken much of the heat for this state of affairs, the Democrats actually receive more money from the PACs and are equally to blame. Congressman Dan Rostenkowski from Chicago, for example, hasn't run a competitive race in years because of all the money sitting in his campaign till. To add insult to injury, the law as it is currently constituted permits him to take that money with him when he retires. A movement that was originally designed to involve the citizenry in local issues—housing, public swimming pools, schools, planning and zoning—has degenerated into a vehicle for stagnation, corruption, and privilege. When we were conducting our seminars back in the 1950s, it was impossible to see how things would evolve twenty to thirty years later. Our intention then was to promote democracy and competition in the political arena; what we have today is a class of incumbents who usually have to be dynamited out of office to remove them from the public trough.

Through it all, the old-fashioned concept of grass roots politics—knocking on doors, visiting people in their homes and offices, discussing issues in town halls and public schools—is as valid today as it ever was. Mario Cuomo employed these tactics expertly in the Democratic primary campaign against Ed Koch for governor of New York. He and his people went from door to door in Queens and Brooklyn, where he was strong, and arranged to drive voters to the polling booths on election day. One reporter covering the race wrote that Cuomo seemed to have discovered a new style of campaigning. There was nothing new about it at all. The observant journalist was just too young to remember what politics was like three decades earlier. Had he been around longer, or done a little research, he would have discovered that Tammany Hall had perfected the technique before he was born. Having grown up in an age of PAC money and televised political commercials, however, he assumed that campaigns had always been conducted that way.

I believe that with the sea changes taking place in the American political system today, we will begin to see more and more grass roots politicking in the future. Lawton Chiles originally got himself elected governor of Florida after having suffered a mental breakdown of sorts by walking across the state. Lamar Alexander did the same thing in Tennessee. While this is more feasible on a local level, Bill Clinton and Al Gore managed to get closer to the voters with their bus tours during their successful 1992 presidential/vice presidential campaign. George Bush was clearly out of touch while the Democrats managed to convey the impression that they were in tune with the people and their concerns.

The fundamental idea behind this type of political campaign is simple: if you let people see you up close listening to their problems and answering their questions, they will respond to you as a human being rather than as a remote image on a television screen. They may not agree with you, but they will at least know that you are not some disembodied monster living in an ivory tower while they are suffering in the real world. It is difficult to hate a *live* human being who has just shaken your hand, while it is far too easy to feel contempt for some distant politician you see only on television.

We took all this for granted back in the 1950s, but it has to be re-learned. It was the sum and substance of what we taught at our seminars—how to organize a campaign, how to get people involved, how to "deliver" the voters if you will. There is nothing sinister about it as long as delivering voters does not become synonymous with "buying" them. My concept of it was diametrically opposed to the PAC idea of buying votes with money.

Three young Republicans walked into my office one day and said they wanted to run a candidate for mayor of Paterson, New Jersey, which had never elected a Republican to that office. I told them the first thing they should do was get me maps of each district, along with the voting tabulations for the past three or four elections. I studied them and discovered that there were indeed a few pockets of Republican strength scattered throughout several neighborhoods. I advised them *not* to spend any money on radio or television in the beginning. "The Democrats will laugh at you, just like they laughed at all the other Republican candidates who went up against them. Instead, assemble a team to go out and meet with every one of those Republican voters, every single one of them, and make sure you get them out to vote on election day. Keep a low profile and let the Democrats think they don't have any real competition. Then, a week or so before the election buy some newspaper and television ads so that the independent voters and disillusioned Democrats know you exist, and pray for a low voter turnout. If the Democrats turn out in large numbers, you're dead. You can't win, the numbers are stacked against you."

They followed the plan I outlined down to the last detail, and managed to eke out a victory. They had to run as liberal Republicans because of the politics of the city, but the basic strategy worked. Once the Republicans were in office, they were careful to govern effectively enough to be reelected several times.

I do not believe that there is a district, a town, or a city in the entire country where that strategy would not work today if it were implemented properly. The key to winning any election with low voter turnout—the norm in this country for a couple of decades now—lies with the nonvoters and the independents who have the power to swing an election in any direction. It is good, sound, fundamental politics that has nothing to do with buying votes.

When we were conducting our seminars in the late 1950s, Bunny and I moved to Rye, New York, in Westchester County just north of New York City. Westchester was filled with young corporate types (the next generation would call them yuppies) who were busy working, raising families, attending PTA meetings, hobnobbing at the country clubs, and they had no time left over for political activities outside of pulling a lever on election day. Conservative by nature, most of them could be counted on to vote Republican—when they voted—but they were badly informed about the various referenda that appeared on the ballot from time to time. I made it a point to hold an open-house cocktail party at my home, usually on the Sunday before an election, to explain the issues and, in effect, tell them how they ought to vote on each one. I went so far as to show them sample ballot forms marked up the way I wanted them to vote.

"Never leave anything to people's imaginations," I used to tell my poll workers all the time. "When you go through a ballot form with voters, mark it up the way you want them to vote."

This way they could take the ballots home with them, and possibly carry them into the polling booth to remind them of their "positions" on the issues without voting the wrong way by mistake. Keep in mind that these were intelligent, successful, sophisticated people for the most part, but they were too busy administering their lives to stay abreast of every local referendum that came up for a vote. They needed someone whose judgment they trusted to tell them what was at stake and why it was important to register their vote. If they had any questions, or harbored any doubts about a particular candidate's integrity, they knew they could come to me for a reliable assessment of the matter. This is what I mean by "delivering the vote." Essentially it is a process of supplying information, letting people know how you feel about an issue or a candidate, and why you think it is in their interests to vote a certain way. The unions do the same thing with their members, and we were performing the same function for the business community.

Another important political lesson I learned during this stage of my life was that people rarely vote on the basis of intellectual commitment; most of the time it is instinct and emotion that sway them. Voters—particularly those who are reasonably intelligent—will tell you that they arrived at their decision through a logical, rational, deductive process. But when you ask them to tell you specifically why they voted a certain way, most of the time you get a vague response about how they agree with a candidate's positions on the economy, or on foreign policy.

"How many people in this room," I would ask a group of voters, "can make a list of the key issues in a campaign, and tell me each candidate's positions on them? How many of you did that, evaluated them, and then voted on the basis of your analysis?"

Invariably, those assembled stared back blankly, or else mumbled something about not having the time to go through all that. After several years of testing voters with this exercise, I concluded that most people voted for the party with which they felt more comfortable emotionally, or for a particular candidate because of a single issue that affected them on an emotional level. Many times it was little more than an instinctive response to the way someone looked or expressed himself. This drove home to me what the role of the local, precinct-level political leader should be—namely, someone who could gain the confidence of his neighbors and make them feel comfortable with his political judgment.

Besides delivering the vote, the second most important role of the local political leader is to *turn out* the vote. Low voter turnout is a major crisis in our society, one we have not yet even begun to address seriously. The trend started back in the 1950s and it has grown worse over the last few decades. I have worked over the years with conservatives and liberals alike, attempting to understand exactly why people do not vote. Sadly enough, there is no definitive evidence to support any of the diverse theories on the subject.

Some have suggested that the logistics of registering and voting is too cumbersome, but our system is a lot more accessible than others where voters turn out in greater numbers than we do. Attempts to simplify the process in different regions have not resulted in increased participation. Others have theorized that poor people don't vote as readily as the more affluent, but here again studies show that the demographics of voters and nonvoters are identical; rich people are no more inclined to utilize their democratic franchise than anyone else. The truth is, no one really knows why so many people stay away from the polling booth on election day.

With no more basis for my theory than anyone else's, it occurs to me that there are two main reasons for low voter turnout. First, there is little question that people have lost confidence in the system and don't believe it is responding to their needs. Accordingly, they have concluded that it doesn't matter whom they vote for, who gets into office. Second, our society appears to be suffering a moral breakdown of sorts. There is a prevailing code in the land that says other people are responsible for everything that goes wrong. More of us are refusing to assume responsibility for our actions, for our family and community. We see this with our tendency to sue others for damage we inflict on ourselves or others, as though third parties were somehow responsible for our own reckless behavior. We don't even want to be held responsible for the candidates we elect to public office.

The political system in the United States is in greater danger of breaking down today than at any other time this century, perhaps longer. We have reached a point where good, qualified people simply will not run because of all the personal scrutiny we put them through. Since we now believe that all politicians are crooks, we demand that those running for office be as pure as Mother Teresa. This is naive at best, and dangerous at worst. No one who has lived a normal life in the real world can measure up to the saintly standards we impose on people running for public office.

It is true that our politicians have brought much of this upon themselves. They've created all sorts of perks and benefits designed to perpetuate their own incumbencies. Members of Congress, in particular, have become an elitist band far removed from the people they are supposed to be serving. The way out of this dilemma is not for voters to stay away from the polls, but rather to turn out in greater numbers and replace their representatives with new blood. We need to revive the public affairs movement to increase public understanding of what politics is all about, to infuse people with a new sense of personal responsibility.

Political education, ideally, should begin in kindergarten. Children in Costa Rica, for example, are taught to conduct mock elections during national campaigns to get them involved early in the democratic process. They learn what a secret ballot really means, as well as the other essentials of a competitive, democratic, electoral process. What I tried to convey over and over at our seminars in the 1950s was that freedom needs constant nurturing; democracy is a living organism, ever-changing, always evolving toward something better or worse. We can't preserve freedom without participating in the process.

If our democracy were functioning the way it was designed to, we would not need special remedies to correct our problems; the system would take care of itself. But since we are arrested in this state of permanent gridlock, with no apparent solutions on the horizon, I have come to the reluctant conclusion that term limits for our politicians may be the only way to get through the impasse. This combined with a law restricting congressional staffs, along with the budgets for newsletters and constituent services, would at least guarantee a turnover in political personnel at regular intervals. While I have always regarded politics as a respectable lifelong profession, we may have reached the point where public service has to be considered a second career reserved for those who decide to run for office after achieving success in the private sector.

A more draconian solution proposed by some is to jettison our two-party system in favor of a parliamentary form of government. This I am adamantly opposed to, as I am to any kind of multiparty democracy. Our Founding Fathers knew exactly what they were doing when they established our ingenious system of checks and balances, with a division of power apportioned among the executive, legislative, and judicial branches of government. The genius of our constitution has been reinforced further by our form of federalism, which reserves certain powers for the various states. You do not have such balances and divisions when the president comes directly from the parliament and requires a majority to govern. The British Parliament does not even

126

have authority in the courts since the House of Lords serves as the Supreme Court.

Any kind of multiparty democracy is loaded with an assortment of pitfalls. It is difficult to attribute responsibility when no single party is in charge. Israel, for example, can barely govern itself because so many splinter parties constitute the balance of power in a tight election. When no one agrees on anything, nothing gets done, government cannot function, and no one is accountable. It does work better in Britain, where there are only three major parties, and most of the governments are elected with a majority. But the general lack of checks and balances I mentioned above poses additional problems.

There is no substitute for an effective, truly competitive two-party system. Our representative republic is essentially a "compromise government" that encompasses diverse philosophies and views. Through the competitive electoral process, compromise inevitably results and keeps absolutist ideologies from gaining control. It is simply not true that everyone's opinions are not represented under the two-party system. If both parties are broad enough, as they are most of the time in the United States, you have room for a Lloyd Bentsen and a Jesse Jackson in the Democratic party, and for a Ronald Reagan and a Mark Hatfield among the Republicans. The spectrum is wide enough for heated debate, and—when the debate is over—for an ensuing compromise on the issues that makes Good Government possible.

19 *A Star Falls*

The public affairs movement that Joe Eley and I launched back in the late 1950s formed the foundation for the political ideals and values I have held over the decades—the same ideals and values I have brought to every campaign I have worked on since. If you look at the Declaration of Independence, the Mayflower Compact, the charters for state governments in the United States, you will find a commitment to God, to the Supreme Being, in every one of them. Each one discusses moral values and the basic responsibility that we as human beings have to one another. Faith in God, belief in the family as the fundamental unit of society, and the assumption of responsibility for our actions, are the common thread running throughout.

My personal philosophy and political views had been developing throughout the previous decade and longer, but now they finally came together in a richer and more complete tapestry with a spiritual foundation. Tocqueville recognized the eternal quality in the American experiment when he observed that it was our spiritual cohesiveness, the quality that bound us together as a community, that would help us survive.

Americans are perhaps the most charitable people on earth; we give a greater percentage of our incomes to worthy causes than anyone else. We also donate much of ourselves—our time and labor. Years ago, when a barn burned down on someone's farm, the neighbors got together and built a new one for the family. When a community needed a church or a school, the townspeople did whatever it took to put one up. We established poor farms, plots of land and living quarters maintained at community expense, for paupers. Through a network of churches and charitable support organizations, we made sure that everyone had enough to eat and a place to sleep. Americans did for one another voluntarily what Europeans and other societies expected government to do, and it worked a lot better. This inherent generosity of the American spirit is the quality that Tocqueville found unique and inspiring.

There is still much of that left today—witness Operation Restore Hope in Somalia, which would not have been possible without the United States—but we have grown a bit more cynical as we have lost touch, to some degree, with God. Impatience with a stagnating political system has led to pessimism in general. Churchill understood that democracy is not utopian, not predictable; he called it the worst system of government except for all the others. It is somewhat messy because it requires choices without offering any guarantees other than personal freedom. And freedom without a sense of personal responsibility, as I stated before, can degenerate into chaos and violence—a condition we are approaching today.

My evolving conservatism recognized the need for government to establish the rules and regulations—the laws—under which we all have to live. My freedom ends at the point where your freedom and your property rights begin. The laws in a civilized society prohibit me from punching someone else, or stealing his possessions by theft or fraud. If two or more people have a grievance, there is an established procedure for due process.

The more informed and literate a people are, the better the chance their democracy will work. Some democracies have survived illiteracy and poor education for brief periods, but they soon collapse. However, we create problems of a different sort when we impose restrictive educational standards on a person's right to vote. The Romans, for example, were concerned that if the masses learned how easy it is to vote themselves largess from the public treasury, the Republic would be destroyed. Ironically enough, our most educated class of citizens, elected officials, have fulfilled that prophecy by giving themselves more largess than anyone else. This is a complicated problem with no easy solutions, but I believe that the broader the voting franchise, the better off we are as a society.

The great experiment in democracy today is taking place in Eastern Europe and the former Soviet Union. It will be fascinating in the years and decades ahead to see what these formerly Communist nations do with their new-found freedom. Democracy will inevitably take on different forms in the various countries—flourishing in one nation and regressing to autocracy and civil war in another. I suspect that the world of the twenty-first century will look far different from the one we grew up in throughout much of the twentieth century.

I continued to conduct the Public Affairs Seminars after leaving the Motor Vehicle Bureau in 1955, and refined my political skills and personal philosophy of government along the way. During this period, Ike's second term, it became more and more apparent that the personal problems between him and Nixon were fairly complex. The two men were so fundamentally different that it is almost impossible to visualize them sitting in the same room together, carrying on a normal conversation. Ike was a gregarious military man who enjoyed playing golf and bridge. He seemed to get along with just about everyone. Nixon was anything but easygoing. You could discuss issues or campaign strategy with him, but never anything personal. He was constantly on guard, his defense mechanisms firmly in place, never permitting any kind of natural warmth or chemistry to take hold with anyone.

When the press asked Eisenhower what contribution Nixon had made to his presidency, I do not believe that Ike meant to undermine Nixon deliberately when he said he might be able to think of one if they gave him a week. Ike was not a malicious man, uncomfortable as he was with his vice president personally. When this more or less offhand remark appeared in print, however, it set off a howl of derisive laughter that cut Nixon to the quick and damaged his 1960 presidential campaign against John F. Kennedy. The big surprise was that the election was as close as it was considering the drawbacks Nixon had going up against the charismatic Kennedy. Many believe to this day that Mayor Daley of Chicago actually stole the election from Dick.

Nixon ran a surprisingly strong campaign and debated the issues well in 1960. Most of those listening to his famous debate with Kennedy on radio thought that Nixon won decisively, while those watching it on television gave the nod to JFK. In front of the camera JFK was poised and telegenic while Dick jiggled his foot nervously and looked worn and haggard. In reality, Nixon was totally intimidated by JFK— as he was by all the Kennedys. Aside from Nixon's pragmatic approach to politics, my main reason for opposing him in 1968 in favor of Reagan was that I thought Bobby Kennedy would be the Democratic candidate, and Nixon was incapable of performing well against *any* Kennedy.

Much has been made of Nixon's vindictiveness, and we will talk about his role in the Watergate scandal later. But I do not think he has been given enough credit for his display of statesmanship after the final vote was tabulated in 1960. The margin of victory was so slim that a handful of votes in Illinois would have tipped the balance to Nixon's side of the scale. Nixon's key people, including Len Hall, Bob Finch, and Pat Hillings, were scheduled to fly to Chicago with the defeated Republican candidate. I sent one of my own staff people up the morning after the election, before they arrived. After examining the evidence he called me up. "There's no question that this is a fraud. Daley stole Illinois for Kennedy and I've got the proof right here."

I called Len Hall immediately and told him what we found out. "I think Nixon should challenge this. This is the presidency of the United States we're talking about. It's worth fighting for."

"I agree. I'm going in to talk to Dick about it now."

The following day Len called me back. "Dick's not going to challenge it. He's made up his mind."

"But—why? We've got proof." I was truly shocked.

"He said, and I quote, 'It wouldn't be good for the United States of America to have questions about who their president was going to be for the next two or three months until we straighten it out.' That's his decision."

It took a lot of character and guts to arrive at this conclusion. The defeat was emotionally and psychologically draining for Nixon, as it would have been for anyone else, yet despite our findings, he refused to challenge the outcome for the good of the country. Nixon handled it well even though the press and everyone else was saying that he was now finished in politics. Kennedy was the bright new face, the shining star of American politics, and Nixon was presumably dead. Many of us had pinned our hopes on him as the representative of the next generation of Republican leaders, and suddenly the hope and the dream were shattered.

Peter Flanigan, who along with Bob Finch was as close to Nixon as anyone else, had recruited me for the campaign in June 1960. Rather than take a leave of absence from the Public Affairs Council, which would have been unfair to my partner, I sold my interest in the business to him. I continued to teach the seminars we had already scheduled in order to fulfill a contractual obligation we had with U.S. Steel, and I moved to Washington where I became the organization director of the Nixon/Lodge Volunteers and traveled home to Rye on weekends. I set up the national volunteer operation, and also the New York State for Nixon organization, which did not exactly endear me to Nelson Rockefeller, who wanted to be president even before he was elected governor of New York. After Dick's defeat in November 1960, I found myself once again without a job.

Nixon traveled to New York in the fall of 1961 with Finch, Flanigan, and Hillings, and I met with them at a suite they reserved at the Waldorf. Finch told me that Dick was thinking of running for governor of California, and he wanted to know what I thought about it.

"I really don't think he should do that now."

"Well, he needs to establish a political base, Clif," some of the others observed.

"Make damned sure that if he runs, he wins it then. If he runs for governor and loses, it'll all but kill his presidential prospects. It's one thing to lose the presidency by less than one-tenth of a vote per precinct nationwide in a crooked election, and another to follow that up with a losing bid in a gubernatorial contest."

They obviously put their heads together after that and decided to ignore my advice. Nixon ran for governor of California and lost, then compounded that disastrous performance with another one of his infamous comments about the press not having Dick Nixon to kick around anymore. It appeared to just about every analyst, including me, that Nixon had indeed succeeded in hammering the final nail into his political coffin. It sounded to me as though he had come close to cracking up under the strain of two successive losing campaigns— particularly one, the Big One, that he knew he had really won. I doubt that any serious observer in the country at the time would have predicted that Richard M. Nixon would one day be president of the United States.

Nixon himself felt personally crushed in the aftermath of the California loss. Insecure to begin with, he had now been rejected not only by the nation at large, but also by the people in his home state. His star, so high and lustrous just a decade earlier when he had been tapped to be Dwight D. Eisenhower's running mate, had fallen precipitously. Once identified as the heir apparent to the Republican party leadership, he suddenly had no clearly defined identity at all.

Part of the problem was inherent in the nature of the vice presidency itself. Vice presidents in general have always depended on their presidents to define the role they are supposed to play within the administration. Many of them came from the Hill, which is where their offices used to be, and therefore were identified more with the legislative than the executive branch of government. Most presidents hired their own cronies to staff the White House, and the vice president who had been put on the ticket primarily for political reasons was looked upon as an interloper at a party.

Franklin Delano Roosevelt, for example, treated his own vice presidents badly. The Constitution of the United States provided for the office, so FDR had no choice but to put up with it. But the only purpose they served for him was to garner delegate votes at the convention and help him win the general election. His first vice president, Jack Garner, was strictly a lure for the state of Texas where Roosevelt had little if any support. In 1940, Roosevelt called upon the services of Henry Wallace because of his popularity with the left wing of the party, but he turned out to be so far to the left that he alienated too many moderates. So FDR turned to good old Harry Truman for his fourth campaign; Harry was a lot safer and never upset anyone all that much. Aside from his value as a running mate, however, I doubt that

Harry Truman was ever invited to dine at the White House, nor was he included in any serious discussion of policy issues.

So Richard Nixon was not unique in his relationship with Eisenhower. Historically, most vice presidents who failed to attain the presidency on their own have faded into political obscurity quickly. Who remembers Jack Garner or Walter Mondale now—to say nothing of those who held the post in earlier generations? When one considers Nixon's 1960 and 1962 debacles, his victory in the 1968 presidential election appears all the more remarkable. Say what one will about his character flaws and other personal failings (and I will certainly have more to add in later chapters when we discuss his presidency), his supporters and enemies alike can only stand in awe of his Lazarus-like political resilience.

20 A New Political Movement

I got actively involved in putting together a conservative political coalition well before Nixon's defeat in California. Kennedy's victory over Nixon in the 1960 presidential race left the Republican party without strong leadership. Dick was the likeliest one to fill the void, and now he appeared to be crippled irreparably—in everyone's eyes but his own at least. Those of us who believed in conservative political principles needed to regroup and mount a new offensive.

As Bill Rusher described the situation in his 1984 book, *The Rise of the Right:*

> One major factor influencing the conservative movement to seek control of the Republican Party in the early 1960s, rather than found a new party of its own, was the sheer disarray of the GOP after Nixon's defeat by Kennedy. The party had not a single leader of truly national dimensions. Eisenhower had retired; Nixon had been discredited by his defeat; Goldwater was the spokesman of what seemed a very narrow segment of opinion; and Rockefeller was the victim of the animosities his liberalism had created ....
>
> As so often, the precipitating impulse to action grew out of a victory for the other side. In the YR national convention in June 1961, the long reign of the increasingly conservative coalition built by Clif White and his allies in the 1950s was ended by the election of Leonard Nadasdy, a Minnesota "moderate," as chairman.

Rusher flew to Washington in July 1961 to meet with some like-minded people in an attempt to devise a political strategy. One of the people he spoke to was Ohio congressman and former YR chairman John Ashbrook. "You know, John, if we held a meeting of our old YR crowd today, I'll bet it would be the third largest faction in the Republican party." Even in that estimate he was being conservative; only Nelson Rockefeller boasted a larger personal organization at the time.

The two of them put together a list of forty or fifty people, averaging perhaps thirty-five or forty years of age, who had cut their political teeth working for me in the YRs. Each one of them was now an experienced political operative whose conservatism, like mine, had developed and matured during the previous decade. With this list in his pocket, and his own considerable political skills sharpened for combat, Bill returned to New York and telephoned me at my home in Rye.

We got together for lunch in the Tudor Room of the old Commodore Hotel (now enjoying a new incarnation as Donald Trump's Grand Hyatt) in mid-July. When he told me about the plan he had in mind for a conservative takeover of the Republican party, it was as though he were reading my mind. Bill and I had worked closely together in the YRs and we were on the same wavelength politically. Indeed, over the years Bill Rusher became my closest political ally as well as one of my dearest friends.

Shortly afterward I flew to Washington and met with Charlie Barr, a businessman from Chicago with conservative leanings of his own. I outlined a political plan that had been germinating in my mind for some time now—one I discussed in general terms with Bill Rusher during our lunch. My grand strategy called for the nomination of a conservative presidential candidate, or at the least the drafting of a conservative platform, at the 1964 convention. Charlie was a level-headed practical businessman, so when he indicated that he might be willing to help, I felt for the first time that the strategy I had in mind was not so fanciful after all.

I had already begun to settle on Senator Barry Goldwater of Arizona as the best of all possible standard-bearers for the conservative cause. Goldwater was a uniquely humble man for a politician, perhaps one of the few people to serve in the United States Senate who was not convinced that he ought to be president one day. He was a rugged individualist to his marrow, a wild westerner in many ways, who was candidly and refreshingly outspoken with his opinions on everything. I don't think Barry has ever tailored his position on any issue to avoid alienating voters—an endearing quality in a politician, as well as a maddening one for those who supported him later.

He entered politics as a city councilman in Phoenix, and then was elected to the Senate in the Eisenhower landslide of 1952. After the death of Robert Taft in 1953, conservatives had no clearly identifiable leader of similar stature; Nixon filled the void as well as anyone because there was really no one else around, but even then conservatives considered him to be more of an opportunist than one of their own. Suddenly, Barry Goldwater burst into public view with the publication of *Conscience of a Conservative,* the best-selling book he wrote with the assistance of L. Brent Bozell. Barry was open and direct, a hard man not to like. He articulated conservative principles unapologetically, and his individualism had a great deal of appeal for Republicans of a more libertarian or classical liberal persuasion as well.

Goldwater was ahead of his time in that he was anti-Washington establishment—an *un*politician if you will—before it became fashionable. His wife Peggy also despised Washington politics as well as the social scene there, and remained home in Arizona a good deal of the time. In addition to his conservative beliefs, his personal appeal, and his best-selling book (which provided him with an ideal platform to promote his ideas), Goldwater had the benefit of his rugged good looks; he looked like a hero in a John Wayne movie. Indeed, the only drawback he had from my perspective, and the perspective of others who wanted him to lead the conservative charge, was that he truly did not want to become the president of the United States. He was, in short, a reluctant leader for our cause.

Rusher and I invited John Ashbrook up to New York after my meeting with Charlie Barr to discuss the possibility of implementing my quickly developing plan. Together we compiled a list of names from the old YR crowd, those whom we felt would be most sympathetic to what we had in mind, and scheduled a meeting in Chicago for Sunday, October 8, 1961. Twenty-two of us in all, including Rusher and Ashbrook, met in the Avenue Motel on South Michigan Avenue. Most were veterans of the YR's like Frank Whetstone, Roger Allan Moore, and Ned Cushing, or solid conservatives like Roger and Gerrish Milliken, and there was one conservative Democrat, James Boyce of Louisiana, who worked on Volunteers for Nixon with me in 1960.

I chaired the meeting and brought up the idea of a concerted effort to nominate a conservative as the GOP's 1964 presidential candidate. For the first time I mentioned Barry Goldwater as the candidate of choice to spearhead our drive—without Goldwater's knowledge I should add. He knew nothing about this meeting or any incipient effort to build a political movement around him. While there was no serious objection to my choice of Goldwater from the group, many present were reluctant to commit themselves to any particular candidate this far in advance of the election since it could stir up political problems in their home states. But the seeds were planted at least, and we adjourned the meeting with a plan to convene again in two months, at which time I promised to have a blueprint for action and a projected budget ready for them to consider.

In the interim, it was necessary to tell Goldwater what we were up to before he heard about it from someone else. Since Bill Rusher knew him better than I, he wrote him a long letter advising him of the existence of what would later become the National Draft Goldwater Committee as well as of the purpose of our organization. Senator Goldwater requested a meeting with us almost immediately. Neither Ashbrook nor Bill was available on the specified date, November 17, 1961, so I flew down to Washington and met him in his office along with Charlie Thone, the Republican national committeeman from Nebraska, who knew Barry quite well.

Goldwater was gracious and courteous throughout the meeting. He seemed anxious to help in any way he could, but he conveyed the impression that he believed Governor Nelson Rockefeller of New York just about had the Republican presidential nomination sewed up in 1964. Barry was anxious to guide the Republican party in a more conservative direction, but he did not yet see himself in the role of party leader, let alone its presidential candidate, so we thought it was premature to share our thoughts on the matter with him. However, we believed that we had received enough encouragement from him for the general goals of our group, to prepare for our next meeting in Chicago with a high level of optimism.

I flew out to Chicago on Saturday, December 9, 1961, the evening before the meeting, to consult with some of the other leaders before the rest of the group arrived. Rusher, in particular, felt that the Republican party was flat on its back. It went with Nixon, its "best shot" in 1960, and there was no one else with whom conservatives felt even remotely comfortable. In the wake of Nixon's loss to JFK (even prior to his disastrous 1962 run for governor of California), Nelson Rockefeller—anathema to those on the Right—appeared to be the GOP's residuary legatee. Rockefeller, we discovered later, had been courting Goldwater behind the scenes in an early attempt to defuse a potential threat from the right wing of the party. There was a sense of urgency in our group, a feeling that we had to "get to" Goldwater first to rescue the GOP from its more liberal elements.

The group of twenty-eight that convened the following morning in the same motel conference room was larger by six than our October 8 conclave, even though several could not fly in because of the weather. I described my meeting with Goldwater and presented a sixty-five thousand dollar budget for the coming year, including a salary of twenty-four thousand for myself, travel expenses, and a small office in New York with a secretary and telephone. Securing the 1964 Republican presidential nomination for Barry Goldwater was going to be my full-time occupation for the next three years. It is worth musing in retrospect that, if Nelson Rockefeller had been a fly on the wall at that meeting, the prospect of twenty-eight conservatives proposing to deprive him of his coveted prize with such a meager budget would not have cost him a single moment's sleep.

I unfurled a map I had prepared beforehand, dividing the nation into nine regions for organizational purposes, and outlined a strategy that amounted to nothing less than a long-term political guerrilla operation. Whereas Rockefeller was employing the traditional tactic of lining up leading Republican officials in every state in which he had support, we would go after the hearts and minds of rank-and-file party members down to the congressional, and wherever possible, down to the precinct level. We would not "write off" any single state since we knew there were conservatives in even the most liberal states who would work hard—harder than those above them in the party's hierarchy—for a cause they believed in. Although I did not express it at the time, I had never been so fired up in my life. This was politics the way it was supposed to be, political combat in the trenches where the battles had to be won. The philosophy behind my strategy rested in the understanding that delegates to the national convention are selected by precinct committeemen who, themselves, are named to their posts as early as two years before a presidential election. Those at the top of the pyramid—governors and other party bigwigs targeted by Rockefeller—name only a few "bonus" delegates, depending on the party's success in the congressional and senatorial races. After all those years of putting the lessons I learned under Dewey to work on the local level, I now had the opportunity to apply them on a national scale.

The headquarters for our still unnamed fledgling movement was a two-room suite of offices in the Chanin Building on East Forty-second Street in New York City—Suite 3505, which became the title of the book I wrote on the Goldwater campaign, originally published in 1967. The lobby directory identified the occupant as "F. Clifton White and Associates, Inc." It was from these small rooms that I would orchestrate and direct a political movement that would be called a revolt by some, and a full-fledged revolution by others. As Rusher put it in *Rise of the Right,* "[I]t was nothing less than a revolution.... The seizure and control of the Republican Party by brand-new forces, based in the Midwest, the South, and the West rather than in the East and dedicated to the fast-growing cause of conservatism rather than to either liberalism or that pusillanimous cop-out called moderation."

What we were doing—although I did not think of it in these terms at the time—was using the intellectual seeds planted by Bill Buckley and his cohorts at *National Review* as the genesis of a new political movement. Bill Rusher, who was closer to Buckley than I was at the time, served as a de facto liaison of sorts between the intellectual and the political camps. As he told my collaborator on this project in 1992, the central thing that Clif White did "was to take the conservatism that had really been pulled together and rationalized and built up into an intellectually respectable movement by Bill Buckley and give it a political dimension. Buckley knew nothing about politics in a practical sense and didn't pretend to. How did you get from the Ivory Tower to the door of the White House, or even to the convention, let alone take over the convention and the party? It was Clif White who did that, more than any other single person."

In all honesty, I have to say that I had no inkling in the cold, gray winter months of early 1962 that any of this was going to take place. When my secretary Rita Bree asked me where I thought we would be at the end of 1964, I told her that I really did not know. I had a wife and a growing family, a son and a daughter; I wanted to leave my children what my father left me—an opportunity. It was idealism that drove our little group, not money or hunger for power or anything else so mundane. Anyone looking for that would have been over in the Rockefeller camp where all the money and ostensible power were evident at that moment. "Getting from the Ivory Tower to the door of the White House" was still a distant and improbable goal in the eyes of everyone, including most conservatives, in the early days of 1962.

F. CLIFTON WHITE   1918–1993

Tom Van Sickle (left) and Clif, inside the famous trailer during the 1964 GOP convention at San Francisco. (Fred Ward, Black Star)

BARRY GOLDWATER'S 80TH BIRTHDAY   Veterans of the 1964 campaign at a United Republican Fund of Illinois event in 1989. From left, Congressman Philip Crane, Sondra Healy, Bill Rusher (rear), URF president Denis Healy, American Conservative Union chairman David Keene, Vic Gold, former URF president Ken Wright, Phyllis Schlafly, Clif and Barry (seated). (Photo by Tom Roepke)

CLIF ELECTS SENATOR JIM BUCKLEY   In a three-way race in New York, Buckley
s elected on the Conservative Party line in 1970.

THE THREE WISE MEN of the conservative movement (from left), Bill Rusher, Bill Buckley, and Clif, uncharacteristically somber at yet another political dinner.

BREAKING UP THE TROIKA   Clif's ill-fated meeting with Ronald Reagan in 1983.
(White House Photo)

ASHBROOK CENTER DINNER 1984   Clif, Bunny and Vice President Bush. (White House Photo)

FOSTERING DEMOCRACY   Clif meets with Secretary of State George Schultz.

The Whites (right) with President Oscar Arias of Costa Rica and Sonia Picado Sotela of IIDH/CAPEL.

Clif with former Venezuelan president Rafael Caldera.

ASHBROOK CENTER DINNER 1990   Senator Howard Baker, Fred Lennon, Clif and Phyllis Schlafly.

PUPIL AND TEACHER   Dan Quayle and Clif at the Conservative Political Action
Conference in 1992. (White House Photo)

21 *The Draft*

It was somewhat disingenuous that Barry Goldwater would be portrayed by the media as a fanatical, fire-breathing extremist during the presidential election, for he came across as the voice of moderation and consensus prior to his nomination. Certainly he did our cause little good when he spoke these words at the Republican National Committee meeting in Oklahoma City in January 1962: "It doesn't help to have our members characterized as western Republicans, or Javits Republicans, or Rockefeller Republicans, or modern Republicans. Nor does it help when some of our detractors get into a particularly vengeful mood and refer to some of us as Goldwater Republicans. We've got to get together and decide just what we are."

I traveled nonstop during the next few months, rounding up support and solidifying our political base prior to the 1962 off-year elections. Periodically I would fly to Washington to brief Senator Goldwater on the progress we were making in identifying pockets of conservative strength across the nation—without once ever bringing up the question of a possible Goldwater presidential candidacy in 1964. His main interest throughout this period remained the structure of the party's platform that year. My own timetable called for the appointment by the end of 1962 of one person in every state who was responsible for the selection of delegates to the 1964 convention. I wanted to garner as much conservative support as possible before confronting Goldwater with our plan to draft him as the next Republican presidential candidate.

Optimistic as I was that we were going to succeed in this effort, there were times during the early months of 1962 when I thought our inchoate movement would grind to a crushing halt. The funds raised by our finance chairman, Roger Milliken, had all but dried up by our April meeting in Bemidji, Minnesota. There was barely enough money to pay the rent on suite 3505, let alone to pay for trips to key areas around the country. The support of people from the old YR crowd—Bill Rusher, Frank Whetstone, and others—helped to keep our little band intact in the absence of adequate financial resources. I was forced to withdraw six thousand dollars from a fund Bunny and I had set aside for our son's college tuition to carry us through the summer. Miraculously we kept the operation afloat through the November elections, which resulted in solid Republican gains throughout the South and West. While the off-year election was a standoff in terms of overall results, it did provide the Goldwater forces with a respectable political base. The results were especially heartening for the Republicans, and conservatives in particular, on the state and local levels where we needed to build up our strength.

Rockefeller had commenced his assiduous courtship of Goldwater for his own presidential ambitions even before his reelection as governor of New York (and Nixon's defeat in California). Goldwater's initial complicity in this political misalliance was made possible by their mutual distrust of Nixon, and it was not encouraging for those working behind the scenes for Goldwater. Party unity was another bond they shared; it was a theme sounded over and over by Goldwater, who had no presidential ambitions of his own as yet, and a powerful argument for Rockefeller, who wanted to neutralize conservative opposition to himself. Their brief but harmonious "honeymoon" was the single largest obstacle I had to overcome.

I planned another Chicago meeting of our group, now expanded to fifty-five attendees, for the first weekend in December 1962 to decide on a firm plan of action. Because of our larger size, we met in more spacious quarters at the Essex Inn on lower Michigan Avenue. Additions to the veterans of the earlier conclaves included Ione Harrington, Republican national committeewoman from Indiana; Pat Hutar, co-chair(woman) of the Young Republican National Federation; Randy Richardson, whom I mentioned earlier; Jerry Milbank and Bill Middendorf from New York; and Congressman William Brock of Tennessee. By this time I had traveled to twenty-eight states and established contacts by mail and telephone in fourteen others. We were close to my goal of achieving organizational support in all fifty states by the end of the year, and the most pressing item on the agenda at this meeting was deciding on our presidential candidate.

It was apparent from the start that the nearly unanimous choice of those present was Senator Goldwater. I submitted a budget of $3.2 million for 1963 through the first half of 1964 leading up to the Republican convention. Much of the money would be for the 1964 primary campaigns, as well as for the drive to line up the necessary 655 delegates to secure the nomination for Goldwater. Other major expenses included rent for a suitable headquarters in Washington and staff salaries. I proposed March 1963 as the target date for the official launching of the National Draft Goldwater Committee. Until this time we had succeeded in keeping the existence of our organization and its *raison d'âtre* a secret from the press. We had hoped to continue this policy until the launch date, but this was not to be the case.

The first notice I received that a spy attended our meeting was a telephone call from Carl DeBloom, correspondent for the *Columbus Dispatch* in Ohio. He called me in my New York office at ten o'clock in the morning of Monday, December 3, less than eighteen hours after the meeting adjourned. DeBloom had little in the way of specific information, and I was not about to provide any for him. (An article published shortly afterward in *Advance,* a liberal Republican journal, contained verbatim quotes from some of the participants, indicating that the pseudonymous author had evidently attended with a hidden tape recorder.) By the middle of the week a media storm had erupted, magnifying our relatively small organization into a "secret" group of "prominent" conservatives who were out to "block" Rockefeller and "push" Goldwater in 1964.

I had known all along that the media had a gift for hyperbole, but they clearly outdid themselves on this issue. The *Herald Tribune* in New York City went so far as to call our meeting a "conspiracy," and the *New York Times* said we were "splintering" the Republican party.

I called Goldwater immediately following my first conversation with DeBloom so that he would get the news from me first. He was courteous as usual, thanking me for letting him know before the media did, and he said he would be straightforward with them. "I don't know a thing about it," he later said, which was true and succinct in typical Goldwater style.

It was not long, however, before the senator's famous temper erupted, this time in our direction. He took me by surprise during a meeting I had with him in his office on January 14, 1963. He was out of sorts to begin with because his colleagues, as punishment for his "defection," had just left him off the party's policy committee where key strategy decisions are made (this was reversed a few days later when cooler heads prevailed). He stared at me directly and said, "Clif, I'm not a candidate, and I'm not going to be. I have no intention of running for the presidency."

"Well, we thought we would have to draft you."

"Draft nothin'. I told you I'm not going to run. And I'm telling you now, don't paint me into a corner. It's my political neck and I intend to have something to say about what happens to it."

I tried reasoning with him along the lines that he was the de facto leader of the conservative movement, and millions of people wanted to see him assume that role as the Republican presidential candidate. Nothing worked. He had evidently made up his mind and his attitude was more than merely intransigent; he had become hostile, or so it seemed to me, for the first time since I had known him. I was stunned and depressed when I left his office that day. Everything we had worked for was about to run down the drain. I did not know it at the time, but Rusher and others found out later that some people Goldwater trusted had gone to him with lurid and fanciful accounts of how I was paying myself a lavish salary and making a career opportunity out of the draft Goldwater movement. He had no way of knowing that I had partly subsidized it with my own savings a year earlier, and that I had passed up a far more lucrative business career to work for the conservative cause, centered inevitably around him. A good deal of the friction being generated between us at that time may well have been due to misperceptions and differing temperaments.

As Bill Rusher told my collaborator on this book:

Clif was on the one hand an inordinately shy person, particularly with the people he was running campaigns for and looked up to—Dewey when he worked for him in New York, Goldwater, and later Jim Buckley .... Goldwater was uncertain about this. He didn't know what he was being confronted with here. He regarded this bunch of young conservative Republicans who insisted on drafting him as a roving band of samurai who came dashing out of the forest and kidnapped him .... He was satisfied with his senatorship, and here he would have to give it up because he was running again and he had teased Lyndon Johnson unmercifully for running both as vice president and senator from Texas. So he was not all that grateful to us for what we did for him.

In addition, when he first noticed the group, he saw that there were very few professionals. Goldwater had a high admiration for the old pros in the party .... Where were they all? All he could see was a bunch of ex-Young Republicans. Whoever leaked our December 1962 meeting to Goldwater told him that White had made a mint for himself promoting Goldwater for his own purposes. Goldwater was furious with White. It was totally untrue. I was trustee of his son's education money, and I know he used that to keep suite 3505 going.

Goldwater totally misconceived Clif and got a lot of wrong ideas, which he later got over. But, all during the key moments then, he relied on his Arizona mafia—Dean Burch, Denison Kitchel, and Bill Baroody, who took things over in Washington and became the guru and gray eminence, and didn't want any "boarding parties" to get anywhere.

With the clarity of 20/20 hindsight, Goldwater's attitude during that meeting in Washington made a good deal of sense. At the time, however, I was puzzled. I felt as though he had unreasonably pulled the rug out from under our feet.

"I'm going to give up politics and go back into business," I told Rusher when I returned to New York. "It's no use. He won't permit a draft. He said he wasn't going to run under any circumstances and that's that."

Once again Bill interceded in the form of another lengthy letter to Goldwater, but the senator didn't reply, and subsequent meetings with him failed to yield anything in the way of hope. There was little to do at this point but get together with others in our group. This time, however, we decided to limit the gathering to a trusted few—Charlie Barr, Frank Whetstone, Robert Matthews, Robert Hughes, Peter O'Donnell, Tad Smith, Andy Carter, John Ashbrook, Dave Nichols, Bill Rusher, and me—in the interests of preventing further leaks.

We met on Sunday, February 17, 1963, at the O'Hare Inn near the airport in Chicago. Our gloomy mood matched the gray weather outside. We had to come up with a way of keeping intact the organizational tapestry we had worked so diligently to stitch together. Word was getting out that Goldwater was not going to run, and it was just a question of time before our committed delegates jumped over into a more receptive camp. As I elaborated glumly on my less-than-productive meetings with noncandidate Goldwater, Bob Hughes, the treasurer of the state of Indiana, came to the rescue with his growled suggestion, "Let's draft the son of a bitch."

"What if he won't let us draft him?" someone responded.

"Let's draft him anyway!"

Bob's mood galvanized the group. His matter-of-fact, let-it-all-hang-out attitude was just the tone we needed to shock us out of our lethargy. We decided to proceed with our original plan of forming the National Draft Goldwater Committee, naming Peter O'Donnell (Republican state chairman of Texas and a "pro" whom Goldwater admired) as chairman and me as national director. When we officially announced the formation of the organization on April 8, 1963, Goldwater's response was not exactly friendly, but at least it was vague enough to invite analysis and interpretation: "I am not taking any position on this draft movement. It's their time and their money. But they're going to have to get along without any help from me."

As far as conservatives were concerned, it was all they needed to hop aboard the bandwagon we had erected and start it rolling in the direction of the White House. We finally had a bona fide political movement of our own, even if it was centered on a man who genuinely did not want to take charge and lead it. The dreaming and planning had come to an end. Now it was time to come up with a detailed political strategy to make it all come true.

22 *Mr. Conservative*

The strategy I designed to secure the Republican presidential nomination for Barry Goldwater was crafted in our new headquarters on Connecticut Avenue in the nation's capital. The individual who was most provoked by it was not the Democratic incumbent, John F. Kennedy, but rather the other contender for the nomination, who wanted to be president of the United States more than anything else, Nelson Rockefeller, governor of New York. It was he who in retaliation against Goldwater, the man he had been assiduously courting for many months, created the issue of Goldwater's so-called political extremism, which the Democrats would use so effectively in the presidential campaign.

What was not widely recognized at the time—or any time since for that matter—was that Richard Nixon also had a strong interest in the nomination despite his disastrous 1962 defeat in the California gubernatorial election. It is an insight into his state of mind during this period, and a comment on his utter dissociation from reality, that he actually believed he had a good chance of getting it.

Nixon was the featured speaker at a hundred-dollar-a-plate Republican dinner in Milwaukee, and later that night one of his people came over and said that Dick wanted to see me.

"I can't meet with him."

"Why not?"

"The press is watching him. They'll be hounding me to find out what we talked about for weeks."

So I met with his associate instead at the bar. He informed me that Dick was thinking of running for president and he wanted my help.

"No way. I'm backing Goldwater in sixty-four. Dick doesn't have a chance this time around. He'll get killed, I guarantee it. The best thing he can do is go to Europe and make himself scarce for a few months so he doesn't get trapped into endorsing anybody."

"Goldwater doesn't have a prayer and Dick's not interested in endorsing Rockefeller or anybody else. He's thinking seriously of going after the nomination for himself."

"You may not believe this now, but I'm going to nominate Goldwater. If Dick sticks his nose into this, I'll beat him to a pulp. He won't know what hit him."

I don't know if it was my advice that convinced him or not, but Nixon did go to Europe for several weeks before the convention and he kept himself out of the nomination battle. Later on, when Goldwater won, Dick went out on the hustings for the ticket; he campaigned as much for himself as he did for Goldwater actually, but at least he played the game like a sport, biding his time until the next best opportunity, which came along four years later to everyone's surprise but Nixon's. He refused to count himself out when everyone else did.

Another little-known fact is that Barry Goldwater and John F. Kennedy were close personal friends despite their political differences. Barry was devastated by JFK's assassination. Beneath the veneer of politics, they were both fun-loving individualists who spoke out bluntly on the issues. Kennedy invited Barry into the Oval Office one day. He arrived a few minutes early and saw Kennedy's famous rocking chair, which he favored because of his back problem. Goldwater sat down in it and started rocking back and forth when Kennedy walked in.

"Trying it out for size, Barry?" JFK kidded him.

"Never thought about it like that. I wouldn't want your job if you handed it to me."

"Go on, Barry. You're right up there at the top of your party. If you ever run, I guess I'll have to agree to debate you even though Bobby would be against it."

Kennedy and Goldwater started joking about what it would be like competing against each other for the presidency. They fantasized about chartering a plane together and flying around the country as a kind of traveling debate team, getting off in different cities and staging their performance before going on to the next stop. They talked about having an open bar aboard the plane so they could unwind and swap jokes and war stories as they jetted around the country. The two men truly liked and respected each other and probably would have enjoyed the friendly competition if it came to that. That's why it was especially vicious when the media tried to portray JFK's assassination as a right-wing coup, planned and executed by conservative extremists of the type who were supporting Goldwater. No one outside of the Kennedy family was more shaken by the tragedy than Goldwater was.

The assassination followed the death of Goldwater's mother-in-law. He was returning home to Arizona from her funeral in Indianapolis when some idiot reporter stuck a microphone in his face and asked him what he had to say for himself, all but accusing him of plotting Kennedy's assassination himself. This theme was echoed over and over until it reached a point where we had to shut down our headquarters in Washington that night because of bomb threats. Senator John Tower, a fellow conservative and a Goldwater ally, moved his family from their house to a hotel for safety reasons. The mood in the country for the first twelve hours or so following the assassination, fueled to a great extent by the media, bordered on hysteria. Everyone was looking for a scapegoat, and the "hate groups on the far right" filled the role for a while—until we learned more about the actual assassin, Lee Harvey Oswald, and his ties to Castro and Moscow.

The single event that helped soften Goldwater's refusal to run for the presidency more than any other had been the Fourth of July rally we staged at the National Guard Armory in Washington in 1963. This extravaganza was successful beyond our wildest hopes. It attracted more than nine thousand enthusiastic conservatives from all over the country, busload upon busload descending on the nation's capital in the heat of summer, all of them vocal in their support of Goldwater for president. Barry, who did not attend, was visibly moved by the display of warmth and affection, which stated our case far more powerfully than all the arguments we had brought to bear on the senator during the preceding months.

My relationship with Barry improved considerably after that, but he continued to feel more comfortable with his inner circle of cronies and confidants. My contacts with him were usually through John Tower, a staunch advocate of our cause; John Rawlins, an Arizona congressman who was elected in 1952, the same year Goldwater won his Senate seat; Paul Fannin, governor of Arizona; and a lobbyist from General Motors named Jay Hall, who was a close friend of Goldwater and worked secretly for him. We used to call this individual "The Mystery Man" or "Mr. X" because he let it be known that he would lose his job at GM if word got out he was a political operative. For this reason I never identified him by his real name before, and I was unnerved when Lyn Nofziger called me up shortly after my book on the Goldwater campaign was published, and told me he knew who Mr. X was.

"Like hell you do," I told him. I was convinced that no one except a handful of people around Goldwater knew the name of the man, let alone Lyn, who was a young reporter then.

"You bet I do." He proceeded to name him.

"What are you going to do with this information?" I didn't confirm or deny it.

"I don't know yet."

"Lyn, if you publish his name, you'll get the guy fired from his job. That's why I never identified him."

To his credit Nofziger never did write the story, which would have been big news at the time. It is hard to imagine a reporter today refusing to take advantage of a headline-making scoop that would boost his career considerably. Nofziger was aggressive and ambitious almost to a fault, so this act of professional self-sacrifice was not easy for him.

Three other close associates of Goldwater in 1963 were Dean Burch, his administrative assistant; Bill Baroody, the director of the American Enterprise Institute; and Denison Kitchel, whom Barry brought on board to serve as a liaison with our Draft Goldwater group. Dean Burch was competent, friendly, and cooperative from the start. I worked closely with him, and he was liked by everyone on my staff.

Baroody and Kitchel were birds of a different feather entirely. Baroody had the mind of a zealot. He developed the notion that he had personally invented Barry Goldwater and had to protect him from everyone else—particularly Bill Rusher, Bill Buckley, and the crowd from *National Review.* Since I was close to Rusher and had got to know Buckley through him, I automatically fell into Baroody's "enemy camp" along with them. Karl Hess was Baroody's protégé, and he was hired to be Goldwater's main speech writer. His unofficial assignment was to follow me around and keep an eye on me under the guise of "helping me." He was friendly and easy enough to get along with, although I did find his role as a "spy" somewhat unsettling.

Denny Kitchel was a nuisance and a hindrance from the start. He was a mining lawyer and a close friend of Barry who knew next to nothing about politics. He rode all the way on the shuttle from New York to Washington, sitting beside a leading Republican senator who identified himself and discussed the forthcoming convention with him. When the plane landed in D.C., Kitchel asked the man what party he belonged to again. This was a leading Republican senator who was undecided as yet about whom to support, who could have been enormously helpful to us.

After that incident, I prepared a booklet containing the names of every national committeeman, and every Republican state chairman and leading power broker in the country for him. "When you get a phone call, Denny," I reminded him on any number of occasions, "look in the booklet so you know who the heck you're talking to. It's important." I don't know how good a lawyer he was, but he never did catch on to politics right through the end of the campaign.

The momentum behind Goldwater kept building after the Fourth of July rally, and he announced officially that he was a candidate for the presidency a few weeks after JFK's assassination. At this point we dissolved the Draft Goldwater Committee and established the Goldwater for President Committee. As so often happens once someone becomes an official candidate, those close to him begin jockeying for positions of influence. Unfortunately for those of us who, more than two years earlier, had created the concept of a conservative movement led by Goldwater, the so-called Arizona Mafia had more clout with him than we did. It wasn't long afterward that Peter O'Donnell, others of our original group, and I found ourselves relegated to lesser roles than we felt we deserved.

The elimination of O'Donnell from the Goldwater for President Committee was a serious strategic mistake. Peter was the Republican party chairman of Texas, with influence not only over delegates, but over some of the wealthiest people in his state as well. He was a wealthy and powerful man himself. To treat a man like him the way the Arizona Mafia did was tantamount to a slap in the face; it was sheer political stupidity.

Barry's people—who now included Richard Kleindienst, former Republican party chairman of Arizona and a lawyer, in addition to the others mentioned previously—held a meeting in Phoenix at which they decided that Kitchel would be Goldwater's campaign director, Kleindienst director of field operations to whom I would report directly, and Baroody a kind of factotum in charge of the speech writers and Goldwater's policy positions. When they informed me of the organizational structure they had developed with the candidate's blessing, I was as aghast that Peter O'Donnell had been cut out altogether as I was at my own new status as Kleindienst's "assistant."

"What are you going to do with Peter?" I asked Kitchel in shock.

"Oh, we'll find something for him," he offered cavalierly.

Peter became disgusted when he discovered that they had no plans to utilize his considerable resources, and he returned to Texas. My initial inclination was to leave the campaign as well, but when I analyzed the extent of the investment in time and energy I had made up to that point, I decided to swallow my pride and stay on.

Kleindienst was decent enough about the relative importance of our roles in the campaign. I was able to arrive at an understanding with him that we would be equal partners in ninety-five percent of the field operations decisions, but he wanted to reserve final judgment over the remaining five percent for himself—similar to the way the senior partner in a law firm would function. This sounded reasonable enough to everyone but Kitchel apparently, who insisted for some reason of his own on regarding me as Kleindienst's assistant.

The issue more or less resolved itself after Barry's disastrous showing in the critical New Hampshire primary, which he lost to Henry Cabot Lodge, who was viewed as a more acceptable alternative to the liberal Nelson Rockefeller. Barry should have won in New Hampshire, but his inner circle failed to rein in the senator's propensity for shooting himself in the foot with off-the-cuff remarks that were easily misinterpreted. By the time election day rolled around in this most critical of all state primaries, Goldwater had been labeled as the candidate who wanted to cut off everyone's Social Security benefits and launch missiles at Fidel Castro—neither of which was true. Immediately following Goldwater's defeat here, Kleindienst and Kitchel both decided to put me in charge of nailing down the nomination for Barry at the July convention. I had suddenly been promoted from Kleindienst's assistant to co-director of field operations with him.

Fortunately for Senator Goldwater and those of us working for him, his performance in the remaining primaries improved considerably. California was close but he managed to eke out a slim victory, convincing analysts that his support carried beyond his own immediate bailiwick in the Southwest and the traditionally Republican states. By then we had enough delegates in our corner to virtually assure Goldwater the nomination at the convention in San Francisco's Cow Palace. The great countdown was finally over. Our "reluctant" candidate would soon have little choice but to accept the role we had created for him—the role of Mr. Conservative, the leader of our movement and the 1964 presidential nominee of the Republican party.

23 Goldwater for President

Even before the primaries had begun, I knew that Goldwater's chances for winning the general election in November had changed after the assassination of Kennedy. Goldwater's rough-hewn southwestern conservatism would have contrasted well with JFK's urbane northeastern liberalism. Lyndon Johnson, a rugged Texan who was perceived to be more conservative than he really was, presented a different kind of a problem entirely. Physically, culturally, and temperamentally he was similar to Barry. Both men were outspoken and direct—John Wayne types if you will. Johnson was a more difficult target to focus on. There was little if any time to think about that in July, however. We had a convention to get through first.

It has been said that the 1964 Republican National Convention in San Francisco was as revolutionary in some regards as was the 1964 conservative takeover of the party itself. "It was at this convention," Rusher wrote in *The Rise of the Right,* "that White introduced various technological innovations that have dominated the management of convention politics in both parties ever since. Previously campaign managers had operated from the convention floor itself, with leg power supplied by aides carrying messages to delegates in distant parts of the hall. At San Francisco, however, White and his regional directors were installed in a spacious air-conditioned trailer, parked just outside the rear entrance of the Cow Palace and protected against intruders by uniformed guards. From this trailer a bewildering array of multicolored wires led to telephones at seventeen strategic locations on the convention floor itself, where state leaders of the Goldwater delegates could pass the word to their troops. In addition, the rival candidates were authorized to have a number of roving representatives, equipped with walkie-talkie radios, on the floor itself. To and from these went messages for key individuals, etc." The days of keeping a telephone line open to a candidate's suite with a pocketful of change, as I had done with Dewey during the 1948 campaign, were clearly over.

Rockefeller had been soundly defeated well before the time the convention got underway. The last best hope of the liberal wing of the party, anxious to stop Goldwater in any way it could, was Governor William Scranton of Pennsylvania. He offered feeble hope at best since we had enough delegates to put Barry over the top well in hand. His strategy, such as it was, consisted of frightening rank-and-file Republicans into abandoning the Goldwater bandwagon by demonizing his supporters as "radicals" and "extremists." When that failed to work, Scranton was reduced to hoping that a last-minute blunder by Goldwater would somehow pry open the door for him. "All that now was left for Scranton," columnist Bob Novak wrote afterward, "was . . . some kind of 'incident' that would miraculously change the mood in San Francisco." It never happened.

I directed the operation from the trailer described above. Beside me sat my deputy, former YR chairman Tom van Sickle, the two of us facing six regional directors ensconced in their own tight cubbyholes. The six regional directors were connected by telephone to delegates in their respective regions on the floor. I had a telephone unit of my own that kept me in touch with the seventeen floor locations mentioned by Rusher—as well as a direct line to Goldwater in his suite at the Mark Hopkins Hotel on the top of Nob Hill. We also had television sets in the trailer that enabled us to monitor network coverage of the convention.

It was all pretty high-tech stuff at the time, right down to a "secret" antenna I had installed in the rafters of the Cow Palace that gave our walkie-talkies better reception than the Scranton forces enjoyed. We also had the capability of eavesdropping on their walkie-talkie conversations, and had taken technological precautions to keep them

160

from listening in on us. All this James Bond wizardry served us well; it was innovative for the early 1960s and, in the final analysis, it amounted to technological overkill. After having come this far in the battle for the presidential nomination, I was taking no chances. We had enough committed delegates lined up to put Barry over the top on the first ballot. The reluctant senator from Arizona received an astounding 883 votes out of the 1,308 cast, 228 more than he needed to win.

"This was a new thing in American conventions—," political historian Theodore H. White wrote afterward, "not a meeting, not a clash, but a coup d'état."

Certainly, no victory was ever sweeter than it was for us who had conceived the quixotic notion of seizing the Republican party from the powerful, heavily financed Rockefeller wing of the party, and installing Barry Goldwater as its undisputed conservative leader. We celebrated long and hard into the night, most of the festivities taking place on the fifteenth floor of the Mark Hopkins Hotel. I finally got to bed about six in the morning for a fitful two-hour sleep before rising at 8:15 to tend to the business of organizing a campaign.

As the one who had orchestrated the drive to victory on the floor of the convention, I logically expected to be named chairman of the Republican National Committee for the forthcoming presidential election campaign. I was in for a shock, as well as a monumental letdown, when I learned later that morning that Goldwater had decided upon Dean Burch as his choice for national chairman.

"Is this thing on Dean Burch a secret or can we let it out?" a member of the Republican Finance Committee asked me. He had just listened to an address by Goldwater.

"I don't know what you're talking about."

"Burch is the senator's choice for national chairman."

I immediately went numb. It was inconceivable to me that Senator—now candidate—Goldwater would pick a different team to run his race for president from the one that had succeeded in getting him the nomination. Neither Kitchel nor Burch mentioned any of this to me when I talked with them later in the morning, but by the middle of the afternoon the newspapers were carrying reports of Burch's appointment as national chairman. Goldwater never did notify me personally of his devastating decision. When the hoopla of the convention was finally over, my wife Bunny asked me if it was worth it.

"I don't know. All I know is that all of us in the group did what we had to do. And we'll keep right on doing what we have to do." Her support was all I had to sustain me through the difficult time ahead.

Bill Rusher and others had more to say about the painful anticlimax to the 1964 convention than I did. I had never felt so low in my entire life. What troubled me more than anything else was Goldwater's refusal to discuss the matter directly with me. "Goldwater acted swiftly—many would later say, brutally—to assert personal control of the party and the campaign," Rusher wrote in *Rise of the Right*.

"After the convention, when [Clif] suddenly, after several years of intense activity, found himself on the outside," Rusher told my collaborator, "he wasn't even able to pack for Hawaii. Bunny called me and tracked me down at a restaurant in San Francisco and said, 'Can you talk to Clif? He can't do anything.' I said I think I knew what the trouble is. It wasn't just that he was upset over the national chairmanship. Naturally he was. I didn't have with me Winston Churchill's statement about how he took up painting when he was ousted from the war cabinet after Gallipoli in the First World War. He said he was left without any ability to influence events and cruelly placed in a front row seat where he had to watch everything that was going on. Clif felt like that when he was made chairman of Citizens for Goldwater/Miller—something like that. Churchill said he felt like a whale on the beach. Clif was suffering from the bends and the squeezes. Finally, he pulled himself together and went off to Hawaii."

Bill's adroit turn of phrase captures my emotional state at the time better than any description I could give. Suffice it to say that this was another one of those critical times in my life when faith in the Lord and his nurturing grace and strength were required to sustain me. We all face these ordeals from time to time, and we all have to learn from them and come away stronger.

The general campaign that followed was a poorly run affair from the beginning, and I say this not with any sense of smugness or satisfaction because I was virtually excluded from the process. Every analyst at the time and after, on both sides of the political divide, was in agreement on this subject. Goldwater may not have been able to win against Johnson, but he could certainly have run a smarter campaign than he did.

The main problem was that Goldwater wanted to run the show himself, and he did to a great extent. Burch and Baroody also had a lot of influence, but there was no coordination among them and the candidate. Baroody prepared a lot of the printed material with Karl Hess's help, but in the end they wound up using a lot of my literature because theirs was sending out the wrong messages. Barry kept raising the wrong issues in all the wrong places—his opposition to TVA in Tennessee, Social Security in Florida, and a disastrous statement about the use of tactical nuclear weapons in Vietnam that made him sound like a warmonger. This opened the door to all sorts of distorted charges against him, including a full-page newspaper ad signed by three hundred psychiatrists claiming that Goldwater was unbalanced. Barry sued the publisher of the ad later and won, but it was too late; the election was already over. Afterward Goldwater did admit that he made a mistake by not appointing me national chairman. I appreciated his honesty and candor, admirable traits that he has always possessed, but my role in his campaign was limited to that of a virtual observer while everyone else stood around shouting at one another.

To Goldwater's credit, he took his defeat well—almost too well it seemed. Those closest to him said that he appeared relieved that he didn't have to assume the highest office in the land. He loved being a senator and he won back his Senate seat later. I ran into Barry at a meeting we held in January 1965, two months after the election, the main purpose of which was to decide whether Dean Burch should be replaced as national chairman.

"Hello, Pete." Flustered about running into me face-to-face again, he momentarily confused me with Pete O'Donnell.

"I'd like to meet with you privately," I told him.

"Yes, Clif. Sorry. Why don't you come to my office tomorrow morning."

The following day I sat down with him and laid my cards right down on the table. "Barry, it's bothered me and a lot of my friends that I was not selected as national chairman. I just wanted to clear the air between us. Did I do anything to irritate you? Did I strike you as incompetent? What was it?"

"Nothing like that at all, Clif. I told everybody I know that if it weren't for you I wouldn't have been nominated and there wouldn't have been a campaign." He praised my abilities lavishly and with apparent conviction, but he never answered my question directly. Over the decades I never did find out exactly what his reason was for passing over me and appointing Burch instead. Perhaps it was something as simple as his feeling more comfortable when he was surrounded by his cronies, or it may be that he never did get completely over the old suspicion he had that I was supporting him for personal reasons. Chemistry has a lot to do with human relationships, and very often it is impossible to understand them logically.

One thing that remains certain is that the draft Goldwater movement was my baptism by fire in the world of major league politics. I conceived the idea of a conservative revolution and brought it to fruition at the 1964 Republican National Convention that resulted in Goldwater's nomination. Never before had a presidential candidate been drafted into the role against his wishes. My prediction that he would get the nomination with 884 delegate votes out of 1,308 cast was off by only one (he received 883). To a great extent I had revolutionized the way conventions are run by both major political parties in the United States. It was an educational process for me, and an achievement I would cherish for the rest of my life.

Now that it was over, it was time to move on. It was time to take the lessons I had learned and put them at the service of a new political candidate.

24 *Filling the Vacuum*

Goldwater's defeat in the 1964 presidential election left the conservative movement temporarily without a leader. Those of us who had worked so hard to forge a marriage between William F. Buckley/ *National Review*-style conservative intellectualism and practical real-world politics were determined not to let it break up because of a leadership vacuum at the top. It was clearly a vacuum that needed to be filled as quickly as possible.

Ronald Reagan had already emerged as one of the likeliest candidates for the role of conservative leader because of his work for Goldwater during the campaign. He had been California cochairman of Citizens of Goldwater/Miller, and a speech he taped on behalf of the Republican ticket turned out to be one of the highlights of the entire campaign. He was big, tall, and handsome with a personal charisma unrivaled by anyone—with the possible exception of John F. Kennedy. Say what you will about his abilities as an actor or the quality of his movies, there was no room for doubt about Reagan's "star" value as a speaker. He had only to stand on a podium to command everyone's attention and light up an entire room.

It was Ronald Reagan as much as anyone who kept the conservative coalition intact by traveling frequently across the country during the mid- and late 1960s, mesmerizing conservative audiences everywhere he spoke. His virtues as the natural successor to Goldwater were sung loudly by Bill Buckley and the writers at *National Review,* as well as by sundry other conservative organizations, including Young

Americans for Freedom (YAF) and the American Conservative Union (ACU). Bill Buckley had, of course, been a leader on the Right since the success of his first book, *God and Man at Yale,* and particularly since the founding of his magazine, *National Review,* in 1955. He ran an eccentric and quixotic race for mayor of New York City in 1965, during which he commented that he would demand a recount if he won. When he was predictably defeated, a roast was held for him in New York and he was asked to speak. His entire speech consisted of two sentences. "I assume you expect me to say something about John Lindsay [commenting on the man who had just beaten him in the election]. Well, I don't believe in kicking a man when he's down."

"That was a perfect place to sit down," I mentioned to him afterward, "because there was no way you could top that line. In a real speech you would have had to save it for the end."

Bill Rusher, as I mentioned earlier, was the one who introduced me to Buckley, and most of my contacts with him until this point were through Rusher. After the 1964 election, however, Buckley asked Rusher if he could get together with me to discuss the future of conservatism. They arranged a meeting at the apartment of an odd fellow-traveler on the Right, a hanger-on of sorts named Marvin Liebman. Marvin entertained certain ideas that were regarded by most mainstream conservatives to be somewhat on the fringe at best, but in the late fifties and sixties he had become the primary public relations adviser to the conservative movement. At the time a budding conservative organization was headquartered in his offices at 75 Madison Avenue in New York City. He had created and sponsored an organization called the Committee of One Million, the main purpose of which was to prevent the recognition of Communist China, led the effort to get Congressman Walter Judd the GOP vice presidential nomination in 1960, and worked closely with YAF from time to time.

Marvin had a strange and somewhat mysterious background. He had begun as a Communist, became a Zionist, and ended up as a conservative and confidant of Bill Buckley. Later, when his mother died and left him some money, he took off for London and attempted a career as a theatrical producer. When that venture failed and his money disappeared along with it, he returned to the states in the late 1970s.

Buckley helped place him, once Reagan was elected, in the government where he remains to this day.

Marvin prepared dinner for Buckley and me the night of our 1965 meeting at his apartment. Only the three of us were in attendance. Buckley was particularly interested in discussing the Goldwater campaign and the significance it held for the conservative movement. He asked a great many questions, which I answered as thoroughly as possible, having to do with the mistakes made during the campaign, whether or not Goldwater's defeat tolled the death knell for conservatism (it decidedly did not as far as I was concerned), and what we should be doing to regroup and grow from that point onward. We talked from about six in the evening until about 11 P.M., with Buckley asking the questions, me doing the responding, and Marvin serving the food and fixing the drinks. Buckley struck me that night as a serious intellectual trying to fathom the inside story of the campaign—how it got started, how it was organized, how it was conducted. This was Buckley the disciplined intellectual, informing himself the best way he knew how about a subject that intrigued and interested him. Along about 11:30 he stood up and said, "Can I give you a lift to the station?"

"Sure." I was delighted at the prospect of not having to flag down a taxi at that hour.

We went downstairs together. Outside I expected to see a long limousine idling patiently at curbside for Buckley and his guest, in keeping with his wealth and circumstances in life. Instead, he directed me to a motorcycle chained to a telephone pole and told me to hop on. Throughout my life I have despised motorcycles, refused to have anything to do with them, regarded them with terror as vehicles straight out of Hades, and here the young intellectual leader of the conservative movement was offering to drive me to Grand Central Station on the back of one. He smiled that broad, famous, toothy Buckley grin, watching to see what I would do. Sucking up my courage as best I could, I climbed aboard with great trepidation and held on with white knuckles as William F. Buckley, Jr. roared down Lexington Avenue at what seemed to me was supersonic speed. Every now and again he turned around to look at me while he talked, never once missing a syllable as we sped along. Bill Buckley, I discovered that night, had a pronounced playful aspect to his nature that contrasted sharply with his erudite public image.

Buckley was not yet sold on Ronald Reagan's potential as the successor to the throne vacated by Goldwater, since it was Goldwater himself who had convinced Buckley of Nixon's merits. If I myself had any doubts about Reagan's prospects, they were dispelled when I saw a televised debate between him and Bobby Kennedy that was filmed at Oxford. Reagan, to everyone's surprise, including Bobby's wife Ethel, Sander Vanocur and his wife, and others not exactly biased toward Reagan, slaughtered Bobby Kennedy. According to Sandy, whose wife viewed the debate at a party, Ethel Kennedy kept shouting at the television screen, "Do something, Bobby! He's killing you, he's killing you!" I obtained a tape of the performance and played it at Republican gatherings so people could see for themselves just how effective Reagan was. It was an education for everyone who saw it.

I was not surprised when a rumor began to circulate about Reagan's interest in running for governor of California. I spoke to him by telephone in December 1965 and asked him if there was any truth to it.

"I suppose so, Clif. Do you think it's possible for someone to run for governor on the basis of one speech?" He was referring to his taped speech for the Goldwater campaign.

"You'd be surprised at how many political careers were launched on a lot less than that. Politics is a moving stream. It's never stagnant. If you see a boat out there going by your dock with the word *governor* written on it, hop in. It won't circle around forever. Sooner or later it'll continue downstream and somebody else will go aboard."

Several of Reagan's California friends—including Henry Salvatori, chairman of the Western Geophysical Company of America; A. C. (Cy) Rubel, former CEO of Union Oil Company of California; and Holmes Tuttle, a wealthy automobile dealer—felt as I did and encouraged him also. Reagan did, of course, go on to win the 1966 California gubernatorial election, defeating the incumbent Pat Brown by a margin of nearly a million votes or 57.8 percent to his opponent's 42.2 percent. This stunning victory for the political neophyte contrasted sharply with Nixon's humiliating loss to the same man four years earlier, and established Reagan as the undisputed leader of the conservative cause.

What struck me most about Reagan at the time was his genuine, fundamental humility. He never lusted after political power, but rather decided to run for public office because he believed strongly in certain philosophical principles. Perhaps one of his great strengths was his ability to find out what he needed to know to do the job. Reagan was not afraid to delegate responsibility and surround himself with people who were experts in various areas of government. Many of his enemies have attempted to portray him as a stupid man, but this is a completely erroneous and dangerous misperception. While he was not an intellectual and never claimed to be, he had an inquisitive mind and a unique ability to absorb and digest information that he later translated into political reality.

Reagan sponsored weekend seminars and invited Nobel Prize economist Milton Friedman and others of that caliber to tutor him in economics theory. He traveled constantly with a stack of books on business, economics, political theory, and history. His memory was sharp to the point of being startling; he frequently caught me off guard with quotes from conversations we had that I had forgotten. He sat back quietly at staff meetings, often not saying much, which led some to believe he didn't have anything to contribute, but absorbing everything that took place and filing it away for future use.

Among all the politicians I have known and worked with, Reagan stands out as the one with the most genuine interest in people. Many presidents and governors smile graciously on receiving lines, shaking hands and saying hello while they are already looking at the next person in line. Not Ronald Reagan. He looked everyone directly in the eye and established personal contact, even remembering intimate details about their lives. Many years later, after he was elected president, my wife and I attended a White House function. We arrived early and milled around outside on the lawn with a large group of other invitees. When we went in to dinner afterward and approached him on the receiving line, he smiled at us with those twinkling, always bemused Irish eyes and asked, "What were you looking for out there on the lawn before?" There wasn't too much that escaped his notice.

As governor of California, Ronald Reagan had to be regarded as one of the leading candidates for the Republican presidential nomination in 1968. Nixon had made his own intentions clear despite his losses to JFK in 1960 and to Pat Brown in 1962. Both Rockefeller and George Romney, representing the liberal wing of the party, were also jockeying for support.

While we regard professional political consultants as indispensable to any serious campaign for public office today, in 1967 they constituted a fledgling profession. It got started, as so many things apparently do in this country, in California, while Reagan was governor. There was a logic to it in this instance, however, because of that state's laws for initiative and referendum. Anyone can start an initiative for just about anything in California. As a result, there are half a dozen or so initiatives on the ballot in almost every state election. This is wonderful for political consultants who attach themselves to an organization of their choice, convince the members that they need to create an initiative and get it voted into law, then charge a consulting fee to get it done. Not even the legal profession has it better.

One of the problems endemic to the profession in the early days was earning a living when the campaign ended. Hundreds of eager young consultants, attempting to capitalize on their success in one campaign or another, opened offices in Washington and filed for bankruptcy six months later. American ingenuity is a wonderful thing, however, and it was only a question of time before professional political consultants figured out a way to make money between elections as well as during them. This, too, was first accomplished in California when they hired themselves out as lobbyists for various and sundry groups, charging hefty fees for the dubious practice of securing special interest legislation for them.

One of the first successful political consulting firms in the country was Spencer and Roberts, founded by Stu Spencer and Bill Roberts. Individually, they had been involved in political campaigns in Southern California, and they decided to pool their talents under a single umbrella. They worked initially on various referenda issues, then did some lobbying for the AMA. Nelson Rockefeller hired them in 1964 to help him in his primary battles, giving them national exposure. By the time Reagan was ready to run for governor in 1966 they had already positioned themselves as the preeminent political consulting firm in the country. They got to know Reagan's so-called Kitchen Cabinet—Salvatori and the others I mentioned earlier—during the course of his campaign, then worked afterward on a number of initiatives dealing with insurance rates, gas regulation, taxes, and other issues of interest to that group. By the end of 1966 Spencer and Roberts's reputation as an effective political consulting firm was well established.

The winning strategy they developed for Reagan consisted first of giving him a crash course in the intricacies of state government and, second, switching him from his stump speech style to a question-and-answer format. The media had already begun to attack Reagan as a grade-B actor who could read a speech well, but couldn't think on his feet. Spencer and Roberts defused that criticism effectively by teaching Reagan how to handle himself in the give-and-take atmosphere of a press conference.

As we approached the primary season for the 1968 presidential campaign, Spencer and Roberts shifted their allegiance momentarily to the Rockefeller camp because—well, because he had the money to finance a major campaign, which included paying a hefty fee to his political consultants. Californians were still a bit provincial in those days and resented their governor running for national office, figuring he had enough to do tending to the state's business, while New Yorkers always felt that anybody they elected governor had the credentials to be president. I had not committed myself officially to Reagan yet, but I was leaning in his direction.

All the leading contenders for the Republican presidential nomination—Rockefeller, Romney, Nixon, and Reagan—offered me jobs in their organizations. Nixon was practicing law in New York City early in 1967, and he had Peter Flanigan, one of his supporters with whom I had worked in Nixon's 1960 campaign, call me up to ask me if I would work for Dick. I told him I would like to talk to Nixon personally, so I met him first at his office in Manhattan.

"What do you think of the upcoming campaign?" Nixon asked me.

"I think sixty-eight is going to be a wide open race. It's really up in the air. The guy with the best organization and the best campaign strategy is going to take it."

"I'd like you to think about coming to work for me. Let's keep in touch."

It was a pleasant enough meeting, and I really did believe that there was no clear front-runner yet. Our next meeting was in his Park Avenue apartment late one afternoon a few weeks later. Nixon was making good money for the first time in his life, but you had the feeling that he was uncomfortable with the trappings of wealth. He seemed somehow overwhelmed by the grandeur of his posh new surroundings. He fixed us both a scotch. "I'd like you to work for me. I want you to be the Republican National Chairman after I'm nominated."

I decided right then and there to turn it down. Nixon startled me by spilling his scotch all over the rug. He knew how badly I had felt when Goldwater passed me by for the post four years earlier. Here he was offering me a second chance at it, and I surprised even myself by saying no.

"Why not?" he stammered. "Why don't you want to be chairman?"

"The power is in the White House," I replied. "If you're elected president you should run the national committee from the White House."

Nixon recovered his composure. "Well, you're right. That's what we'll do."

Life is full of ironic lessons for all of us, and the lesson I learned myself that night was that even the jobs you want the most are not worth having at any price. Richard M. Nixon had tempted me with the prize I craved most during the Goldwater campaign, but it suddenly lost its appeal under these new circumstances. I had not committed myself to working for Ronald Reagan prior to this second meeting with Nixon, but I was committed to his candidacy from that moment on.

25 Not Our Turn

When Ronald Reagan assumed the office of governor of California early in 1967, his first chief of staff was a fellow who was caught in a homosexual tryst at Lake Tahoe and was forced to resign his post as a result. Bill Clark replaced him and Tom Reed, who had been Northern California campaign manager for Reagan, joined the administration as the head of personnel—basically, director of patronage responsible for filling all the staff jobs. Tom's father was Gordon Reed, CEO of Amax who many years later got both himself and Tom in a bit of trouble with the SEC. Tom was a nuclear physicist who was involved in the invention of one of the nuclear devices dropped over the Pacific during World War II, shortly after he had graduated from college.

Gordon Reed had been a substantial backer of Reagan's gubernatorial bid, personally contributing $100,000 or so and sponsoring a fundraising party for the campaign. Afterward, Reagan came east to help Reed develop the Blind Brook Country Club in Greenwich, Connecticut. The only members of it in the beginning were Ronald and Nancy Reagan, Gordon and Tom Reed and their wives, and Bunny and I. It was at the first dinner there in 1967 that I told Reagan that many of us regarded him as the heir apparent to the role vacated by Goldwater, and that if he wanted to run for the Republican presidential nomination in 1968 I would be happy to support him in any way I could.

Not too long afterward, Tom Reed called me and asked me how much it would cost to put together a Reagan for president campaign, and if I would be interested in heading the effort. I told him I would look into it, and then developed a strategy whereby I would serve as consultant to the California delegation to the Republican nominating convention in 1968. We decided immediately that Reagan should not actively seek the nomination because of the attitude of voters in that state, as I mentioned earlier. If word got out that he was interested in the presidency while he was a sitting governor, it could hurt his chances for reelection if he lost. In effect, Tom Reed became the director of operations for Reagan, raising money and serving as liaison between Reagan and me and others active in the effort. The entire operation at that point was conducted in utmost secrecy.

Maintaining secrecy entailed my flying out to California frequently to meet with Reagan and his people under an assumed name since the media would have been able to figure out what was going on if they knew about my visits. Our meetings were limited to a trusted few—Reed and Bill Clark, of course, as well as Lyn Nofziger and a few others on the staff. Careful as we were to keep the fledgling Reagan for president effort confidential, we found ourselves undermined by an unlikely source.

A leak had developed, and we couldn't figure out who was responsible for it—at least not at first. Tom Reed was tough and determined, and he set out to find out where the leak originated; the evidence he unearthed led him directly to the door of Stu Spencer, Reagan's ostensible political consultant. All along many of us felt that Stu was not as committed to Reagan as the rest of us were. Evidently Stu had been calling George Hinman, Rockefeller's national political consultant, and feeding him information about what we were up to, what Reagan's plans were, what his schedule looked like, and so on. Ordinarily, this type of "intelligence" doesn't really bother me; it goes on all the time in campaigns and a lot of the "inside information" gets garbled in transmission. What did bother me, however, was that a trusted member of our inner circle turned out to be the spy. He was privy to everything we were doing, including the most guarded information of all—Reagan's interest in the presidency.

There was no question in Tom Reed's mind that Stu Spencer had been consorting with this colleague in the Rockefeller camp. Tom called a meeting, which I attended, along with the governor himself, and Bill Clark. We decided it would hurt our cause more than help it if we fired him outright. Somebody would hear about it and begin to wonder why Stu was working for Reagan in the first place. The more effective maneuver would be to "disinvite" Stu from all the key meetings and leave him in charge of rounding up delegates for Reagan. As long as he was successful at that, he was contributing toward the campaign and there was no reason to get rid of him.

(In a footnote to this episode, Stu told me a couple of years later that the Reagan inner circle—Reed, Clark, some of the Kitchen Cabinet, others—really went after him when the 1968 convention was over. They cut him off from clients and did everything they could to put him out of business. Personally, I have always gotten along well with Stu; I believe he just got a bit too greedy in this instance, possibly believing Rockefeller had more to offer him, and it backfired on him. There was a time when we even talked about merging our consulting businesses. But Stu decided to remain in California, working on local issues, and he ended up prospering reasonably well when everyone's emotions cooled down.)

Not knowing that I was working sub rosa for Reagan, George Romney, governor of Michigan, tried to interest me in his own presidential aspirations. Romney was a handsome, silver-haired, well-built man who seemed to have great appeal at first, until you got to know him better. He was such a devout Mormon that his critics used to say he wanted to use the presidency as a stepping stone. He was dynamic, full of vitality, but unfortunately not generously endowed with high intelligence.

Romney was endowed with a high energy level, however. His idea of a golf game was to play three balls at once, then run through eighteen holes with them for exercise. He was also a domineering man who liked to force his views on people, even to the point of intimidating them. He suffered from the moderate Republican delusion at the time that, in order for Republican politicians to be successful, they had to position themselves left of center on the issues. His liberal attitudes were further enhanced by his religion, which requires Mormons to tithe and establish social programs for those in need, sometimes regardless of the efficacy of those programs. Then, too, much of his liberalism may have been due to his notion that he was the de facto leader of the Rockefeller wing of the party.

George really did think Rockefeller was going to support him for the presidential nomination in 1968, and Rockefeller in his inimitable fashion did nothing to disabuse him of that delusion. In the end, Rocky double-crossed him royally. He kept saying that he himself was not a candidate, that Romney would make an excellent candidate as the guardian of moderate Republican values, and Romney took him at his word. He went so far out on a limb, anticipating Rockefeller's full backing, which never materialized, that when his cumbersome campaign finally collapsed of its own dead weight Rockefeller was the only moderate left to pick up the ball and run with it. The only problem for Rockefeller, however, was that Romney self-destructed early—on February 28, 1968—before Rocky was ready to launch a full-fledged primary campaign of his own. He was secretly hoping that Romney would fall apart closer to the convention so that he could be *anointed* as the candidate, rather than have to earn it in the primaries.

All this political maneuvering and subterfuge created a scenario tailor-made for the craftiest political survivor of them all, Dick Nixon. I believe to this day that if Ronald Reagan had been willing to seize the moment and strike in the spring of 1968, he could have gone on to win the prize at the summer convention. But he hesitated, and Nixon stepped right in and positioned himself just so—just far enough to the right to convince conservatives that just maybe he was one of them, and just far enough left not to frighten away the Rockefeller liberals.

Until this point my strategy was for Reagan to go into the convention as California's favorite son—strategically significant since California's eighty-six delegates were second only to New York's ninety-two. As the favorite son from a powerful state, he was a force to be reckoned with, yet he was not an "active" candidate, a fact which might have alienated California voters. This game plan seemed to be working well until a bombshell, in the form of Lyndon Johnson's withdrawal from the race two weeks after Bobby Kennedy entered it, exploded on March 31.

This was the perfect time for Reagan to abandon the favorite son ploy, throw caution to the winds, and enter the breach boldly. Immediately the old questions about whether Nixon could beat a Kennedy—any Kennedy—started to make the rounds. Reagan, as I mentioned before, had debated Bobby in Oxford and beaten him decisively. He was anything but intimidated by the Kennedy mystique, while Nixon was. The old conservative coalition was Reagan's for the taking; all he had to do was step forward and announce his candidacy. Instead he hesitated, and that moment's indecisiveness cost him the Republican presidential nomination, which Nixon won by a narrow margin in Miami.

Many delegates who would have cast their lot with Reagan had he declared his intentions unequivocally were left with Nixon as their only viable choice. Only on Monday afternoon, August 5, just hours prior to the opening of the convention, did Reagan abandon his favorite son status in favor of open candidacy. Our only chance at this late stage was to deny Nixon victory on the first ballot in the hope that a loss of momentum would give committed delegates the opportunity to reconsider Reagan. Toward this end, I was accused ironically enough of conspiring with Rockefeller to stop Nixon. This was true only to the extent that we had similar goals; I *did* assign several of my people to the Rockefeller camp primarily to keep me abreast of the running delegate count. We had an arrangement to keep each other informed of any defections—which way they were shifting and so on. The big difference, however, was that Rockefeller believed he would win after the first ballot, whereas I *knew* that Reagan would be the main beneficiary of a fading effort by Nixon.

I remember a conversation I had with Strom Thurmond after he came out for Nixon. "Senator, what are you doing? Ronald Reagan is your kind of candidate."

"Mr. White," he answered in his courtly southern manner of addressing everyone formally, "if we don't get behind Dick now, that fellow Rockefeller's gonna make it."

"That's not true, not true at all." I was visibly agitated. "I know most of these delegates and they'll swing over to Reagan."

"Well, you may be right, son, but we just cain't take that chance and let Rockefeller slip in."

Many other conservatives felt as he did; they feared Rockefeller more than they distrusted Nixon. Many on the Right still maintain that Reagan could not have won the general election in 1968. Only west of the Rockies, they say, was he viewed as a governor at the time; everywhere else he was regarded as a movie actor. I've always disagreed. There is no way to prove it now, of course, but I still think he would have sparkled in debates against Hubert Humphrey, who was a nice man, but a monotonous blabbermouth when you got right down to it. Reagan would have come across like a statesman in comparison. Actually, Reagan had a similar "image" problem with the media in 1980, but he was able to overcome it then, and I have little doubt that he would have done the same twelve years earlier.

Those too young to have lived through the period have no sense of how frustrated the average voter was in the late 1960s. The war in Vietnam was still going strong, middle-class kids were rioting in the streets and seizing college campuses, there was a total lack of respect for authority, and a breakdown in moral values. The times were perfect for a dynamic candidate with strong leadership qualities, but instead we ended up with a somewhat clownish and uninspiring drone like Humphrey and an old gutter fighter like Nixon whose presidency ended in disgrace. Considering all this, I have never agreed with those who think I launched Ronald Reagan before he was ready. I was not in it as a political exercise or to take control of the party, which is a process some people go through in this business.

In the end, considering Reagan's late entry as a bona fide presidential candidate, the margin of victory for Nixon was embarrassingly slim. I had obtained secret pledges from many southern delegates to switch to Reagan if Nixon failed to win on the first ballot. Many were aware of Dick's well-known penchant for retribution, and were afraid of what might happen to them if they threw their support to Reagan prematurely and Nixon won. Nixon's people even went so far as to circulate rumors that Reagan would be their candidate's choice for vice president in an effort to keep the delegates in line. After all, if Reagan were going to be on the ticket anyway, what was all the fuss about? This proved to be a clever and effective tactic. It forced Reagan to state repeatedly that he would not consider the vice presidency under any circumstances to keep his presidential bid alive.

"Even if they tied and gagged me I would find a way to signal 'no' by wiggling my ears," Reagan said, delivering the best one-liner of the convention.

Another thing working against us was that the Nixon team did a superb job of organizing the convention by following the working plan I had established for Goldwater four years earlier. One newspaper commented that we were up against a "small army." It wasn't so much that we were terribly outnumbered as that most of the people I had with me in 1964—Strom Thurmond, John Tower, Bill Timmons, and others—were now working for Nixon. When we added up the delegates on Wednesday, August 7, the situation was less than promising.

"We have only one option left," I told Reagan during a meeting in our trailer. "We can fold the tent now, or we can keep working and hope for a break."

"Well, that's what we're here for, isn't it?" Reagan decided without hesitation. "Let's get back to work."

Work we did, right up to the roll call of states, but there was little we could do at this late stage to keep the inevitable from happening. It was all over when Wisconsin cast its thirty votes for Nixon, giving him the edge with 692 votes, only twenty-five more than he needed to win. Contrast this with Goldwater's 228-vote margin at the Cow Palace in San Francisco in 1964. A near miss like that is more difficult to accept than a resounding defeat; you can't help but wonder whether a smarter move here or there would have tipped the balance to your side. All of us were shaken by the loss, but none more so than my daughter Carole, who was fifteen at the time. She came to me weeping as though the end of the world were at hand because her father and his candidate had lost. Nothing I could do or say was able to comfort her. Calming down my daughter seemed beyond my capacity as a father, but Ronald Reagan, the defeated candidate for the Republican presidential nomination, rose to the occasion. He entered my suite, put his arm around Carole's shoulder and said:

"Carole, the good Lord knows what He's doing. This just wasn't our turn."

26 *The Tragic Flaw*

Nixon ran a poor campaign, turning what should have been an easy victory in the general election into a closely contested race. Elected along with him as his vice presidential running mate was Spiro Agnew, who became governor of Maryland in 1966, the same year Reagan won in California. He was not widely known before Nixon plucked him from obscurity and put him on the ticket, but I had gotten to know him early in 1968 when I was courting governors for the Reagan camp. My rule of thumb was: governors control delegates, senators don't. For this reason I had spent much of my political life since 1952 dealing with politicians from the state level on down to win support for my candidates, rather than chasing after big-name congressmen and senators.

Agnew was not high on my list before the convention for the simple reason that Maryland is not that critical a state. I was more concerned about lining up delegates from states like Pennsylvania, Illinois, and Ohio. But I knew that Agnew was furious with Rockefeller, whom he had openly supported, for withdrawing abruptly from the race without so much as informing him beforehand. I spent a fair amount of time talking to him about Reagan. He struck me as a moderate Republican, decidedly closer to the center than Rockefeller was. I heard that he was leaning toward Nixon at this point, and I scheduled an appointment with him in his office in Baltimore to see if I could deflect him, possibly talk him into remaining neutral or going into the convention as a favorite son candidate.

Ted Agnew was a tall, strapping man, dapper and smoothly handsome, and extremely articulate. He was still livid when I met with him, nearly frothing at the mouth every time the name Rockefeller came up. He was obviously determined to strike back at him in any way he could. Reagan was a long shot and Nixon was a fairly sure thing, as far as he was concerned, so nothing I said could change his mind. He made it clear that he was going to back a winner this time, and that meant coming out unequivocally for Dick Nixon. I thanked him for his time and went on my way, then virtually forgot about him until Nixon stunned the convention by tapping him as his running mate.

Many have forgotten just how obscure a figure Agnew was prior to the 1968 general election. Governors are generally not that well known outside their own states, and Agnew was one of the lesser-known figures among them. I am convinced that Nixon's primary reason for picking him was to even up the score a bit after being humiliated by Eisenhower. He wanted someone who would not overshadow him, someone he could dominate, perhaps send off on some remote errand and promptly forget about. The strategy backfired to a great degree when Agnew became the darling of conservatives, thanks to one-line zingers written for him by his speech writers at the time, Pat Buchanan and Bill Safire.

"Nattering nabobs of negativism," was a definition of liberals in the media that earned him a lot of free publicity. "Effete snobs," was another. Agnew became an eager and skilled deliverer of provocative punch lines.

He stole a lot of Dick's thunder with conservatives who never completely trusted Nixon and saw a more kindred spirit in Agnew. And Agnew delighted in this unexpected turn of events that suddenly transformed him from an unknown governor and a faceless vice president into a conservative hero. It was almost as though there had been a feisty right-wing provocateur lurking beneath his bland moderate facade all along. He joined Ronald Reagan and Bill Buckley as the favorite featured speakers at assorted conservative functions, particularly those sponsored by youth groups such as Young Americans for Freedom.

I attended a governor's conference in Hot Springs, Arkansas, shortly after the new administration took office. A lot of business and industry types flew in for the occasion, and Agnew came down from Washington to speak at a VIP dinner in the evening. Reagan was there as well, and the three of us were chatting by the hors d'oeuvre table during the cocktail hour. Suddenly, Agnew and Reagan put their heads close together and started whispering. I noticed that many in the crowd were backing away in unison, forming an ever-widening circle of space around the two men. It was as though those nearby were afraid to be caught eavesdropping on what they presumed to be a sensitive, high-level conversation about matters of national, and perhaps international, consequence. When one of the executives asked me afterward what they had been talking about, I didn't have the heart to inform him that they had been telling each other jokes.

What happened to Agnew in the aftermath of the 1972 election was a horrible tragedy. Watergate was the beginning of the ruination of the Republican party for years to come. One week Agnew was addressing the New Jersey Republican Women and the National Republican Women's Federation of California, leaving them with tears in their eyes as they stood on tables cheering themselves hoarse. A week later it was all over. He was gone. It was as though someone had cut their hearts right out of them.

The problem was Agnew's home state of Maryland, which was regarded as notoriously corrupt by many. Agnew was accused of accepting cash payments in return for state contracts when he was governor, a way of doing business in the state that had existed for decades. He pleaded *nolo contendere* to the charge and resigned—some might say, was hounded from office. The main issue, I believe, was not whether he did or did not take the money as his accusers claimed. It was the way the media went after him. They staged a personal vendetta, determined to drive him out of public life even while he was still presumed innocent, and prepared to wage war against the man they were really out to get, the president himself. It was the media's turn to get even (if not one up) after playing straight man to Agnew for four years. In doing so, they destroyed the public career of a man who, although flawed like the rest of us, was fundamentally decent beneath it all.

The real tragedy of Watergate and all that followed rests squarely on the shoulders of Richard M. Nixon. First and foremost, he let his family down—particularly Pat, who was always a dedicated wife and mother. He also let down the nation he was chosen to serve as its chief executive officer and moral and political leader. It is still almost incredible to me that he could have permitted himself to get caught with the tapes as well as the cover-up. Richard Nixon was smarter than that; he knew better.

There was nothing in the Democratic headquarters that he needed to know about to win reelection. I can't imagine what he and his advisers thought they would come up with. A sense of paranoia develops in many campaigns, particularly closely contested ones, where one side starts to believe that the opposition has all kinds of secrets that will tip the balance to its side. There is always a con man who shows up at campaign headquarters, usually looking for money or a job, who claims to have secret information that you can use against your opponent. I can't remember a campaign I've been in where that did not happen. But the 1972 campaign against George McGovern was anything but tight. Nixon didn't have to get involved in anything as spurious as that, and he later admitted as much to me.

The only thing that makes any sense is that Dick was looking to protect his brother Don. Donald Nixon had never been particularly successful, and the little success he did have was connected to his brother's status as one of the country's leading politicians. Many of Dick's close associates had been concerned about Don and his activities for some time. I went down to the Dominican Republic to give a speech one time, and I ran into Donald. There was a rumor afoot that he was on Howard Hughes's payroll, working for a shadowy character named Mayhew who was a key Hughes associate at the time, possibly hired to see what influence he could exert on the government's nuclear testing program. I doubt that there was anything illegal in what he was doing, but it's possible that Dick may have been worried about Don's relationship to Howard Hughes and the effect it might have on the campaign if it got out. This was a fundamental weakness in Nixon—his insecurity, his concern about being personally embarrassed about something he had nothing to do with. It clouded his judgment at times.

(It is worth noting here that Howard Hughes once tried to hire a group I belonged to during this period called Public Affairs Analysts. I was the only Republican in the organization, which also included Larry O'Brien, a JFK strategist and cabinet member under Lyndon Johnson; Joe Napolitan, Democratic campaign consultant; and Martin Ryan Haley, a close friend of Hubert Humphrey and campaign manager in Eugene McCarthy's first bid for the presidency. Nothing came of the offer and I only mention it here because of the Nixon connection to Hughes. Public Affairs Analysts was an eclectic group to be sure. As Joe Napolitan told my collaborator, "That Clif managed not only to survive but to thrive in this sociodemographic stew is a tribute to his tolerance, patience, and perhaps befuddlement at what we had wrought.")

Richard Nixon's monumental insecurity was the tragic flaw that brought him down. It is all the more tragic in that he is a gifted, highly intelligent man with a wealth of knowledge at his fingertips. The press always gave him a hard time, which only reinforced his lack of self-confidence. However, notwithstanding his uneasy relationship with the media, I remember him receiving a standing ovation from the Association of Newspaper Editors when he stood before them for two solid hours without a single note, holding them in thrall with a brilliant analysis of world events. One by one he dissected every leading country in the world with a detailed accounting of who was in control, who was out of power, and what was likely to develop in the months and years ahead. It was a dazzling performance, acknowledged even by those who were not among his most ardent supporters. Nixon had that kind of depth, which makes his role in Watergate all the more unfathomable.

I mentioned earlier that Dick Nixon succeeded in politics despite his being an introvert. Most people drawn to politics are extroverts, although there are noted exceptions. The introverts who make it, however, usually exude a palpable warmth and love of people that override their shyness. Nixon was atypical in this regard, as he was in so many others. He never developed a circle of close friends, and I never met anyone who felt he truly knew the man. Supposedly, Bob Haldeman was closest to Nixon during his first administration, and yet

Haldeman claims he has yet to hear from his old boss since serving time in jail because of Watergate. I did meet someone in 1968 who considered himself to be one of Nixon's closest friends going back to the 1950s, but even he said that he was never invited to the White House after Nixon's election. I don't think anyone has ever really been able to penetrate Richard Nixon's defensive facade.

It is interesting to speculate on what draws introverted people to public life where they are so closely scrutinized. One explanation is that they are a lot more complex than the media realize. The more idealistic ones genuinely want to make an impact on public policy, even at great personal cost. There was something of that in Nixon; despite Watergate, he did have a sense of his role in history. He was dedicated, and he was capable of putting the interests of the country ahead of his own—his decision not to contest the vote count in Illinois in the 1960 election attests to that. Then, too, some high-achieving introverts have a personal, psychological desire to overcome their basic shyness through public exposure.

In Nixon's case there was also a need to redeem himself after his less-than-satisfying years as Eisenhower's vice president. In this country we have never clearly defined what the vice president is supposed to do, other than cast his vote in the event of a deadlock in the Senate. In the 1950s the vice president's office was not even in the White House, but rather up on Capitol Hill—safely removed from the executive decision-making process. I remember an old joke about two brothers; the first was a crook and the second became vice president. The second brother was never heard from again. Well, Dick Nixon was determined to be heard from again. Say what you will about him, he kept getting back up off the floor every time he was knocked down until he finally attained the presidency. His tragedy (and the nation's) is what he did with it after he got it.

Even though I cast my lot with Reagan in the 1968 election, I did have access to the White House afterward. Dick's chief of staff Bob Haldeman and I had always got along, and I said to him afterward, "Bob, I'll call you three times if I have to when you're in Washington. If you haven't returned my phone calls after the third time, I'll assume I'm not welcome there and I'll find another way to solve whatever problem I have."

Only once did I have to go to three phone calls, and that was when Haldeman was out of town on business. I kept busy with Public Affairs Analysts during most of Nixon's first term, working on various campaigns, including Jim Buckley's successful bid for the Senate in 1970 (more on this later). I was able to get Dick's endorsement for Buckley through both Haldeman and Attorney General John Mitchell, a further indication that Dick had decided to let bygones be bygones. Then, in 1972 Mitchell called me up. "What are you planning to do during Dick's reelection campaign?"

"I've been running a business." I told him about my involvement in Joe Napolitan's "sociodemographic stew," Public Affairs Analysts.

"Well, we'd like to have the benefit of your service."

Mitchell and the others set up the Committee to Reelect the President (CREEP), and they provided me with an office in Washington as the senior adviser to the organization. In the summer of 1972 Nixon came up to New York for a campaign kick-off dinner, and he sent word before his arrival that he wanted a lot of young people there to demonstrate that he had support among middle-class youth despite all the anti-war protesting that was going on. I rounded up close to seventy-five Young Republicans from Queens and the Bronx primarily, and told them that if they attended they'd get a free dinner and drinks, and get to shake hands with the president.

The night of the dinner when they arrived at the hotel in Manhattan, Haldeman ushered them up to a large suite on the top floor—and *locked* them inside. They started banging on the door, yelling that they wanted to get out, but the staff up there had orders to keep them inside. Finally, one of them escaped somehow and came downstairs for me. "You can't believe what they're doing to us. They've got us locked upstairs and won't let us out. We can't go *anywhere*."

At that moment I saw Bob Haldeman getting out of an elevator, and I ran over to him. "What's going on with my kids, Bob? Why're they locked upstairs?"

"It's a precaution. Dick wants us to be sure they're here when he arrives."

"That's a lot of crap!" I exploded. "I want them out of there now!"

To make the situation even more ludicrous than it was, a Secret Service agent saw us arguing and he walked over and asked to see our IDs. I showed him mine, but Haldeman did not have his with him.

"I'm sorry, sir. You can't stay here," the agent said.

"Oh yes I can!" Haldeman shot back.

"You'll have to leave, sir." The agent was firm.

"Do you know who I am?" Haldeman was almost frothing at the mouth by now.

"I don't care who you are, sir. If you don't have an ID you can't stay here." The agent was a young local fellow who obviously did not recognize Bob and had no idea that he was the president's chief of staff. Deciding that this was an opportune moment to do Bob a good turn, I told the agent whom he was speaking to. After a few moments we straightened things out, and Bob agreed to go upstairs with me and let the kids out of the suite. With all the free food and drink available downstairs, there was little chance if any that they were going to scurry off into the night before it was all gone. The entire episode was totally ridiculous. It almost defies comprehension, but it is indicative of the atmosphere of paranoia that surrounded Nixon and his people at the time.

Paranoia and cynicism. Later in the campaign, Nelson Rockefeller held a reception for Dick at his Pocantico estate in Westchester County. Earlier in the day John Ehrlichman had made a speech during which he stated emphatically that the president would not raise taxes under any circumstances. This was clearly a sop for conservatives who had grown disenchanted with Nixon for a number of reasons. When John flew in later in the evening for the reception, I mentioned to him, "That was a great speech you made today."

"Yeah, and I'll bet you believed every word of it, didn't you?" he replied in that cynical way he had.

Things began to unravel quickly after the Watergate break-in, which occurred during the campaign. The media were calling CREEP every day, and I spent most of my time on the phone with them, trying to answer their questions as best I could. I was in my office one evening at about six o'clock when Jeb Magruder, Mitchell's assistant, walked in. "Do you have time for a drink, Clif?"

"Sure."

We went out for a drink, and I could see he was troubled about something. "If you were running the show around here, what would you do about this Watergate flap?"

"I'd find the guy responsible and fire him," I answered without hesitation.

"What level would that have to be to make it credible?"

"Well, I guess that would be about your level." I was joking.

"I was afraid you'd say that." He was deadly serious. My joke had obviously struck a raw nerve inside him.

Later, of course, it came out that Jeb Magruder, the head of CREEP directly under Mitchell in the chain of command, was a major player in the whole sorry affair. He ignored my serendipitous advice and tried to blame the break-in on low-level functionaries, a tactic that backfired in the end. Quite possibly if he had admitted his responsibility from the beginning, instead of engaging in a whitewash and an attempt to cover up the truth, Nixon's presidency might have been saved. Then again, perhaps justice was best served with Nixon's resignation. His was a presidency that did not deserve to be saved.

Nixon let down his family, the Republican party, and the nation. It bothered me then, and it still does, that he did not level with everyone and admit his culpability. I knew many people who had worked and sacrificed for Nixon since 1960 who were devastated in the aftermath of Watergate. Most appalling of all was the way Dick let his daughters defend him tearfully in public—only to tell them in the end what really took place. I knew those girls from the time we provided the Nixons with baby sitters at YR conventions. They were crushed by the truth when it finally emerged.

Pat Nixon, too, was deeply wounded by the whole sordid affair. She had been beaten up by the press for a long time. She was not enthusiastic about her husband's campaign for reelection in 1972, yet she went along as a dutiful wife—only to see her family torn apart by the disgrace. She had survived in the nasty world of politics since 1946, and she was tired of it all. Richard Nixon victimized many people because of Watergate, but he victimized no one more than his own wife and family.

27 Jim Buckley

No less of an introvert than Dick Nixon, but a different kind of a man entirely, was James Buckley, the older brother of author and syndicated columnist William F. Buckley, Jr. I got to know the entire Buckley clan in 1970 when I ran Jim's campaign in New York for the U.S. Senate.

Interestingly enough, while most conservatives opposed the Panama Canal Treaty, which returned ownership of the canal to Panama, Bill Buckley and I both supported it; we may well have been the only two conservatives in the country who did. My reason for doing so was a longstanding relationship I had with the president of Venezuela. I respected him and his administration, and he likened our ownership of the Panama Canal to a foreign nation owning the territory between Lake Michigan and Lake Erie. I viewed the situation from the perspective of a Latin American head of state, a democratically elected pro-U.S. one at that, and I actually helped develop a program supporting the treaty. I never discussed with Bill his rationale for supporting the treaty, but I suspect it had something to do with his family's varied business interests in South America.

It is hard to imagine two brothers as different as Bill and Jim Buckley. Bill, as everyone knows, is a gifted writer and speaker, a lively debater and polemicist. Jim is somewhat withdrawn, almost shy, and he jokingly referred to Bill as his "precocious younger brother." He decided to run for the U.S. Senate in 1970 out of a genuine sense of duty and responsibility. We had an unusual situation in New York at the

191

time. The incumbent senator, Charles Goodell, was a liberal Republican, and his major opponent, Dick Ottinger, was an equally liberal Democrat. Goodell, who had been appointed to his seat, was running to retain his seat, while Ottinger was a congressman looking to unseat him. I faced a daunting task with Buckley. He was running on the Conservative line as a third-party candidate, and I needed to establish him as a serious candidate who had a chance to win.

This would have been difficult enough with a polished campaigner, but Jim Buckley was anything but that. He had a professorial manner, and he was given to long, studious discourses on the issues that would have been fine in a college classroom, but were anathema on the campaign trail. He didn't have the vaguest idea of how to work a crowd for votes.

"You mean you want me to go up to total strangers, introduce myself, shake hands with them, and ask them to vote for me?" he asked me once in all innocence.

"That's what you do, Jim, if you're running for public office," I explained as patiently as I knew how.

His naiveté was somewhat disconcerting since he had made it clear beforehand that he would not run at all unless he had a chance to win. His only previous campaign for office, also as a Conservative party candidate, was a half-hearted attempt to unseat liberal Republican Jacob Javits in the 1968 senatorial election. He was not interested in another quixotic third-party effort. I asked my friend and colleague in Public Affairs Analysts, Joe Napolitan, to conduct a poll to see what Buckley's chances were.

As Joe explained it to my collaborator: "In the early seventies Clif got me involved with a Republican candidate. I never work for Republicans and I salved my conscience in this instance because he was a Republican running as an independent—Jim Buckley, candidate for the United States Senate in New York. Clif had this idea that Buckley could win a three-way race, and he asked me to take a poll to see if his theory was sound. Since Buckley would be running against a Republican, Clif didn't want to go to any of the Republican pollsters, and I guess I was a Democrat he felt he could trust. He didn't have to worry; I sure as hell didn't want anyone to know I was taking Jim Buckley's polls either."

Joe's poll indicated that Buckley had only a sixteen percent recognition factor among New York voters, but there was enough there for me to feel that he had an outside chance to win as the only conservative in a race against two liberals, assuming he waged an effective campaign. I ran this by him, and he said he would think it over and let me know. Several days later he called me back. "You have a candidate."

Our strategy—the only one that would work as far as I could see—was to portray Goodell and Ottinger as birds of the same feather despite their party allegiances, and have them split the liberal vote evenly so that Jim could squeak in with a bare plurality. Toward this end I engaged Bill Rusher in an unpaid capacity to help me flesh out the campaign staff. We hired David Jones, a conservative from Tennessee who had been active in YAF and other organizations, as my chief of staff; Arnold Steinberg, another YAFer and former editor of the *New Guard,* as press chief; and Leon Weil, a Wall Street broker, as chairman of the finance committee. We located our campaign headquarters in an office building on the southwest corner of Madison Avenue and Thirty-eighth Street, a few blocks northwest of brother Bill's *National Review.*

The odds against us seemed daunting, but not overwhelming. For one thing, Nelson Rockefeller was up for reelection as governor that year, and he wanted as little as possible to do with the unpopular Goodell, who had started off as reasonably conservative, and then alienated rank-and-file Republicans by swinging abruptly to the left. Goodell was not even permitted to get close enough to Rockefeller for so much as a photo opportunity. Dick Nixon was also disgusted with Goodell for lining up against him with liberals in Congress against the war in Vietnam. While Dick could not break party ranks by openly endorsing Buckley, he did fly into New York State and allow himself to be photographed with a group of YAFers carrying NIXON & BUCKLEY posters. It was a typically devious Nixon ploy, but in this case at least it worked in our favor.

The big battle of the campaign—the one that finally put us over the top—centered on the issue of debates. Don't debate if you're ahead. That's been the rule of thumb in politics from time immemorial.

Debates only serve to further the cause of the underdog. They've become unavoidable to a great degree because the public has come to expect them, so the basic idea has been modified to limiting debates to as few as possible if you are ahead in the polls. Since Buckley was the underdog in 1970, naturally I screamed bloody murder for debates—as many and as frequently as possible. They were the best and the cheapest way to give my candidate exposure. David Garth, who ran Ottinger's campaign, was predictably against them. However, the New York television stations wanted them, as the media always do, so I created a fait accompli by telling them to "set aside the time and we'll be there. The debate will take place, with or without the other candidates."

Part of the game in politics is for the party opposed to debates to conduct a debate *about* the debates. You bicker over dates, location, the size of the podium, the format, anything you can think of. The idea is to play for time by postponing the debates as close as possible to the election when they're least likely to sway the voters. In this regard I was able to thwart Garth by agreeing to everything he demanded. We were "available" on every date he suggested, no matter how inconvenient. I made it clear that if anyone was stalling, it was the opposition.

I sensed that the debating forum would be a good one for Jim, as the campaign trail was not. He was far more comfortable in front of a camera and an audience enunciating his positions on the issues than he was in a crowd, shaking hands and kissing babies. Most of all I wanted him relaxed. He had all the facts and details he needed to know inside his head. The structured format of a televised debate was a perfect opportunity to accentuate his strengths while playing down his weaknesses.

The first debate among the three major candidates was televised on WABC, and the results could not have been better for us. Buckley came out the clear winner—not only by our estimate, but according to polls taken afterward. Goodell was smoother than Ottinger, and the consensus was that he came in second and Ottinger third. I watched it in the studio with David Garth and others. When it was over Garth walked up to me. "What do you think?"

"We won, clearly." I responded without hesitation.

"You won as soon as your man walked out on the damned platform with the other two guys."

"You got that right."

He shook his head in disgust and walked away, essentially acknowledging our tactical victory in cornering him into a debate in the first place. The first debate was such a hit among the voters that both CBS and NBC asked for equal time for their networks. I accepted immediately for Buckley, and told them he would be there no matter what the two other candidates decided. They had little choice but to accept. Each debate resulted in an increase in Buckley's standing in the polls. We picked up the endorsements of twenty-seven newspapers around the state, many of which had initially dismissed Jim's candidacy as a third-party exercise in futility. Then we got a call from the dean of Columbia University, at the time a hotbed of left-wing antiwar activity, asking if we would be willing to debate before the student body.

"Absolutely."

"Clif, are you really serious?" He was obviously surprised. "You know where these kids' sympathies are."

"I guarantee you Jim Buckley will be there whenever you want to put it together."

This was a calculated risk on our part; I viewed it as a win-win opportunity from Jim's perspective. Just holding his own in such a hostile environment would be perceived as a victory. And if the kids hooted him off the stage, it would only serve to increase his "sympathy vote" with the middle class whose patience with privileged youth taking over entire campuses and setting fire to buildings had run out long ago. Ironically enough, Ottinger (who was ahead of Goodell in the polls, registering strongly with liberal voters) was the one who decided not to show up for this final face-off. Jim handled himself well in this forum also, and was roundly cheered by a large contingent of YAFers and other conservative students who had attended in large numbers.

In the final days before the election I was fairly confident that we were going to pull off an upset victory. I flew upstate to visit Jim in

Rochester, where he was feeling ill and showing some signs of exhaustion after an arduous campaign. We held a briefing for half a dozen reporters in Jim's hotel room, and one of them asked me if we really thought we had a chance to win.

"We are going to win, and we're going to do it with 38.7 percent of the total vote."

I think Jim was as stunned as anyone with my prediction, but this was not a figure I just picked out of thin air. Our staffers had polled many of the key districts throughout the state, and the percentage I came up with was based on an assessment I believed to be valid. We virtually held our collective breath until election night. When the final tally came in it showed that Buckley had won with 38.5 percent of the vote, two-tenths below my estimate. He had received 2,288,190 votes; Ottinger was an extremely close second with 2,171,232 votes; Goodell came in a distant third with 1,434,472 votes; and there was a smattering of votes for an assortment of fringe candidates. Our strategy of splitting the heavy liberal vote (approximately sixty percent of the total) enabled Jim Buckley to become the first third-party candidate in New York history to win a statewide election.

Buckley's election to the U.S. Senate in 1970 (the last campaign I planned and managed myself) proved to me that successful candidates for public office do not necessarily have to be stamped from a particular kind of mold. They come in all forms, and Jim Buckley was as atypical a candidate as I have ever had to work with. The essential element in winning any campaign is to exploit your candidate's strengths while simultaneously taking advantage of your opponent's weaknesses. In many regards, planning a political campaign strategy is similar to drawing up a battle plan in a war. You look at the terrain, at the enemy's strengths and weaknesses, and you devise an appropriate strategy. Each campaign is different. In politics, whoever captures the most votes in the end is the winner. That's the goal—getting votes, not winning debating points—and it is something you have to keep in mind at all times. You must never lose sight of what it is going to take to get voters to pull down the lever for your candidate when they enter the voting booth.

Sadly enough, Jim Buckley, who was an unlikely political candidate from the start, turned out to be a more effective campaigner than he was a senator. To some extent, I blame myself for his failure to win reelection six years later.

Jim Buckley's problem as a senator was related, in a sense, to his idealism; he was more concerned about developing good legislation than he was in cementing political relationships. After his election he brought David Jones to Washington with him as his administrative assistant. David had good political savvy and he got Jim started in the right direction. But David left after a while to take another position, so Jim was left more or less on his own to figure out the art of survival in Washington politics. He spent his time drafting legislation that he felt was needed, instead of working with other New York politicians to form a consensus and gain support for what he was doing. Politics, as I stated earlier, is the art of compromise, and Jim Buckley failed to understand that politicians can't get anything done on their own.

Had I been more attentive to what was going on, I would have been able to see the hole he was digging for himself. But I was busy with other activities, including Public Affairs Analysts, and I assumed he was in good hands. I found out that I could not have been more wrong when I got a call from Jim Cannon, a Rockefeller aide and an old friend of mine. He asked me what Jim intended to do about a federal revenue sharing bill that would have allowed New York to balance its budget.

"I have no idea." I was surprised at the question. "Didn't anyone ask Jim what he intends to do?"

I called Buckley myself and broached the subject. "I guess you've been getting as many calls from Albany as I have. People want to know what you plan to do about revenue sharing."

"Are you concerned about it?"

"Not me personally, unless you care to tell me."

"Well, I'm drafting my own bill."

I called Jim Cannon and told him he had better get down to Washington as soon as possible to coordinate things with Buckley since he didn't seem to know what was going on. He took my advice, and when he returned he called me. "Buckley's bill is great, it's excellent. But it'll never go through. We made the necessary compromises with the other senators and put together a bill that can pass."

In the end Jim Buckley introduced his own bill, which predictably was soundly defeated and made him look ineffective. He ended up voting for the Rockefeller bill. His embarrassment could have been avoided if only he, or someone in his office, knew enough to communicate with other politicians in New York and coordinate his efforts with them. I am sure he would have been willing to play the game by the rules, if only he had known what they were. But there was no one on his staff with the political expertise to advise him properly and, to some extent, I felt that I had let him down. He trusted my political judgment, and he assumed I would follow up after his election and make sure he got the guidance he needed.

Finally, about eighteen months before his term expired, Jim called me up. "Shouldn't someone be taking charge of my reelection campaign?"

It was obvious by this time that he was floundering badly, and I agreed to fly down to Washington to discuss the matter with him. I met with his staff, which was filled with some of the brightest and most gifted young people in Washington. They were all dedicated intellectuals with a string of academic degrees that would have put any other senatorial staff to shame. But we had one overriding problem: there wasn't a single politician among them. I promised to do what I could to put together some semblance of a campaign for his bid for reelection, but it was already clear to me that there was little if any chance for him to save his Senate seat.

One of the most disheartening moments for me took place in Grand Central Station when I ran into Jim's secretary, Dawn Cina, who later married Tom Winter of *Human Events*. She was almost in tears. "Mr. White, we're going to lose, aren't we?"

"It doesn't look very good, Dawn."

"I said a prayer that if Jim wins, we'll keep our lines of communication open with every county chairman in New York."

The Almighty, however, was not inclined to work miracles in 1976. Jim lost, and the U.S. Senate ended up losing one of its most idealistic and dedicated members because he was not a good enough politician.

28 A Bad Campaign

A while back I mentioned Stu Spencer in connection with Reagan's 1968 bid for the Republican presidential nomination. Stu, as I said, was somewhat less than wholeheartedly committed to Reagan at the time, and as a result he was ostracized from Ron's inner circle of advisers. In 1976 Gerry Ford and his advisers, Dick Cheney and Donald Rumsfeld, selected Bo Callaway as Ford's campaign manager in the presidential campaign. Bo was a former congressman from Georgia and secretary of the army. He asked me if I would be interested in working in the campaign, so I scheduled an appointment in Washington to discuss the matter with him, Cheney, and Rumsfeld. Cheney was serving as chief of staff and Rumsfeld was secretary of defense at the time.

"I've lined up a good guy to help us in the campaign," Bo told me when I went in to see him. "I think you'd get along just fine with him."

"Who is it?"

"I think you know him. Stu Spencer."

"I've worked with Stu before. He's a good man. I'm not interested myself in running another campaign, but I'll be happy to talk to Stu about it."

When I first met with him he seemed hesitant, perhaps recalling what happened in 1968. I tried to put him at ease. "Look, I don't have any hard feelings. This is a great opportunity for you, running a campaign like this. So why not do it?"

He thanked me for the advice and signed on as deputy campaign manager. Shortly afterward, a magazine implicated Bo in a scandal involving a ski resort he was developing in Colorado, claiming that he used political influence to get the zoning he needed. He had little choice but to resign from the campaign, which stirred up all sorts of internal dissension among Ford's campaign people. Stu needed help, so he phoned me. "Clif, why don't you come down here and run this damned campaign? You've got more experience than anyone. You can be campaign chairman and I'll work for you. Together we can make this thing go."

"I really couldn't do that, Stu. I'm not prepared to make a full-time commitment to this campaign. But if you need to call me in as a consultant from time to time, I'd be glad to help out on that basis."

We left it at that. Shortly afterward, Gerry Ford brought in Rogers Morton as campaign manager, Bill Timmons to work the floor of the convention, and Jim Baker as the delegate counter to make sure they had the necessary votes to secure the nomination for Ford.

As far as I was concerned, my loyalties were still with Reagan, who had expressed some interest in going after the nomination himself that year. I expected to be called in to help out in his effort, not realizing that a rift of sorts had developed between his people and me. Reportedly, some of them had convinced Ron that "Clif has enemies in the Republican party," and for that reason they would be better off with someone other than me running his campaign. I was shocked when I heard of it, and joked, "If you've been in politics as long as I have, and you don't have enemies, then you haven't stood for very much or accomplished very much."

Bill Rusher had a clearer view of the situation at the time and explained it this way: "Reagan noticed that the campaign Clif waged in 1968 did not work. This was because Reagan himself put too many limitations on it. If Clif had been allowed to run him instead of conducting a hesitation waltz, it would have been different. He came close as it was. But after that, Reagan did not feel that he had any great obligation to latch himself to Clif White for the rest of his life. That remark about Clif having enemies, as I found out later, was a reference to some politician—a governor or political leader in one of the Carolinas—who had something negative to say about White. Look, nobody's universally liked. And he may have impressed Reagan that maybe Clif did have enemies. Reagan was being sold a bill of goods on John Sears then, and he was getting all sorts of bad advice. I think it was a mistake that he didn't take White again."

Fortunately, the rift between Ron and me was healed later on, but not in time for me to be of any use to him in the 1976 campaign. So when Stu Spencer asked me to help him out of a tough situation in Iowa—ironically enough, with some delegates committed to Reagan—I flew out to see what I could do. Stu was the ranking Ford adviser there, and he just couldn't bring himself to make a big decision when the chips were down. I spent some time going over the situation with him, and said, "You've got to make a deal with them. You don't have enough votes here to have it all your own way."

"Let me think about it."

I knew most of the people in the Reagan camp out there; most of them had worked for me going back to the Goldwater days, and they were tough, savvy politicians by this time. The following morning, when I went in to the negotiating session, Stu pulled me aside. "I offered to compromise with them. I think they'll go for it."

"I told you they would if you're willing to bend a little. Hell, I know these guys. They can count delegates as well as anyone else can—*better* than anyone else can. Grab the deal while you can. If you don't, they'll fight you tooth and nail and beat you in the end."

"Well, I'm not sure." He was still hesitant, afraid to make the decision.

"What's the problem?"

"If I come away with only five or six delegates, I'm not sure how it'll go down with Gerry and Rogers Morton."

"Well I'll make the decision then, if you want me to." I lost my patience a little. "If you need somebody to take the responsibility, go back to Washington and tell Rogers Morton and Gerry Ford that Clif White made the decision. Just go back in there and make your deal now before they cut us down two more delegates. Tell them you've spoken to the president and he was opposed to it, but he's agreed to accept their offer in the interest of harmony. I'll take responsibility for it if you want me to."

So that's what he did, and it worked to our advantage later on. Stu was fine in the broad strategy areas, but he lost his self-confidence when it came to the tough negotiations.

The Republican National Convention opened in Kansas City on August 15, 1976, and I accepted President Ford's invitation to serve as the de facto manager of his convention campaign. Again I set up headquarters in a specially outfitted trailer just outside the arena, connected to the events inside by a network of electronic gear. I took it as something of a compliment that my good friend Andy Carter directed the Reagan effort from a similar rig a few feet from my own. The innovations I had introduced during the Goldwater campaign had evidently caught on.

Ford and Reagan were the only two serious candidates for the presidential nomination, and this time around Reagan decided to mount a credible challenge to the incumbent president. Bill Timmons ran Ford's campaign on the convention floor, and Dick Cheney presided over the staff meetings. One of the big issues that arose concerned the selection of a running mate by the presidential nominee. Cheney selected me to negotiate with Reagan forces, who were in favor of full disclosure of the nominee's choice for vice president, and I met with Paul Laxalt, Reagan's campaign manager, and Roger Allan Moore in this regard.

"I'm not interested in fighting over a whole bunch of platform issues and dividing the party," I told them, basically agreeing to go along with them on the issue.

Both Dick Cheney and Gerry Ford accused me of caving in to the Reagan people. "You're damned right I gave into them on that. You didn't think I was going to let them trap us into a fight with conservatives over a conservative platform, which would only play into their hands, did you? I've been through so many of these smoke-screen platform issues, I can't count them anymore. The way it works is, the president decides what he wants to do and, essentially, he ignores the platform. Once you're nominated, it doesn't really matter what the platform says. The president runs things the way he wants to."

At first they didn't see it that way, but when Reagan announced his choice of liberal Republican Richard Schweiker as his running mate, and challenged Ford to do the same, it backfired on Reagan. Gerry refused to take the bait, and we defeated them on the platform amend-ment, 1,180 to 1,069. After that, the outcome of the convention be-came an academic exercise. With 1,130 votes needed to win the nomination, the vote on the platform amendment was a clear indica-tion of the candidates' relative support within the party. The final vote on the nomination was 1,187 for Ford, and 1,070 for his challenger. Reagan put up a good, tough fight, but he only came as close as he did to wresting the nomination away from an incumbent president because Ford had not been elected to the office in the first place.

The Republican party was in shambles after Watergate and Nixon's resignation, and its leadership was up for grabs. Perhaps Reagan would have campaigned more effectively than Ford did and gone on to win against Jimmy Carter in the general election. It is also possible that the nation was not yet ready for Reagan in 1976, that it had to heal the wounds of Watergate and suffer through the Carter stagflation malaise of the late 1970s to appreciate the kind of change that Rea-gan offered. It is inconceivable to me, however, that Reagan would have campaigned as badly as Ford did in the general election.

Simply put, Gerry Ford's campaign was a disaster from the start. He had been a congressman before becoming president by accident as it were, and he never stopped thinking of himself as a congress-man. On the campaign trail he comported himself more like a man struggling to retain his seat in Congress than like an incumbent pres-ident. A case in point, which no one talks about any longer but which for me was the turning point in the election, occurred during the first debate between Gerry Ford and Jimmy Carter.

A fuse blew at some point in the debate, and the power system failed. For seventeen painful minutes, two men who were seeking to hold the most powerful office in the world stood speechless at their podiums like dummies, afraid to open their mouths and take charge. Neither one of them understood the power of the presidency. If you're the most powerful man on earth, you're supposed to act the part, not stand by helplessly while technicians fiddle with the electrical system. The president of the United States is supposed to take charge when things break down and assume control of the situation. But both can-didates' advisers had briefed them beforehand, telling them in effect,

"You can't win a debate, you can only lose it. So don't do anything out of the ordinary and take any chances."

The television cameras remained fixed on the two of them for all that time, demonstrating to everyone watching—to the entire world—that neither one of these dummies knew how to be the president. Whichever one moved first and acted as though he were trying to get to the bottom of the problem would have won the election in November, I am convinced. Whichever one said, "What's going on? What are you doing to fix it? How long do you expect me to stand here like this?" would have soared in the polls the following day. The opportunity was there for the taking—but neither man moved or said a word for seventeen excruciating minutes. This had to go down as one of the most incredible incidents in American political history. Yet no one even *talks* about it today. It has inexplicably become a nonevent.

Although not many pundits discussed the incident in depth afterward, which is itself a comment on our so-called political experts, the big question that had to be running through the minds of most viewers was, How can either one of these candidates take charge of the fate of the western world if they can't control a situation like this? Since Ford was the incumbent president, he was the bigger loser of the two. He was the one who presumably was supposed to know how to handle the problem. But he failed to act.

I don't mean to come down too hard on poor Gerry Ford, who is basically a decent guy and who had been an effective congressman. We all have our limitations, and Gerry just could not rise to the office of the presidency and the stature it demands. For most of his political life he had been not only a congressman, but a congressman from the minority party, accustomed to dealing with the problems and concerns of his local constituents. Suddenly he was thrust into the role of the presidency, where he had to start dealing with issues of national and international importance. It is a different level of politics, requiring a higher level of thinking and problem-solving. Gerry just didn't have it.

To make matters worse, he allowed himself to be portrayed by the media as a clumsy, bumbling idiot, tripping and banging his head when he got off an airplane, or hitting someone with a golf ball. This was a man, perhaps one of the most athletic ever to occupy the White House, who had been a gifted football player, a graceful natural athlete, who for some reason failed to display his fluidity of movement in public. All he had to do was arrange some photo sessions showing him tossing a football on the White House lawn, and the image would have been emblazoned permanently on the public mind: a quarterback, leading his nation expertly through difficult times. Kennedy, who was *not* an athlete and who suffered from severe back pain, created that image with his well-publicized touch football games and by allowing photographers to take pictures of his trim body in a bathing suit. Ford should have been able to accomplish as much without even trying, yet he incredibly came across as a man who tripped over his own feet.

In the final analysis, I reject the notion that Gerry Ford lost the election to Jimmy Carter because of Watergate and the stain it gave the Republican party. There is some truth to that, but Carter's victory was by an extremely slim margin—40,830,763 to 39,147,793. The shift of a few thousand votes in two states, Ohio and Mississippi, would have given Ford the edge in the electoral college. Carter was definitely beatable, but Ford ran a dismal campaign and, in the end, that was what cost him and the Republican party the presidency. Carter did not *win;* Ford *lost* the election largely through his own ineptitude.

$\mathcal{29}$ *A Revolution Begins*

Perhaps the most amusing thing to happen during the two brief years Ford was president, before the 1976 campaign, involved his vice president, Nelson Rockefeller. Conservatives, of course, had never been happy with Gerry's choice of Rockefeller for the job, figuring it put the liberal New Yorker only a heartbeat away from the office he had coveted all his life, the presidency of the United States. But now that Nelson was as close to the job as he would ever get, he discovered that he could not get in to see his old friend Gerry Ford in the Oval Office. I was shocked one day when I visited Washington, and Nelson approached me before I went in to see Ford, asking me to deliver a message to the president. Later on I asked Rumsfeld, Ford's secretary of defense, what it was all about.

Rumsfeld responded with a hint of a smile behind his deadpan expression, "It's not true that Nelson can't get in to see the president. I just told him that he would have to schedule an appointment through me first, that's all."

Rummy would never admit it openly, but this was his way of putting a barrier between Ford and his vice president. He knew that the proud Rockefeller, one of the most powerful governors in New York history as well as one of the wealthiest men in the world, would never demean himself by requesting an appointment to see Ford—a former congressman whom Rockefeller had once considered beneath him.

After the 1976 election, I sat down to reflect on what I had accomplished so far in life. There was much I had done that I could be proud of, but there was one major goal I had yet to fulfill: to see a bona fide conservative elected president of the United States. As I surveyed the political landscape following Ford's defeat, it struck me that there was only one conservative capable of attaining the White House, only one man with the ability, the perseverance, and the talent. That man was Ronald Reagan.

By 1978, two years into the Carter presidency, I was determined that Reagan had to make a serious bid for the office in 1980. He was already well into his sixties, and the country was reeling badly from soaring inflation, skyrocketing interest rates, and rising unemployment. It was now or never.

Feeling as well as I ever had in my life, I decided to have a routine checkup at the Mayo Clinic in Rochester, Minnesota. It had been a while since my last physical and I was long overdue. My health was something I had taken more or less for granted all my life. Like most people, it just wasn't something I thought much about unless there was a reason to do so. While I was in the clinic waiting to see my doctor, however, I was struck by a massive heart attack and rushed immediately into an oxygen tent.

The doctors put me in intensive care for a few days until they had stabilized my condition. Bunny was there constantly at my bedside, and the nurses instructed the staff not to let any phone calls come through unless she was there to take them. One day she turned off the phone before she went out for some fresh air. A nurse came into my room and said some politician had called while Bunny was out.

"Who was it?"

"Some governor or something."

"It wouldn't have been Ronald Reagan?" I somehow knew who it was before she mentioned his name.

"Reagan? Yes, that sounds like the name. I told him he wasn't supposed to be calling you, but he said he'd call back to find out how you're doing."

A call from Reagan at that point was the best medicine imaginable for me. He had been on my mind for some time now, and there was no one I wanted to speak to more.

He called again the following day. This time he managed to get through to me even though Bunny was not in the room. "My brother Neil had a bad heart attack some years ago," he said, "but now he can play eighteen holes of golf and I'm sure you'll be doing the same."

He put Nancy on and she also wished me a speedy recovery. I was smiling when Bunny got back, the first time since entering the clinic. I didn't know what my health was going to be like in 1980 but, God willing, if I had the strength I knew I would do whatever I could to help elect Ronald Reagan to the presidency.

My heart attack occurred at an unfortunate time in another respect as well. I was involved with one of the organizations established by my friend Joe Napolitan, the International Association of Political Consultants. Michel Bongrand of Paris was its first president. He was followed by Joe. Then I became the third president of IAPC. Just before my heart attack, I organized an international conference of political consultants in London. I'll let Joe Napolitan tell the rest of the story.

> Clif was conference chairman and said he wanted no committees; he would arrange the program, invite all the speakers, handle all the details. We all thought this was fine. Clif organized a fine conference, making arrangements for speakers to fly in from California and Washington and Paris and other places. Unfortunately, a few weeks before the conference, Clif was stricken with a heart attack while at the Mayo Clinic and obviously was unable to attend the conference.
>
> While we were meeting in London we discovered that while Clif had invited a gaudy list of speakers and agreed to pay their expenses, the conference generated much less in fees than we needed to pay all the bills. Thus, in order to bail out of the Hyde Park Hotel where the conference was held, we literally had to pass the hat to raise enough money to pay the hotel bills. Six of us wrote personal checks for a thousand dollars apiece to get out of the place. I'm sure that had Clif not had his heart attack he would have found a way of getting the money to cover the conference expenses. In the end, all of us were paid back by the association.

I am not sure Joe is right in his optimism about my ability to dig everyone out of that hole in London, but I am happy that those who anted up the money were reimbursed later on. Joe also founded the American Association of Political Consultants, which has grown larger over the years than IAPC. Its membership reached five hundred in 1992, and it is widely accepted as the preeminent organization of its kind. Joe was the first president of AAPC and, since the bylaws call for the presidency to rotate between Democrats and Republicans, I succeeded him there as well.

I was convinced as early as September 1979 that the Republican presidential nomination and the election were Ronald Reagan's to lose. I said as much in a speech I made before an audience of political scientists at the University of California's Long Beach campus. Judging by the skeptical response from those who heard it, I was apparently in the minority in my assessment. Yet my conviction was not based on personal preference alone. The country was overwhelmingly anxious to get rid of Carter; not even the Democrats were excited about him. Reagan's main rival in the primaries would most likely be George Bush, who struck me as a weak candidate, not up to Reagan's caliber at all. Philip Crane, John Connally, Howard Baker, Bob Dole, and John Anderson were also interested in the nomination, but none of them could go the distance against Reagan, in my judgment.

No one had to teach Ronald Reagan how to look and act the role of president. It came naturally to him; it was almost as though he had been subconsciously grooming himself for the job from the time he became governor of California. He understood the importance of maintaining a presidential image at all times. He exuded a presidential presence from the moment he entered political life. After he was elected, Mike Deaver walked into the Oval Office one afternoon. It was blazing hot, and Reagan was attired as always in a dark suit and tie.

"Why don't you take off your jacket?" Deaver asked him in surprise.

Reagan stared at him for a long moment. "In this office? No way. You don't run around the Oval Office in shirtsleeves."

His commanding presence set him apart from most politicians in other ways as well. Most candidates today give a speech in the morning with fifteen-second sound bites and quotable quotes packed in for easy excerption for the evening newscasts. It is understood that the public will allot you only a few seconds or so to make your point, so you have to get your zingers in quickly before people tune you out. Sometime during the 1970s the rule became: no half-hour shows. They were a waste of time and money since no one would focus that long on a politician.

(This changed somewhat in the 1992 presidential election when the public grew so disgusted with the political stalemate that Ross Perot was able to command the public's attention for his own thirty-minute telecasts. Perhaps we have reached a point today where the voters have become willing to concentrate for lengthy periods, as long as substantive issues are discussed.)

However, during the 1970s no audience would listen to any politician for more than a few seconds at a time—with one exception: Ronald Reagan. I noticed that voters of all ages, from their early twenties to senior citizens, would sit enraptured for as long as an hour at a time during a Reagan speech. It was an incredible thing to see; he had a commanding presence, a charisma about him that was unique among politicians.

"Turn him loose," I told his advisers. "He can hold them for a half hour and longer. Nobody ever turns him off in midstream."

My role in Reagan's 1980 presidential campaign is chronicled in detail in the first two chapters. In the beginning, there was great concern about the so-called age issue: Ron was approaching his seventieth birthday. However, he was remarkably youthful for his age, energetic and alive with the importance of his mission. He defused the age issue successfully in his first debate with Jimmy Carter. When questioned by a reporter about whether or not this was an important issue, Reagan tossed out a one-liner about how he wouldn't hold his opponent's youth against him in the campaign. The remark drew the laughs it was intended to elicit and, suddenly, age was no longer an issue.

The old rule about keeping debates to a minimum when you're ahead in the polls was another that did not apply in Reagan's case. As far as I could see, any opportunity to match Reagan against the deadly serious and downbeat Jimmy Carter could only work in Ron's favor. For the first debate with Carter in Cleveland, I flew in a panoply of dignitaries including Henry Kissinger and Jeane Kirkpatrick. Their primary purpose in being there was to nod affirmatively whenever Reagan was speaking and the camera was on the audience, and afterward to affirm that Reagan had clearly won the debate.

"Dress it up any way you want to," I told them. "Henry will probably want to talk about how solid Reagan is on foreign policy, and Jeane about why Democrats should vote for him instead of Carter. But the key message is, Reagan won."

The media were all set up in the hall, and I had assigned advance men to work with Kissinger to make sure he got the media's full attention. I had actually "casted" the entire Reagan side of the audience with superstars so that they were fully visible when the cameras panned the audience. I seated Nancy where Ron could see her as soon as he walked out on stage. When he did, and then smiled and winked at her, I turned to somebody next to me and said, "It's all over. I don't care what else happens tonight, we're going to win."

I had stacked the audience pretty much the same way in Baltimore for Reagan's debate with Independent candidate John Anderson, but the stakes were higher for this one against the incumbent president. After it was over, reporter Mary McGrory came up to me. "Everyone is saying Reagan won tonight, Clif."

"If everyone's saying it, it must be true then." I couldn't restrain my smile.

Poor Bob Strauss, who was usually effective in these situations, was running around trying to get the media to give him equal time to explain why he thought Carter won, but without success. My "superstar" strategy had worked even better than I hoped.

The debate in Cleveland was the ostensible turning point in the campaign. I believe Reagan had victory firmly in his grasp prior to the October 28 debate, but the public's reaction in the days that followed reaffirmed our own assessment of who had come out ahead. The momentum built afterward, adding to the margin of Reagan's landslide victory in November. When the votes were finally tabulated— 43,899,250 for Reagan, 35,481,435 for Carter—the Reagan Revolution of the eighties was ready to begin. Conservatives had waited a long time for one of their own to be elected to the White House. They could not have found a better or more ardent spokesman for their ideas than Ronald Reagan.

30 *Persona Non Grata*

There is no question in anyone's mind that Reagan's first term in office was more successful than his second. I've already mentioned some of my activities in and observations of Reagan's first term in chapters 3 and 4. Reagan's second administration was hampered by the Iran-Contra situation, which occupied everyone's attention to the point where it was difficult to accomplish anything. Ron worried a good deal about it. Our involvement with the Contras in Nicaragua sidetracked him from his domestic agenda and put him on the defensive much of the time.

The major problem, however, was his staff, which undermined him more than anything else. Jim Baker was the worst culprit. He and the others over-briefed the president for his press conferences and generally would not let him relax and be himself. They corrected his statements afterward to the point where he was almost afraid to say anything. Baker was convinced that Reagan was a dummy, and he felt a need to second-guess every statement he made. For example, when Ron said something to the effect that trees emitted more carbon monoxide than automobile exhaust did, Baker responded immediately with a press release saying that the president didn't really mean it. Yet I had read the environmental report that supported Reagan's conclusion, and I told Baker he should have backed him up on it. He should have told the media to study the report if they didn't believe it, and figure it out for themselves. Baker corrected the president so often that the media picked up on it and perpetuated the myth of Reagan's alleged stupidity.

Baker did not appreciate my calling him on it, and as a result I became persona non grata at the White House during Reagan's second term. In 1985 I was instrumental in drafting some legislation that led to the creation of Radio Marti, a sort of Radio Free Cuba broadcast from Miami. I had hoped to lead the program, but John Herrington, who was head of White House personnel at the time and later became secretary of energy, called me up and said apologetically, "Clif, I don't know how to tell you this—"

"The best way is usually to tell the facts as they are." I was trying to make his job easier.

"Well, I took your name in to Deaver and Baker this morning. I thought it was logical that you should be chairman of the advisory committee of Radio Marti and told them so. But both of them told me, 'Don't ever put his name in front of us for anything again.' If you want, I can go over their heads and take it to Reagan."

"No, but thanks. I don't want to present the president with problems he doesn't need."

"We can fight it you know. I'm willing to go around them for you. If the president knew about this, I think you'd get it."

"No, thanks again. Let's just leave it alone."

It turned out that I did become a member of the advisory committee a couple of years later, although not its chairman. But this was typical of how Jim Baker operated. He was friendly and cordial when it suited him, particularly when he thought you might be of some use to him, but he was manipulative and vindictive underneath.

The question arises, Why did Reagan permit Baker and Deaver to wield so much power in his White House? I believe the answer to that is, he really didn't have a lust for the exercise of power himself. He did not have a personal need to be president, as Kennedy did. He believed that his role was to serve his cause and the country at large in the best way possible. Reagan was guided primarily by his conservative ideals, which called for the reversal of the statist direction the country had been heading in for decades. He knew exactly what he believed in and where he wanted to go.

Toward that end, he put a great deal of trust in the people around him, people he thought were guided by the same principles he was.

Part of the problem was that many of the true conservatives who staffed his administration in the beginning had left for one reason or another, many out of frustration with the entrenched liberal bureaucracy. This created a vacuum that was promptly filled by the pragmatic types—Baker, Deaver, and others—who were guided essentially by political expediency rather than by commitment to principle. Expediency dictated that it was easier to compromise with the bureaucracies than to dismantle them, it was easier to perpetuate the status quo than to slash spending and trim budgets, easier to accommodate Congress on almost everything it wanted than to do battle over pork-barrel legislation.

Perhaps Reagan's greatest weakness was that he delegated too much authority to people like Baker, who he thought would carry out his programs, but who actually had their own agenda which was at variance with his.

Reagan did fight back more effectively during his first term in office, but by 1985 Baker managed to convince him that it was next to impossible to get most of his programs through Congress. Any president depends on his staff and his party leadership to let him know what is attainable and what is not. It did not take long for the Democrats to realize that Reagan was not prepared to go to the wall for much of his legislation. The leadership of his own party was worried about stirring up too many bad feelings with their Democratic colleagues; they all belong to the same club after all.

The president also has his own congressional liaison staff advising him to be careful and avoid unnecessary battles. It's easier for them to keep their jobs if they win than if they stick their necks out and end up losing. More often than not, the careerists on the Hill will come down on the side of caution. "We really don't want to risk losing a big one," they're apt to tell him. "Let's go along with them on this bill, and keep our ammunition dry for when it really counts." The net result of this approach is that little if anything of importance ever gets accomplished.

The pressure Reagan faced with the Democrats controlling the House (and Senate in his last two years), and the pragmatists in his own party telling him not to pick a fight, was overwhelming. He allowed himself to get trapped by that kind of thinking, particularly when he found himself preoccupied with the Iranian and Contra situations. Without the original conservative stalwarts there to tell him, "You'll never know whether the battle is winnable or not unless you fight it," Reagan succumbed to Baker's middle-of-the-road, let's-not-rock-the-boat approach throughout much of his second term in office. It is easy to argue that Reagan should have taken a firmer stand, but it is difficult for anyone continually to resist the advice of people telling you, "You can't pass it, you haven't got the votes, we'll never get it through, the press will beat up on us if we try it."

Reagan's second term was a dramatic departure from his first. His first hundred days in office were superb, and most of what Reagan will be remembered for occurred during his first four years in the White House: his outstanding 1981 tax bill, which lowered the top tax bracket from seventy percent to twenty-eight percent, reduced the number of brackets from fourteen to three, and indexed the rates to account for inflation; his federalism program, which returned many decision-making powers to the states; deregulation of much of the economy; making free enterprise and entrepreneurship respectable throughout the world; and creating much of the atmosphere that led to the demise of the Communist empire. On balance, Ronald Reagan launched a genuine revolution and presided over nearly a decade of prosperity, economic growth, and the expansion of individual liberties. This is his legacy not only to his nation, but to the world at large. The decade of the eighties was one of the most dynamic periods in recent history, particularly since the depression of the thirties and the end of World War II. Reagan ushered it in, and no attempt to rewrite history (as many have attempted to do) can deprive him of that accomplishment.

31 | *The Ashbrook Center*

In 1982 Bill Rusher called to say that I would be receiving a telephone call from Tom Van Meter and Fred Lennon to ask if I would be interested in helping them establish a public affairs center at Ashland University in Ashland, Ohio, in memory of our good friend Congressman John Ashbrook, who had died unexpectedly at the age of 53.

"For God's sake, Clif, don't say no to them."

Bill explained to me that Lennon and Van Meter had approached the university about locating a center for the study of public issues there, but they were concerned about having someone with experience in the area to head it up. Bill and Tom had hit on me as the right person for the job, and Bill wanted to make sure I understood the importance of establishing a public affairs center dedicated to teaching democratic, free market principles. He believed it was a sorely needed enterprise that would be extremely instrumental in imbuing new generations of college students with democratic ideals and a thorough understanding of the principles of a free society. Bill was his usual persuasive self, and I accepted when Lennon and Van Meter called to offer me the directorship of the center.

Throughout the rest of the decade, I worked hard to turn their dream into reality and help bring it to fruition. The goal was nothing less than to plant the seeds that would help produce the next generation of political leaders in the United States. As director of the Ashbrook Center, so named because John Ashbrook exemplified the ideals we wanted to instill, I was able to return to some extent to my first

219

love in life—teaching. I wanted to build the center into a highly respected forum for the study of public issues and American democratic principles. Toward that end, I was fortunate in being able to attract President Reagan, Vice Presidents Bush and Quayle, and many other prominent politicians to the center, where they shared their insights with both students and faculty—and with my Ashbrook scholars, who made the entire venture worthwhile.

Our $1,000 "Ashbrook scholarships" were made available to qualified full-time Ashland University students who were interested in public affairs. Students from every discipline were considered, and our scholars came from the social sciences, the humanities, education, broadcasting, business and economics, as well as other areas. They were required to have a minor in public affairs, which consisted of specified courses in political science, history and economics. They also had to complete an application and review process, have a minimum grade point average of 3.0, and submit an essay of 500 words or less on the subject, "The Relevance of Public Affairs in Our Lives." Scholarships were reviewed annually, and depended on the maintenance of the 3.0 grade average, satisfactory progress in their public affairs minor, and full participation in Ashbrook Center Activities.

It is interesting to contemplate how life has a way of coming full circle from time to time. I started out as a teacher, left it for a career in politics for several decades, then suddenly found myself teaching politics to a new generation of bright, energetic, eager young college students at this late stage of my life. I certainly hadn't planned it that way, so I attribute these ironic developments to the Supreme Being— who apparently has a well developed sense of humor—continuing to play an active role in our lives. In any event, this involvement with dedicated young scholars, after working for decades in the more cynical world of political maneuverings, was a breath of fresh air that helped me understand the importance of bringing the right people into public affairs in the first place. I thoroughly enjoyed every minute of it, and looked forward to my frequent trips from Connecticut to Ohio with more and more enthusiasm as the decade wore on.

The people we assembled to serve on the board of advisers of the Ashbrook Center comprised a Who's Who of prominent figures from the political arena. They included industrialist Fred A. Lennon, Bill Rusher, Ohio State Senator Thomas A. Van Meter, Illinois Congressman Philip M. Crane, Ambassador William Middendorf, former Treasury Secretary William E. Simon, Senator Steven Symms of Idaho, economist Walter Williams, presidential assistant Lyn Nofziger and others. President Reagan, Vice President Bush, Vice President Quayle, and many members of the Reagan and Bush Administrations addressed the Center's annual dinner. In addition, Henry Kissinger, Alexander Haig, Barry Goldwater, and many others have been featured speakers at the center's Major Issues Lecture Series dinners over the years. The Ashbrook Center has also sponsored a series of seminars and discussion programs on various public affairs issues, featuring prominent representatives from the political, business, and media worlds.

I cannot end these grateful acknowledgments, however, without paying a particularly heartfelt tribute to Fred Lennon, the first chairman of the Center's board of advisors and our mainstay from the beginning. This wonderful man, who in his eighties still runs a major business, has long been a financial supporter of the Republican Party and the conservative movement, and in the case of the Ashbrook Center was our founder and chief advisor as well. To him, primarily, we owe its survival and, in large part, its success.

Nor can I forget to recognize the immense contributions of Dr. Peter Schramm, Dr. Bradford Wilson, and all the other members of the Center's staff who have worked for it so energetically.

Because of the continuing activities of the Ashbrook Center, and the involvement of so many idealistic and dedicated students from every academic discipline in the major issues affecting our country and the entire world, I remain optimistic that the principles I have believed in all my life—democracy, liberty, free enterprise, the precepts of our Judeo-Christian heritage—will survive and flourish long after I am gone.

32 *IFES*

It was around the beginning of Reagan's second term that I created an organization that was to occupy much of my time and labor for the rest of the decade. In 1985 I had a drink with Peter MacPherson, director of the Agency for International Development (AID), whom I had known for some time. His organization was dedicated to the promotion of democratic reforms in developing countries, an area in which I had become increasingly interested. "You're spending a lot of money around the world," I observed,"but you don't have any way of measuring whether it's effective or not."

"You're right. Maybe you should do something about it."

"I'm too old. You need some young guy with a lot of energy to do it."

He took me seriously enough to hire a young fellow named Eddie Mahe, who had served as executive director of the Republican National Committee. His claim to fame—or infamy if you prefer—was that John Connally had hired him in his 1980 attempt to get the Republican presidential nomination. Mahe spent a million dollars and secured one delegate—probably the most expensive delegate in American political history. I don't intend this to be a reflection on Eddie's talents, which are actually quite considerable.

Eddie organized some observer missions to determine if AID's money was having the desired effect of fostering democracy around the globe. After about a year and a half, he produced a comprehensive report that was typically bureaucratic in nature. It weighed a ton and was filled with more appendices and footnotes than anyone could possibly count. I may well be the only person on the planet who has ever read it in its entirety. The conclusions were something less than startling. The first was that AID needed to hire a consultant—Eddie Mahe—who would teach AID how to spend its money properly; the second was more constructive—namely, that a private independent foundation ought to be created to assist AID in accomplishing its goals.

Peter called to see if I would be interested in establishing the foundation. I told him I would, and I went to work recruiting a bipartisan board composed of people who I felt would make a genuine contribution in this area. I wanted people with intellectual capability and commitment to democratic ideals, as well as a knowledge of international politics. Among my board members were Richard Scammon, director of the census under Jack Kennedy; Richard Stone, former Democratic senator from Florida, who had been Florida's secretary of state prior to that; Chuck Manatt, former chairman of the Democratic National Committee, a member of the board of the National Endowment for Democracy, and president of the Democratic Institute for Democracy; James Cannon, a former aide to Nelson Rockefeller, director of the Domestic Council under Gerry Ford, and special assistant to Howard Baker when he was Senate majority leader; Patricia Hutar from Illinois, who had been president of the National Federation of Republican Women, co-chairwoman of the Young Republicans, and vice chairwoman of the Republican National Committee; and Robert Walker, vice president of Coors for public affairs and director of Republican Associates in Los Angeles, who had also worked closely with Reagan when he was governor of California.

I named the organization the International Foundation for Electoral Systems(IFES), with headquarters in Washington, D.C., and a branch in San Jose, Costa Rica, established under the Court for International Human Rights. The United States is not a signatory to the court since our policy is not to relinquish any judicial powers to other bodies. But the Court for International Human Rights did create a subsidiary organization called (in English) the Center for Electoral Promotion and Assistance (CAPEL), and asked me to serve on its advisory board. Essentially, CAPEL functioned in a capacity similar to that of IFES.

I made it clear from the inception of both IFES and CAPEL that the two organizations would not compete with each other, but rather cooperate with and complement the work the other was doing. The seed money for CAPEL was a million-dollar grant from AID spread out over five years. I hired the staff for CAPEL, as I did for IFES, with the combined objective of making both organizations nothing less than the primary sources of knowledge on how to run a democratic election anywhere in the world. Toward that end, we sent technical teams to observe elections in every country that would let us in, and compiled on our computers the most comprehensive record of election law for virtually every nation on earth.

We established strict criteria for the observers we sent out. First, the chairman of each team had to speak the language of the host country, and have a working knowledge of its history, traditions, and culture. The number-two person on each team was usually a political expert with an understanding of the political ins and outs of the country being visited. Next, I always tried to include a team member who was well known in the host country—a senator, representative, former ambassador to the country, someone of that ilk. The purpose of the team is to observe the country's election, then prepare a detailed report to supply us with a case study of how it was done in that particular time and place. Then, if a country with similar demographics at a comparable stage of development wanted us to help it run an election of its own, we had the necessary information to advise it on what worked and what did not. Most of the time we held briefings for congressmen in Washington, the State Department, AID members, and other interested parties to keep them abreast of what was going on in each nation.

Many foreign countries asked us to help them establish democratic procedures right from the start. Paraguay conducted its first election in quite a few years in 1988. The opposition party, fearing fraud on the part of the government, refused to participate unless voters were required to ink their fingers before they cast their ballots. They wanted voters to actually stick their pinkie fingers in an ink bottle down to the cuticle, where it can't be washed off for two or three days, to eliminate repeat voting. It sounds absurd, but we actually had to go down there and test various kinds of inks before we found one from Venezuela that was suitable for this purpose.

Sophisticated Americans and others accustomed to a century or more of democratic freedoms might not think it takes much training to stick one's finger in a bottle of ink, but we discovered otherwise on our trip to Paraguay. One community in particular, apparently after watching too much American television, tried to make fingerprints on their ballots instead of dipping their pinkies all the way into the bottle. As a result, the election was declared null and void because the ink had not penetrated into the cuticle, so we had to go back and conduct a training program on the proper inking technique when the election was rerun a month or so later. We learned that you could not take anything for granted when establishing democratic electoral procedures in developing countries. Our efforts paid off, however, and many nations around the globe today use this "inky pinkie" procedure, as it has come to be known, to eliminate fraud in their elections. IFES has also worked on several projects with the National Endowment for Democracy, including one in Nicaragua in which we assisted in the creation of an organization called Via Civica, designed to educate the people about the voting process from a nonpartisan viewpoint. We recruited more than 2,500 dedicated individuals, who did an outstanding job of instructing the citizenry on the mechanics of an election—where to vote, how to get there, how to cast a ballot, how to ensure privacy and safeguard the democratic process—things that we take for granted in the United States and other advanced nations, but that were unheard of until recently in most of the countries on earth.

The Mott Foundation provided IFES with a grant to work on exchange programs between the Supreme Electoral Council of Russia and other former Soviet Republics, and the Federal Election Commission of the United States. During the late 1980s delegates were sent to one another's countries to observe and learn how things were done in each locale. Many Eastern European nations had some experience with democracy in the past before communism suppressed it, but the Russians never did. They've lived under one autocratic system or another for centuries, and the concept of a free, competitive electoral system is alien to them. They need to learn from scratch what a ballot is—what it looks like, what it symbolizes, what its purpose is.

In May 1990, IFES conducted a conference in Caracas, Venezuela, co-sponsored by CAPEL and the Supreme Electoral Council of Venezuela. Participating in the conference were the supreme electoral councils of every nation in the Western Hemisphere. This was the first time that the entire hemisphere has ever had a meeting of this magnitude. This was a working conference, with papers presented, workshops, and discussions taking place. A manual was published containing all the elements we had determined to be essential to the conduct of a free, competitive, democratic election process: the type of constitution required, a supreme electoral council and its functions, civic education, establishment of political parties and how they work, registration, what happens on election day, how to tabulate the vote, poll workers, voting station procedures, security at the polling station, voting material and literature, and more.

IFES is not in business to tell people how to run an election. There is no single blueprint on how democracy works. Democracy is a dynamic process, contingent upon social and cultural traditions. What works in one country will not necessarily work elsewhere. What IFES does do is provide information on what has worked in various countries, and what has not.

Following the success of the Venezuelan conference, IFES made plans to hold similar conclaves all over the world, particularly in Eastern Europe, which gave birth to the greatest flowering of democratic reforms in recent history. IFES was asked as soon as the Berlin Wall came tumbling down to send people to Hungary to answer their questions on how to proceed. We sent a team there whose chairman was Dr. Peter Schramm from the United States. He had left Hungary during the 1956 uprising, studied at the London School of Economics, and later got a Ph.D. in the U.S. IFES also sent a team to Romania in the spring of 1990, headed by a woman who was a professor in Romania before she fled to the U.S. In addition, we developed programs for other countries in the area, such as Czechoslovakia, and sent some of our own people with a U.N. team down to Haiti to report on conditions there.

IFES has already made a serious contribution to the development of democracy throughout the world, and its influence, I suspect, will grow during the years ahead. I kidded the president of Venezuela, who is an old friend of mine, that of the twenty-two participants in the Venezuelan conference, only three were gringos—one of whom was myself, the chairman of the conference.

33 *A Center of Knowledge*

While democracy is beginning to flourish and develop its own dynamic in so many areas of the world, it is growing increasingly stagnant in the United States. The American political parties no longer work the way they should, they are less responsive to the needs of their constituents, and our Congress doesn't function properly; during the last ten years, the Congress passed a budget on time only once. You can't run a country with that kind of performance, and the last thing Eastern Europe needs now is American political consultants running over there giving them advice on how to run an election.

Unfortunately, the rest of the world is fascinated by our political consultants because we are the most advanced users of modern technology for political purposes—communication, propaganda, advertising, whatever you want to call it. Everybody thinks we know what we're doing. When I first went into international consulting, one of my first major campaigns was in Venezuela in 1973. The Adeco party had lost an election for the first time since their revolution. They blamed the other side for fraud, but refused to contest the election in an effort to make democracy work in the country. Adeco also believed that another major reason why it lost was that the opposition, the Christian Democrats, used a sophisticated political consultant from the Christian Democratic party of West Germany. Adeco concluded that the consultant gave the Christian Democrats a decisive edge. In the next election Adeco decided to get the "best" political consultant available, an experienced one from North America. My partner in the venture,

Joe Napolitan, doesn't like me to say this, but I believe it's true that Adeco would have won the 1973 election anyway, even if he and I had never ventured south into Venezuela. I'm sure we helped a bit; we showed them some other ways of doing things, some of which they adopted and some of which they didn't. Ever since then, American political consultants quickly learned that the way to get rich and stay that way, between U.S. elections, is to run all over the world selling advice to other nations. During the last election in Venezuela there were more U.S. and German political consultants on the scene than I had ever seen in one place before. I don't like this trend, and I believe it's fraught with danger as far as Eastern Europe is concerned right now.

If we have anything to teach these countries it is philosophy and a system of values. It would be more important for them to learn and understand the ideas espoused by Thomas Jefferson, Benjamin Franklin, Tom Paine, and James Madison. Most modern consultants have never read *The Federalist* and they don't even know what federalism is. American political consultants are media experts, nothing more. They know a lot about advertising campaigns, but nothing about politics and political principles. The danger in Central and Eastern Europe is that it has always been a difficult part of the globe for governance. Today, that part of the world needs help in learning how to govern itself—how to put democracy to work.

The role IFES will play is a practical one. We can show them where to get ballot paper that can't be counterfeited, where to get the right kind of ink and how to use it, where to get voting machines, how to establish competitive political parties, the elements required for viable constitutional provisions, how to create a supreme electoral council that functions properly, and other critical ingredients for a free and democratic political process. But I don't think that IFES or anyone else should be telling them how to conduct their campaigns.

At our conference in Venezuela in May 1990, we had a trade fair for the first time. The participants were so excited that they wanted us to open it a week early so they could see the actual tools used in an election: voting booths, scanning machines, ballot cards, paper, ink, and the latest electronic equipment. The vendors of those products were on hand to display their wares, and they were well received.

One of the big hits of the fair was a portable cardboard voting booth that could be transported to remote areas of a country where the citizens would otherwise have difficulty voting. These are the crucial concerns of poorer countries and Third World nations with limited transportation services—making sure the people have the ability to vote, and ensuring the secrecy of their ballot.

It had always been my contention that only amateurs steal elections on election day; pros steal them well in advance. I use "steal" here loosely to indicate which party or candidate has done his homework properly, and laid the necessary groundwork required for any successful political campaign. That's why I like to send a team in well in advance of an election, then again on election day. In Brazil I had my team in six months before the election, then about six weeks before, and again on election day.

About two-and-a-half years ago, Nigeria said it wanted to create a democracy and write a constitution. I sent a man over to talk to the Nigerians about it. He came back and reported that they had written a pretty good constitution, but what was most interesting was that they didn't have any political parties.

"How will the political parties evolve?" I asked him.

"They had no set ideas, except to count off. 'You two are Party A, you two are Party B.' Just divide the candidates up like that."

"That's not going to work," I concluded. I was going to send somebody back to follow up on that, but the Nigerians decided to reevaluate the entire process in 1989, and it appears as though democracy is not about to rise up there any time soon. I doubt we'll go back there until they change their minds.

We sent people to India and got a thorough report from them. It's an incredibly complicated situation. India is the largest democracy in the world. They use vats and vats of ink, and vote over a period of three days, the country is so populous. India proclaims itself to be in one time zone, which is stretching things a bit, but they can proclaim anything they want. During the three-day voting period, cumulative voting is continuously reported.

IFES has been all over the globe, and we're growing all the time. I make the somewhat immodest claim that the goal of IFES is to become the center of all knowledge on how democratic elections can be run. We're collecting all kinds of data and information and storing it in our computers. Countries keep changing election laws, so we've got a big job keeping up with them and plugging the changes into the computers. But we've got the base and the people, who are there in the countries, so we can stay on top of things. IFES keeps getting inquiries from different countries, and a lot of projects come our way through AID, which helped create us. The State Department also asks IFES for information, briefings, and people to be sent to different countries. The White House requests information from IFES from time to time. The National Endowment for Democracy (NED) calls on us for various projects, and we also get calls from the U.S. embassies abroad that want to know whom they should contact for various reasons in their host nations. The chairman of the Supreme Electoral Council in Venezuela called to ask us about paper for ballots in his country. We located an Indian reservation in Utah that has been using paper ballots since the beginning, and he came up from Venezuela and went to Utah to speak to the Indians there and learn about their system. We also helped him get information about electronic vote scanners by directing him to a county in Florida that uses them. That's the sort of thing IFES is really good at, aside from its function as an observer.

IFES is a service organization and, along with CAPEL, is positioning itself as *the* expert on democratic elections—the organization people turn to when they want to get the final word on what is happening anywhere in the world. I had originally said I wanted to raise at least a third of our money on my own, and I'm ahead of that projection. The problem with public funding is that a good deal of it is spent inefficiently, or else it is totally wasted. That's why I prefer to raise as much money as I can privately, so we have better control over where it goes and how it's used.

From the beginning, Richard Soudriette has been the director of IFES. Richard spent some time in the Peace Corps prior to that, then went into local government in Oklahoma before becoming administrative assistant to Jim Inhofe, at that time a congressman from Tulsa. The greatest challenges democracy faces today, and the greatest potential it has to evolve in exciting new directions, lie in the nations that have recently thrown out dictatorial regimes of one sort or another. Those who carry on my work after I am gone will most likely achieve their biggest successes in foreign countries.

34 *The Election Process*

I don't know if everyone fully appreciates what a revolutionary period we are living in. Self-government is really what the electoral process is all about. It is only in this century that the concept of man's capacity to govern himself, along with the acceptance of that concept, has become a *universal* dictum. The idea that there must be an election process for a government's actions to be legitimate has been accepted only within the past twenty-five years or so.

Even in a one-party dictatorship, such as the one the Soviet Union had until recently, the government deemed it necessary to establish some sort of a voting process to give the appearance of legitimacy to its actions. As we approach the end of this century, virtually everyone everywhere considers self-government to be a legitimate concept; each one of us has a responsibility and a right to engage in an election process to establish the kind of government we want.

Equally important to the democratic process is the fairly recent establishment of world opinion as a major factor, thanks to the power of technology. Because of modern technology, the events that took place in Tiananmen Square appeared on everyone's television sets as they actually happened; just a short time ago that was not possible. With the advent of communications satellites and the transmission of information across the globe, governments everywhere have to be concerned about world opinion as it affects the legitimacy of their own actions.

We have seen the collapse of communism, fascism, and other forms of dictatorship all over the world in recent years. Latin America has

235

been on the cutting edge of this movement toward democracy, and the entire Western Hemisphere—with two notable exceptions—has instituted some form of democratic election process in its system of government. In Central and Eastern Europe, parts of the Orient and Asia, virtually everywhere the flag of freedom is flying more proudly now than ever before in human history. This is truly an historic moment in the course of human events.

Today we send observers everywhere, under all sorts of auspices: the United Nations, the Organization of American States, CAPEL, IFES, and an assortment of special committees. We are finding that, in many countries today, observers are being invited in by the governments themselves to ensure that they will be legitimized by the international observer teams. Countries such as Costa Rica, which are proud of their political and election systems as they should be, have been inviting observers in for years now.

Witness the number of observers present during the February 1990 election in Nicaragua; hundreds of independent observer teams were there to oversee exactly what was taking place. In Central and Eastern Europe observers are present to see history being made. Tied in with all this is the magnifying effect of the media. Media representatives from all over the world are on the scene to report on the activity, to interview the observers, and disseminate their conclusions. The resulting publicity further serves to legitimize the election process taking place in these countries.

This leads us to the subject of the election process itself, its importance and significance, and why it concerns us. I believe we have learned that, if an election process is going to provide its citizens with real freedom, it is critical that it must be competitive.

What is the purpose of the election process? I submit it is threefold. First, it populates government with various people, such as senators, congressmen, and governors. Second, it provides for public discussion of public policy. What kind of policies are going to be carried out by this government that you're going to populate? What sorts of rules will it establish under which its citizens live with one another? Competition among various public policies allows the voters to decide what they should be.

Third, the process supplies the country with an institution that, ideally, will imbue the citizens with confidence. This is a process they can trust, it has a foundation, people recognize it and accept it. It provides a sense of community. I believe it was Aristotle who said that society must create a trust between thee and me so that power can be transferred without apprehension. To the extent that it is competitive, the election process accomplishes that end.

Next we come to the question of how the election process is implemented. The first essential ingredient is a clearly defined set of rules and regulations that the public is aware of. If people understand these rules and abide by them, that serves to minimize any confusion that may ensue, not to mention any opportunities for distrust and perhaps even violence.

Second, the election process must be truly competitive if it is to have any meaning. There must be competition at all levels; as someone commented, you need a process that allows the devils to watch one another. This is the most effective means possible of avoiding fraud. Two candidates with an equal chance of winning will watch each other more closely than any disinterested party will. The law doesn't make men honest. Observing their actions does. Without competition the voters will not have any real choices to make regarding the individuals who populate government, and carry out public policy. Conversely, if a country does establish a truly competitive process, the need for an overwhelming amount of rules and regulations is eliminated. Competition is itself the best regulator in the world.

As the world stands today, a large number of systems have been created in an attempt to achieve these objectives. Democracy is a dynamic enterprise; there is nothing static about it. The various democratic systems ought to be changing, evolving, moving ahead in accordance with their own internal momentum. The systems that function best will be determined in due course by the people who participate in them, who make them happen. As we observe these various political systems, we search for clues to what is and what is not working. I do not believe that you can impose one system of government on another culture, and expect that it will work there the same as it did elsewhere. The various political systems must evolve from the culture of each individual society.

As we enter the final years of this century, we find ourselves faced with two phenomena that have begun to affect the political process. Both deserve to be examined in the light of whether they contribute positively to the process and, if so, how, or whether they are a hindrance and a liability. These phenomena, which entered the political arena within the past quarter of a century, are the emergence of both political consultants and political polls. Unfortunately, they both developed in the United States and professionals are now trying to infect the rest of the world with their viruses.

Political consultants, within whose circle I once traveled myself, can be found running around anywhere you care to look. They represent a serious problem in the election process. In the United States, if you are serious about running for public office, you get yourself a political consultant who has achieved a maximum amount of "success". (Usually, he can boast of one major victory to his credit; he will never tell you about his defeats.) After the would-be candidate has retained the political consultant, he can then go out and raise a lot of money. The consultant will spend this money for the candidate on a supposedly effective public relations campaign composed mostly of thirty-second television commercials and five-second media bites. Then the consultant disappears. He has no further concern about or responsibility for public policy once the candidate is elected. His only concern was getting the candidate elected, and getting paid for the effort.

As a result, political parties in the United States are in a serious state of disrepair today. Their effective influence is minimal at best, and there is a distinct danger that this will happen elsewhere if political consultants are permitted to take over the political process in other countries. Having said this, I should admit to the fact that I was president of the American Association of Political Consultants when it was founded, and I have also been president of the International Association of Political Consultants.

Let me make it clear that I am not opposed to the existence of political consultants, per se. The need for them arose originally because of the development of technology in the political process—television, computers, etc.—about which politicians knew absolutely nothing. You may remember the famous election between Richard Nixon and Jack Kennedy for president of the United States in 1960. A good case can be made that Nixon lost that closely contested race because of a lousy make-up man. Nixon looked terrible on television, although those who only listened to his debates with Kennedy on the radio actually thought Nixon had won them.

After 1960, every politician in the country decided that was not going to happen to him, so all of them went out and hired lighting men, sound men, make-up men, and anyone else who could teach them how to use the media properly. Unfortunately, over the years the media consultants assumed more and more power until they reached a point where they orchestrated everything, *including* the substance of the campaign: the issues that would be discussed, the topics to be debated, and so on. As a result, political campaigns in the United States have been reduced to mere entertainment; nothing of substance gets discussed because it could be too risky. Roger Ailes, it can be stated with a great degree of accuracy, actually elected George Bush president. Michael Dukakis's political consultant was not as effective as Ailes was. All of this has a deleterious effect on the election process itself. It tends to trivialize the entire concept of democracy.

The political consultant who operates as a gun for hire is not presenting to the public a clear idea of what the candidate or his party stands for. What is his program? What are the basic values? What are the philosophical parameters of the candidate's party? These are the sorts of things that ought to be presented in the election process if it is to have any meaning. How else can the voters make a rational decision about which party and which candidate they want to set public policy for the country? These decisions should not be based on how good a candidate looks on television, how he smiles, the cut of his suit, how well he has mastered the art of speaking in five-or ten-second sound bites, but rather on values and ideas. All too often now, elections are determined on superficial nonissues.

The political consultant does have a genuine role to play, but it is a role that has to be clearly and carefully prescribed. The technical consultant who coaches the candidate on the best way to express his views, the best way to present them to the television or radio audience, to the print media, or on the debating podium, is one thing. Within those constraints, the role of the political consultant is constructive. But to allow a consultant, whose only claim to fame is that he can create a better-tailored nonentity than the next guy, into the political process is a policy fraught with danger.

The second fairly recent phenomenon concerning the election process that I mentioned a moment ago is the emergence of the political poll as a significant factor. There is almost an effort, as most of us have experienced, to determine the outcome of an election before it is held. The major media organizations spend a lot of money conducting public opinion polls before an election, announcing who the likely winner is throughout the campaign, and then again the day before the election.

The tendency these days is to challenge the results of an election if it does not conform to the projections made by the pollsters. The attitude is that something must have gone wrong in the election process, not the polling process. This is an insidious development, one which threatens the integrity of the election process itself.

It is incumbent upon those of us who work within the electoral process to put these procedures in their proper perspective. Public opinion polls when used in elections should be seen as technical devices in guiding the conduct of the campaign, not as definitive instruments for determining the outcome of an election.

To accomplish this we need to do a better job of explaining to people exactly what a political public opinion poll is. Anyone who has conducted a poll knows how easy it is to skew it in such a way that you get precisely the results you want. I can get you whatever result you want from a poll if, first, you let me ask the questions and, second, allow me to select the sample. I might even be able to accomplish this with the first criterion alone. But if you let me select the sample, too, I can guarantee that I will get nine out of ten people to answer the questions the way you would like them to.

People who conduct polls—newspapers, television stations, other media, various institutions—have an overriding responsibility to explain exactly what their polls mean. In my judgment, this is a responsibility that is largely unrecognized. Recently, some small degree of progress has been made in that some pollsters will reveal the size of their sample, and the exact phrasing of the questions asked. To the extent that this is done, they have taken a step in the right direction. But hardly anyone involved in the political polling process has done an adequate job of pointing out the potential for error.

A good recent example of this is what occurred in Nicaragua preceding that country's general election. Not a single poll conducted by North American pollsters—newspapers and media people primarily—came close to being accurate. Many polls are inaccurate, even when the winners are picked; when you say someone is going to win by sixty percent to forty percent, and the results come in fifty-one percent to forty-nine percent, you might have gotten the victor right but that's still an inaccurate poll. Unfortunately, most observers overlook that fact because all they remember later on is that the poll picked the winner. But, in Nicaragua, the esteemed pollsters didn't even get the winner straight. This, to me, is a classic example of an abrogation of responsibility on the part of the media. They couldn't pick the winner because they conducted slanted and inaccurate polls. The questions and the samples were both bad. So, in the end, the forecasts made by the pollsters in Nicaragua turned out to be as valid as the polling process they used.

To be fair, I should mention that two polls conducted by Central American pollsters were notable exceptions. Both of them understood the culture and asked the right questions in the proper manner. They alone were able to accumulate the necessary data to predict more accurately the outcome of the election.

Perhaps even more dangerous is that the polls have actually become a determining factor in the election process itself. Politicians use polls to plant the idea in the public's consciousness that they are going to win. Based on that spurious finding, they can then go out and raise campaign money and create a so-called last-minute bandwagon effect. Their polls, skewed to show the results they want, indicate that a "groundswell of support" is flowing to their camp. There is sufficient evidence to suggest that voters will stay home if they are convinced beforehand that their candidate and their party are heading for defeat, and, ironically enough, those same voters will also stay away if they're convinced their party will win big. The notion takes hold that their votes are not needed. In many elections, this "stay-at-home" vote can be significant in affecting the actual outcome. This can be, and often is, a negative side effect of the polling process.

Obviously, this is less critical in those countries where voting is mandatory and a ninety percent turnout of voters is ensured. But in countries that permit people to vote or stay home, as they choose, we have seen voter turnout drop to dangerously low levels, and the polling process is one of the primary causes of it.

In light of all these concerns, it behooves all of us who work in the voting process to make sure that the polls are properly understood to begin with, and that they are correctly used. They cannot and, I think, should not be totally eliminated. West Germany attempted to restrict the use of polls by prohibiting the publication of poll results within three days preceding an election. So the pollsters went out and purchased time on British radio and television and got their information out to the world anyway. International communications being what they are, it would seem to be all but impossible to eliminate this type of end run around an individual country's rules and regulations. Any attempt to do so would probably create more problems than it solved.

The final responsibility for proper polling procedures falls on the shoulders of those of us working within the process. We need to ask the pollsters to work with us, and we need to follow up to make sure that their procedures are being used correctly. No one should be given carte blanche to distort the results of an election. The election process that we have discussed in this book is both vital and critical. I believe that we have come up with several techniques and procedures that will imbue the people with confidence that their particular process is both honest and objective.

These are the critical elements: the preservation of the secrecy of the ballot, the institution of constitutional provisions, and competitive political parties. Without these ingredients, the election process cannot work the way it is intended to. Democracy cannot prevail. With them, you create an atmosphere that permits democracy to flourish, and allows government to provide its people with the maximum amount of political and social freedom.

When the Founding Fathers of our country left Constitution Hall in Philadelphia, Ben Franklin, the oldest member of the group, was approached by a woman who asked him, "Dr. Franklin, what kind of a government have you given us?"

Ben, who was then over eighty years of age, looked at her over his homemade bifocal glasses. "A republic, madam, if you can keep it."

That is the essence of what we are dealing with. We need to develop systems that will allow people to govern themselves. These systems are in a constant state of checks, balances, and reappraisals. The primary purpose of IFES and similar organizations is to present all of the methods that have been found effective in establishing a competitive, democratic, and pluralistic election process. To the extent that we have succeeded in accomplishing this end, the cause of freedom and democracy will be advanced throughout the world.

35 *Promoting Freedom*

There is no question in my mind that the Reagan administration was perhaps the greatest catalyst for democratic change that the world has seen since the days of Ben Franklin.

In a speech he gave to the Houses of Parliament in London on June 8, 1982, President Ronald Reagan said: "No, democracy is not a fragile flower. Still, it needs cultivating. If the rest of this century is to witness the gradual growth of freedom and democratic ideals, we must take actions to assist the campaign for democracy. . . .

"The objective I propose is quite simple to state: to foster the infrastructure of democracy, the system of free press, unions, political parties, universities, which allows a people to choose their own way; to develop their own culture; to reconcile their own differences through peaceful means."

One could almost say that Ronald Reagan was prophetic in that speech. He provided the leadership that made it possible for nations throughout the world to cultivate democracy and grow it on their own soil. Historians in the middle of the next century are likely to say that Ronald Reagan's greatest contribution to world society was his fostering of democratic principles and ideals. Certainly, the results of his commitment to freedom started to become evident during the early years of his administration, and they blossomed fully as the 1980s drew to a close.

Reagan embodied the essential qualities that are necessary for any major movement to build up momentum. The first of these was his leadership ability. President Reagan will be remembered as a great leader. Perhaps the two greatest American leaders of the century were Ronald Reagan and Franklin Delano Roosevelt. Roosevelt addressed the fears and concerns of society, and Reagan fulfilled his country's hopes and aspirations. They articulated the paramount feelings of their countrymen, perhaps the world at large, during their administrations. As a result, the public was inspired and followed them willingly.

Ronald Reagan took two major steps to create an atmosphere conducive to the growth of democracy in the world. He understood that the antithesis of democracy is dictatorship, and the most powerful dictatorship on earth was that of the Soviet Union. Communism had been imposed on the people by force; no country had ever voted for a Communist dictatorship. Knowing this, and understanding that the growth of Communism had to be curtailed by force, President Reagan began building U.S. military forces until they were superior to those of the Soviet Union. Russia could no longer impose its will on another country with total impunity. This was the first step Reagan took to foster democracy, and it was largely a defensive strategy.

The second step he took was of a positive nature, and it consisted of several elements. He articulated the principles of freedom and free markets perhaps better than any American president of this century. He truly believed in individualism, entrepreneurship, and capitalism, and he used every opportunity he had to promote those ideals, not only domestically but in the international arena as well. Reagan was not afraid to give history lessons to those he thought needed them. When he went to the Soviet Union and spoke to students and intellectuals at Moscow State University on May 31, 1988, he charmed his audience with a discourse on American history and civics, and received a standing ovation. Standing under a bust of Lenin, President Reagan declared, "The growth of democracy has become one of the most powerful political movements of our age."

He went on: "Democracy is less a system of government than it is a system to keep government limited, nonintrusive, a system of constraints on power to keep politics and government secondary to the important things in life, the true sources of value found only in family and faith. But, I hope you know, I go on about these things not simply to extol the virtues of my own country, but to speak to the true greatness of the heart and soul of your land."

The president discussed the communications revolution in the West, and said that the Soviet Union could not join the revolution unless it allowed "freedom of thought, freedom of information, freedom of communications." He spoke of the existence of thousands of newspapers and television stations in the United States, all of them "fiercely independent of the government," and of our legal system in which "the word of a policeman, or any other official, has no greater legal standing than the word of the accused. . . .

"As I see it," Reagan continued, "political leadership in a democracy requires seeing past the abstractions and embracing the vast diversity of humanity, and doing it with humility; listening the best you can, not just to those with high positions, but to the cacophonous voices of ordinary people, and trusting those millions of people, keeping out of their way; not trying to act the all-wise and all-powerful; not letting government act that way. And the word we have for this is freedom."

Ronald Reagan was a salesman for democracy, a promoter of freedom, and his leadership in this regard played a significant role throughout the world. His speeches were heard on Voice of America, Radio Free Europe, and Radio Liberty, and they had an impact on people living behind the Iron Curtain who listened to them. An American president articulated their own dreams of freedom, and gave them the hope and the strength to fulfill those dreams in their own time. It is sad that very few of us have been able to learn about this side of Ronald Reagan.

Another element of President Reagan's second and more positive step in the cause of freedom was his ability to persuade the U.S. Congress to establish the National Endowment for Democracy. This was a direct result of his speech in London, cited above. This organization has contributed in a major way to the support of democracy throughout the world. At the same time, money was made available from the Agency for International Development to promote democratic movements in the world, thanks to Ronald Reagan. The agency had been active trying to build up Third World countries, but under Reagan's guidance there was more emphasis put on the simultaneous development of democratic institutions in those nations—free elections, a free press, and economic freedom.

If the world is indeed on the threshold of a New Age of Freedom and Democracy, no single individual deserves more credit for this state of affairs than Ronald Reagan. Many people gave Gorbachev a good deal of credit for moving his country away from totalitarianism and toward a semblance of democracy. But his actions were precipitated by necessity. Russia's economy was collapsing and it became impossible to keep up the arms race with the U.S., so Gorbachev had little choice other than to do what he did. Ronald Reagan had no such burden imposed on him. His actions were taken out of choice. He promoted democracy because he believed in it. He believed that the peoples of the world had a right to fulfill their dreams of freedom.

Another quality embodied by Reagan that allowed him to launch this great, international democratic movement was his commitment to philosophy and political ideology. Unlike many other leaders who govern by efficiency and expediency, Ronald Reagan knew what he believed in. He moved his nation and the world in a particular direction. He knew where he was going all the time. Richard Nixon said as much during a television interview in 1990. In responding to a criticism of Reagan, Nixon replied that Ronald Reagan always knew where he was going, and this may have been his greatest strength. People have criticized Reagan for not being a "hands-on" manager, but what was overlooked was that he had a clear sense of direction, and he expected those around him to carry out his vision.

Leadership. Salesmanship. Philosophical commitment. President Ronald Reagan embodied all these qualities, and they enabled him to articulate the hopes and aspirations of people throughout the world more effectively than any political leader of our time. The practical results of his vision in the domestic arena were an increase in federalism—a return of more power to the states; the appointment of judges to the federal judiciary who believe in interpreting the U.S. Constitution, not making law; the promotion of workfare as an alternative to welfare; tax reform that saw the top tax bracket drop from seventy percent to twenty-eight percent; economic decentralization, and the development of entrepreneurship and freer markets. Internationally, we've seen a marked decline in the number of military dictatorships in the Western Hemisphere, with one country after another—Nicaragua, Argentina, Chile, Brazil, etc.—adopting democratic governments. Communist Cuba stands as the preeminent example of one country in the hemisphere that has so far refused to go along with the trend.

The Reagan years witnessed an outstanding commitment to the principles of freedom and democracy—a commitment whose legacy resulted in an outbreak of democracy throughout the world. Despite the attempts in some quarters to discredit the Reagan years, the goals achieved by President Reagan cannot be denied. Future historians will have little choice but to recognize the Reagan era as one in which tyranny and dictatorship were overthrown by an outcry for liberty and democratic forms of government. These revolutionary winds of freedom were set in motion by the president himself, and his unyielding commitment to an ideology.

Unfortunately, the Bush administration took a sharp detour from the direction established by Reagan. To understand fully what happened, it helps to view Bush's election and his four years in the presidency against the backdrop of history. The twentieth century witnessed the rise of socialism (and its extreme political application, Communism) as well as its subsequent demise. Much of the world experimented with a system where government was viewed as the solution to all our problems, only finally to reject that view in favor of letting the free market and the private sector make the necessary economic decisions. The Reagan era, as I mentioned, was largely responsible for this sea change in world thinking.

Beginning in 1964, with the conservative takeover of the Republican party, it began to function for the first time in many years as a distinct philosophical and ideological alternative to the Democratic party. Perhaps even more important than that, the Democrats commenced the virtual destruction of their own party in 1972 with the presidential campaign of George McGovern. While the Democrats maintained control of the Congress and many state legislatures, they lost their ability to elect a candidate to the White House; the Republicans mastered the art of presidential politicking, but forgot how to operate in the precincts and congressional districts. The result by the end of Reagan's second term was gridlock at the highest level of government, a virtual standoff between the executive and legislative branches of government that precluded much of value from being accomplished.

While Reagan and the philosophical alternative he offered to the American people came as a breath of fresh air, the American political system itself had ground to a standstill. The Congress had become an entrenched bureaucracy whose members made careers out of fattening themselves at the public trough. Representatives and senators couldn't be blasted out of office. The new president, George Bush, who had essentially ridden into the White House on the coattails of Reagan's popularity, provided little if any leadership or sense of direction. The result was a stalemate in the nation's capital. The world's most dynamic democracy suddenly was not functioning the way it was supposed to.

The Congress of the United States was largely responsible for this sorry state of affairs, but much of the blame also has to be laid at the doorstep of George Bush. Perhaps the most eloquent statement on the Bush presidency and Bush's pathetic campaign for reelection was made by my old friend Bill Rusher. "When Bush got in he wanted to distance himself a little from Reagan. Unfortunately, he did it all too well. His campaign for reelection was dismal. His attempt to invoke family values was just plain laughable. He blared the term 'family values' into a microphone and paraded his grandchildren across the stage. But that's not what it's all about. . . .

"Reagan understood that the social issues, which are real issues, are not like the economic issues on which you can often pass a bill in this session. Social issues deal with great fundamental beliefs as to what America is about. American opinion moves slowly and the president's job is to be, in a sense, almost our spiritual leader—not to expect a bill to go sailing through Congress in this session, or even to demand that. Reagan pleaded for the great social issues. A lot of these ideas are going to take time to work their way through the system. Whoever understands that, and still stands for the social issues and for the economic issues and the libertarian issues, is going to be the one who will pull us together again."

Mine is the last generation, I think, that had total confidence in the United States. We fought the "Good War" where the issues were clearly good versus evil, democracy against totalitarianism in the form of both Nazism and Communism, and we won. There was no nonsense about shades of gray in between. It was a clear moral victory. Reagan was part of that and he portrayed the United States and the free world as a clear alternative to the Evil Empire, as he called it. He got a lot of criticism from the media and the liberals in Congress for using that terminology, but he was right; atheistic Communism embodied in the Soviet Union *was* an evil empire—as was Hitler's Germany—and Reagan was not ashamed to identify it as such. Reagan lived in a time of clearly defined black-and-white issues, and his generation—our generation—had little doubt about who the enemy was or about the need to defeat it.

George Bush was also a member of the generation that fought in World War II and lived through the cold war, but his failure to articulate the great and important issues of the present time hastened his demise. He was on to something during Desert Storm when he talked about the new world order; it was the germination of a grand theme. The problem is that George didn't have the foggiest idea of what the new world order was. If he had possessed the vision (which he trivialized as "the vision thing" in his reelection campaign), he could have used this theme to formulate a great concept of where the world was heading throughout the rest of the decade and beyond, and the role the United States would play in this evolving new world order. Instead he let the opportunity slip by. What could have been a spiritually and morally uplifting battle cry for his presidential campaign became nothing more than a public relations slogan penned by one of his speech writers. Incredibly, George Bush followed up a decisive victory in the Middle East with a thoroughly inept and disgraceful campaign for the presidency.

36 *Remaining Optimistic*

In the shock of defeat following the 1992 presidential election, it appeared at first as though the Republican party was in disarray. A new generation of Democrats had taken control of the White House for the first time in twelve years. They had a clear majority in the Congress, as they had had for some time, and the Republican party in the wake of Bush's uninspired leadership seemed to be floundering with no sense of direction or cohesiveness.

After careful reflection, however, I believe the Grand Old Party was not in nearly as bad shape as it seemed. Some political analysts compared the Republican party in 1992 to that of 1960 following Nixon's loss to John F. Kennedy. But the differences far outweighed any similarities on the surface. For one thing, there was an absence of leadership in the GOP following Nixon's defeat. After Nixon there was—nobody. We had to go searching for a leader back then, and in the process of doing so we forged a strong conservative majority that rebuilt and strengthened the Republican party over the decades, culminating in the Reagan Revolution of the 1980s. That coalition is still intact, and there are any number of strong leaders of a conservative or moderately conservative bent within the Republican party whose voices will be heard as we progress through the decade.

A lot depends on how Clinton responds to the public's demand for substantive change in the way we do business in this country. If his policies work and he succeeds in cutting down the budget deficit while simultaneously rejuvenating the economy, he could be the Democrat's first two-term president in half a century. If his taxing and spending programs make things worse, then we will most likely have a political free-for-all by the time 1996 rolls around. The public's contempt for politicians is as high right now as it has ever been in my lifetime. Ross Perot is not just going to disappear. He—or some other politically independent gadfly—will be there to present himself as an alternative to the major political candidates in the next presidential election. For better or worse, we could be on the threshold of a complete overhaul of the American political system, the first since the Republican party was founded prior to the Civil War.

I think the key to the future is finding people to run for office who are dedicated to public service rather than to accumulating wealth and power. Now that the cold war is over, the focus will be more and more on solving the problems of the people in our own country. The United States will most likely continue to get involved to one extent or another with conflagrations in various parts of the world, but the threat of a cataclysmic worldwide nuclear holocaust that we lived with for decades has receded. The country is hungry now for leadership that will address the considerable problems we have at home, and define the role the United States will play in the so-called new world order that will continue to take shape throughout the rest of this century.

Whether that leadership will come from the Republican or Democratic party, or from some independent political movement, remains to be seen. It is certain that Clinton will have government doing more than it should, that taxes and government regulation will increase, and many of the Reagan reforms of the 1980s will be dismantled. This will be unfortunate; it goes against everything I believe in, and I don't see how Clinton can succeed in the long run. The question then becomes, how will the Republicans respond to this? Constructively or negatively? Will they get bogged down by fighting amongst themselves over the social issues Bill Rusher referred to earlier, or will they go to work formulating viable solutions to the basic issues people are concerned about—the economy, health care, the budget deficit, the environment, and so on?

Who will emerge from the crop of Republican presidential hopefuls in the aftermath of the 1992 election to lead the way in 1996? Will a new face, a new name, a dark horse candidate enter the fray seemingly from nowhere? It is still too early to say as I ponder these questions in the late fall of 1992.

I would like to believe that the John M. Ashbrook Center, which Thomas A. Van Meter and Fred Lennon established at Ashland University in Ashland, Ohio, in 1982, would be instrumental in helping to produce the next generation of political leadership. The Ashbrook Center is dedicated to perpetuating the conservative, democratic principles that John Ashbrook fought for during his lifetime of public service.

Through it all I remain optimistic. There is nothing human beings cannot accomplish, with the help of Almighty God, if they come together united in principle and persevere to attain just and noble goals. The ideas I believed in and fought for all my life—freedom, democracy, the faith that we are all created equal in the image of Almighty God—are not ephemeral notions to be casually tossed aside in the aftermath of one election or another. These are everlasting truths, which will abide long after those alive today have passed from this earthly place and ascended into the eternal Light. As long as men and women are free to speak their minds, to worship openly and freely, and to reap the rewards of their commerce and labor—and as long as we treat one another with dignity and respect—our republic will not perish. It will continue to serve as a beacon of hope for peoples everywhere looking to throw off oppression and live their lives under the banner of liberty.

Postscript

In his introduction to a recent edition of Clif White's book, *Suite 3505,* the distinguished American historian Forrest McDonald wrote: "In 1961 three young men who devoutly loved their country—F. Clifton White, William A. Rusher, and John Ashbrook—got together out of concern for the way America was headed. The federal government had not yet become Leviathan, but it was unmistakably drifting in that direction. Their determination to do something to stop it was unfocused at first, but it soon evolved into a plan to form a nationwide network of volunteers committed to electing Barry Goldwater president in 1964. Operating on a pathetically small budget, but supported in due course by scores of thousands of dedicated grassroots volunteers, they pulled off an utterly awesome feat: the first genuine draft of a candidate in the history of America's two-party system. As Clif White wrote, they proved that good people can join together and, 'through dedication and fortitude,' accomplish the impossible."

This was essentially what Clif White's life was all about: accomplishing the impossible. His conservative convictions, so unfashionable in the Camelot days of the early 1960s, were more spiritual than ideological. They emanated from him like an irrepressible outpouring from his soul. He was innocent enough to say that he preferred his history to have heroes in it, and there was certainly no shortage of heroes in Clif's life—Dewey, Goldwater, Reagan, others. But this book of history, this memoir and political how-to guide all in one, has its own hero as well; that hero is none other than Clif White himself. Clif

White was a quintessentially American hero, a common man of the people who rose to uncommonly lofty heights.

Clif passed away on Saturday morning, January 9, 1993, when we were approximately halfway done with this book. By then I had already taped him for over thirty hours and reviewed all my notes and transcriptions with him.

In his final days, Reagan, Nixon, Bush, and Goldwater—men who had played such important roles in his life—telephoned Clif to pay their final respects. He died after a lifetime of dedication to a profession he truly loved. He left behind his wife of over fifty years, Gladys (Bunny); his son F. Clifton White, Jr. (Kip); daughter Carole (Mrs. G. Graham Green III); and seven grandchildren. Clif's loss is deeply felt, but family and friends alike take some comfort in the knowledge that Clif has passed over to a greater place than this temporary home we all share in common.

In June 1992 Clif was honored with a "roast" in the nation's capital for his "unswerving commitment to the genius of constitutional democracy." Proceeds from the affair were for the benefit of the F. Clifton White Chair at the Ashbrook Center and for the International Foundation for Electoral Systems. The dinner committee boasted such names as William J. Bennett, Charles Black, William F. Buckley, Jr., Midge Decter, Newt Gingrich, David Jones, David Keene, William Kristol, Richard Lugar, Joseph Napolitan, Lyn Nofziger, George Romney, Donald Rumsfeld, Richard M. Scammon, Randal C. Teague, Frank Whetstone, and many others. President Bush, Vice President Quayle, former presidents Ronald Reagan, Richard Nixon, Gerry Ford, Senator Barry Goldwater, and others who had known and worked with Clif over the years all contributed words of praise for the man who had touched their lives in a unique fashion.

Ronald Reagan called Clif "one of democracy's great benefactors" who was an "inspiration to me and millions of others whose lives you've touched."

George Bush said, "I'll always be grateful [to Clif] for all you have done to make politics and service more noble."

Dan Quayle claimed to be "one of the activists first attracted to politics by Clif White's efforts."

Richard Nixon praised Clif for his "lifelong commitment to the democratic system."

Barry Goldwater mentioned that Clif "had done so much for his country that I couldn't begin to list his contributions."

Columnist and political commentator Bob Novak called Clif White a man "whose courage has made him a source of inspiration to everyone."

In his postmortem, "F. Clifton White, RIP," written for the February 1, 1993, issue of *National Review,* Bill Rusher summed up Clif's career with these words: "Politicians come in two varieties. Some are born candidates, addicted to applause and adroit at winning it. These are the men and women who run for public office, and whose names are therefore familiar to everyone. Others, equally devoted to the 'great game,' may never run for office at all, preferring to work in the campaigns of others, or to serve their party and their country in ways less visible still. F. Clifton White was one of the latter, and his career puts to rest forever the notion that a politician of this type cannot hope to have as much influence on events as a successful candidate.... Few Americans, if any, have done more to hammer the high-test ore of conservative principles into the gleaming metal of political victory."

Clif White's influence on the American political system, and on the expansion of democratic processes into many countries throughout the world, cannot be overestimated. In the few years I knew him before his death, I found myself inspired by a man who refused to be bowed by the cancer that was soon to take his life at age seventy-four. He pressed on, as diligently as he always had throughout his life, his loving wife Bunny by his side to bolster his strength when it inevitably began to fail. His belief in our eternal Lord and Creator carried him through the difficult times right to the end. His dedication to the principles of freedom and democracy never faltered. He refused to grow bitter and pessimistic as the end approached, and the work he dearly loved became increasingly difficult to perform.

Sadly, he did not live to see the great Republican sweep in the elections of 1994, "Ronald Reagan's third national victory," as George Will called it. It was nothing less than a rebuilding of the Reagan coalition that had come undone, briefly as it turned out, during the Bush years. However, Clif had predicted after the Goldwater campaign of 1964 that conservatives would govern the United States before the turn of the century, not knowing that his prescient forecast would perhaps be realized six years ahead of schedule.

A well-lived life is perhaps the greatest legacy any of us can leave behind. A life that serves as a model to others, one devoted to high principle rather than to self-aggrandizement, is perhaps the rarest gem of all. Clif White lived such a life, and those who came in contact with him are enriched because of it. In addition to the impact he has had on the democratic system of government, both in the United States and worldwide, Clif gave birth to several books that will help us remember the ideals he fought for all his life.

This book is one of them.

Any failings in it are not his, but mine. I intended it to capture the essence of a man—his life and time and place in American political history. Clif did not live long enough to see it completed and pass judgment on it. But I take comfort in the knowledge that he will look down forgivingly on any gap between what was intended and what has come to pass.

Jerome Tuccille
January 15, 1995

Index